Diet–Behavior Relationships

FOCUS ON DEPRESSION

Larry Christensen

AMERICAN PSYCHOLOGICAL ASSOCIATION • WASHINGTON, DC

Published by the
American Psychological Association
750 First Street, NE
Washington, DC 20002

Copies may be ordered from
APA Order Department
P.O. Box 2710
Hyattsville, MD 20784

In the United Kingdom and Europe, copies may be ordered from
American Psychological Association
3 Henrietta Street
Covent Garden, London
WC2E 8LU England

Typeset in Century by EPS Group Inc., Easton, MD

Printer: Kirby Lithographic Company, Inc., Arlington, VA
Cover designer: Berg Design, Albany, NY
Technical/production editor: Valerie Montenegro

Library of Congress Cataloging-in-Publication Data
Christensen, Larry B., 1941–
    Diet-behavior relationships : focus on depression / by Larry Christensen.
        p.   cm.
    Includes bibliographical references and index.
    ISBN 1-55798-325-9 (pb : acid-free paper)
    1. Depression, Mental—Nutritional aspects. 2. Mental illness—Nutritional aspects. 3. Depression, Mental—Diet therapy. 4. Mental illness—Diet therapy. I. Title.
    RC537.C487   1996
    616.85′27—dc20   96-4665
                                                                      CIP

British Library Cataloguing-in-Publication Data
A CIP record is available from the British Library.

Printed in the United States of America
First edition

Contents

Introduction v

PART I HISTORY AND METHODOLOGY **1**

1 Historical Development of the Field of Study 3
2 Research Strategies and Methodological Issues 11

**PART II THEORETICAL BASES OF DIET–BEHAVIOR
RELATIONSHIPS** **35**

3 Metabolic Mechanisms Underlying the Effects of
Carbohydrates on Behavior 37
4 Psychological Mechanisms Underlying the Effects of
Carbohydrates on Depression 55

PART III BEHAVIORAL EFFECTS OF FOOD **71**

5 The Effects of Diet on Mood and Task Performance 73
6 Nutrition and Depression 89
7 The Role of Carbohydrates in Seasonal Affective Disorder,
Obesity, and Premenstrual Syndrome 109

PART IV THE USE OF DIET AS THERAPY **125**

8 Efficacy of Dietary Interventions for the Treatment of
Depression 127
9 Efficacy of Dietary Interventions for the Treatment of
Disorders in Children and Adolescents 147
10 Recommendations for Applying Diet Therapy 163

Appendix A: Christensen Dietary Distress Inventory (CDDI)
Administration Booklet 169

Appendix B: Dietary Instructions and Sample Diet 179

References 183

Index 205

About the Author 209

iii

Introduction

Throughout history there has been a continuing interest in the effect of food on behavior. In the past, it was thought that certain foods contributed to mental and physical health. The ancient Greeks used food to treat disorders such as diarrhea and to increase the libido. We now know that the associations made by the ancient Greeks have little if any utility. Interest and belief in the food–behavior connection is as dominant today as it was during ancient times, although the nature of the beliefs has changed. Today, for example, rather than believing that ox-grease can be used to eliminate coughing or that turnips can increase sperm count, many people believe that sugar is the cause of hyperactivity. Such beliefs are promoted by radio and television programs that purport to inform us about the way in which different foods influence behavior.

Scientific studies have demonstrated that diet and various nutrients can have an effect on behavior and that this effect is, in some instances, quite dramatic. The primary purpose of this book is to summarize the scientific data. This information is particularly important because, although diet and certain nutrients do influence certain behaviors, they have little, if any, influence on other behaviors. For example, the persistent belief that sugar contributes to hyperactive behavior in many children runs contrary to the findings of scientific studies, which have consistently demonstrated that sugar seems to have a calming effect on hyperactive children.

It is important to know the type of dietary substances and nutrients that influence behavior and the type of behavior that is influenced. For example, evidence is consistently demonstrating that depressed individuals not only alter the type of food that they eat when they become depressed, but also that this change in dietary intake may contribute to the maintenance of their depression. Similarly, it has been demonstrated that children with attention deficit hyperactive disorder (ADHD) may be sensitive to certain foods and that the type of food to which a child is sensitive may be unique to the child. When the diet of some depressed individuals or children with ADHD is changed, their behavior improves or their depression ameliorates. Consequently, diet and nutrition seem to have therapeutic benefit in certain individuals. In such instances, diet can be used as an adjunctive therapy to more standard therapeutic modalities.

In this book I focus primarily on the relationship that diet has to depression, because this seems to be one of the strongest relationships. You, the reader, will gain information regarding the nature of this relationship and will become aware of the fact that diet can have therapeutic benefit for *some* of these individuals. You will also become aware of the fact that our knowledge of the diet–behavior relationship is still in its infancy. There are many questions that remain to be answered. The book is, therefore, directed to both the researcher interested in investigating the diet–behavior relationship and to the practicing clinician. For clinicians who want to try including diet as an adjunctive therapy, this book will not only provide information as to some of the types of disorders that may be responsive to diet, but will also give some guidance in terms of the type of diet to use and some of the cautions that must accompany a dietary treatment. For researchers, it will provide a summary of information on the relationship between diet and behavior and a list of issues and methodological concerns that must be incorporated when conducting a scientific study in this area.

The book is divided into four parts. The two chapters in part 1 provide an overview of the development and design of research pertaining to diet and behavior. In part 2, I discuss the theoretical underpinnings of the research, focusing on physiological constructs (chap. 3) and on psychological constructs (chap. 4). In part 3, I turn to reviewing and discussing the extant scientific literature on dietary effects on mood and performance (chap. 5), on depression (chap. 6), and on three disorders—seasonal affective disorder, obesity, and premenstrual syndrome (chap. 7). I assess, through a review of the research, the efficacy of dietary interventions that have been implemented to treat depression in adults and a variety of conditions for children and adolescents (chaps. 8 and 9, respectively). Part 4 concludes with my suggestions for how to apply dietary approaches in a variety of situations (chap. 10), illustrating some approaches with several case studies.

Part I

History and Methodology

1

Historical Development of the Field of Study

The topic of food and its effect on our physical and mental health has attracted considerable interest throughout recorded time. The belief that certain foods and nutrients will either increase or decrease our mental and physical capacity has persisted. The ancient Greeks believed that treatment of both physical and psychological disorders should include dietary manipulation. During the Middle Ages, there was a perceived unity between food and health. Physicians of that era believed that a good diet helps cure the body. Inappropriate or inadequate attention to medical nutritional care was considered sufficient justification for a malpractice suit (Cosman, 1983). Belief in the curative power of food is as prevalent today as it was in the Middle Ages, although the exaggerated belief in the power of food seems to reside more within the general public than in the medical profession.

Belief in the healing power of food is promoted by the proliferation of self-help books, magazine articles, and "nutritional therapies," all of which claim that changing one's diet will cure a variety of physical or psychological disorders. Books written for the general public have claimed that the consumption of certain foods such as sugar and artificial sweeteners can cause a variety of both physical and psychological problems ranging from depression and diabetes to schizophrenia and alcoholism (Duffy, 1975; Roberts, 1990a). Specific diets have been proposed for treating disorders that range from arthritis to multiple sclerosis (Scanlon & Strauss, 1991). These diets run the gamut of possibilities, including high-protein, low carbohydrate, and high-fat diets to single-food diets such as a rice or grapefruit diet (Breland, 1974).

Similarly, there are claims that eating the right food can increase a person's mental and physical prowess. Nutritional supplements, such as bee pollen or special concoctions, have been promoted as enhancing athletic performance (Wolf, With, & Lohman, 1979). Vitamin C has been promoted as a medicinal for the common cold as well as a contributor to health and longevity by Nobel Prize Laureate Linus Pauling (1970).

In the extreme, claims of the effect of food on physical and mental health lead to food faddism or the exaggerated belief in the effect of nutrition on one's health. Food faddists praise certain foods (e.g., raw or organic foods) for their desirable benefits and decry others (e.g., sugar or white flour) for their adverse effects. However, the foods being condemned are never as bad as the faddists claim nor the good foods as beneficial as claimed (Jarvis, 1983). There tends to be an underlying kernel of truth to the claim that is exaggerated and generalized far beyond the scientific data, exaggeration that is frequently promoted by our own mortality and human vulnerability.

We expect to live long and productive lives free of any major illnesses. Not only have we come to expect good health, but also our society places emphasis on youth and regards aging as undesirable. As we age and begin to show the typical accompanying characteristics of graying or loss of hair, wrinkles, diminished vigor, and failing senses, we become prime targets of food faddists with their lure of restoring our youthfulness. When medical science fails and does not provide a cure for a physical or mental disorder, we are ripe for the food faddists with their promises of cure or relief from pain and suffering (Bruch, 1970).

Although beliefs founded on such faddism greatly exaggerate the importance of nutrition on one's health, we would be wise not to throw the baby out with the bathwater. Nutrition obviously does affect physical and mental health. It is well established that diet has an impact on a variety of physical disorders. Diets rich in saturated fats and cholesterol have been shown to contribute to the development of heart disease (Levy, 1981) and certain cancers (Doll & Peto, 1981), a fact that is well accepted by the medical community (Secker-Walker, Morrow, Kresnow, Flynn, & Hochheiser, 1991).

The effect of diet on psychological health was vividly demonstrated by Keys, Brozek, Henschel, Mickelsen, and Taylor (1950) in their semistarvation study. This study revealed that a 25% weight loss was accompanied by extensive psychological changes including depression, insecurity, lack of interest in the ideas or activities of others, and an obsession with food. The appeal of this causal relationship is pervasive and has even permeated the psychotherapeutic setting. Burks and Keeley (1989) revealed that 68% of psychotherapists surveyed have suggested that their clients follow a specific diet or have referred clients to someone else for dietary counseling. Although diet and nutrition can influence one's psychological health, scientific evidence demonstrating this causal relationship is scattered and has only recently been systematically investigated. In the remainder of this chapter, I will present a selective history of events leading up to the current scientific investigation of the relationship between nutrition and behavior.

Historical Survey and Analysis

Food has always been recognized as one of the most vital components of life. The Bible, for example, not only makes repeated reference to various foods, but also provides detailed and specific information concerning those animals (e.g., fowl, fish, and other species) that could and could not be eaten by the Jewish people. Animals that chewed the cud and had cloven feet were clean and could be eaten, whereas animals who were not ruminants and did not have cloven feet were forbidden (Arrington, 1959).

Ancient documents and art work reveal that food and beliefs about food played important roles in medicine (Cosman, 1983). This association between food and medicine probably developed from observations that consumption of certain foods seemed to contribute to an individual's health. In 400 B.C., Hippocrates stated,

> The art of medicine would never have been discovered to begin with, nor would any medical research have been conducted—for there would have been no need for medicine—if sick men had profited by the same mode of living and regimen as the food, drink and mode of living of men in health. . . . (cited in Schneider, 1963)

Without the use of systematic experimentation or the field of biochemistry, the Egyptians and Greeks could do little more than observe and speculate.

The dominant role played by food in all periods of Egypt is reflected in its numerous recorded therapeutic uses. Ox-grease was consumed to eliminate coughing, was placed on burns, and was applied to the eyes to treat night blindness. Egg yolk was used to control diarrhea, and salt was used to stimulate passion (Darby, Ghalioungui, & Grivetti, 1977). The ancient Greeks were also staunch believers that diet could be used to treat physical and mental disorders. Their belief was based on the assumption that the body was made up of four basic "humors" (i.e., the bodily fluids of blood, black bile, yellow bile, and phlegm) and that an imbalance in these humors produced a variation in temperament. Because food contained the characteristics of heat, cold, moisture, and dryness, and because these characteristics were associated with the four humors, it was assumed that food could be used to correct a humoral imbalance (McCollum, 1957). During the middle ages, food was used to maintain and restore health as well as to excite and to dampen the passions. Lettuce, for example, was supposed to serve as an erotic tranquilizer that dampened and slowed the passions, whereas vegetables nourished the libido. Turnips increased sperm and stimulated desire, and meat increased seminal flow and incited sexual urges (Cosman, 1983).

The ancient Egyptian and Greek use of food for medicinal purposes seems humorous by today's standards. However, even today there are numerous individuals and companies that make unfounded and unscientific therapeutic claims for the use of food. In the 1970s, E. R. Squibb & Sons promoted the use of the vitamin supplement Theragran. Advertisements mentioned the product's endorsement by the U.S. Olympic Team, a sales pitch that capitalized on the myth that athletes profit from nutritional aids. This endorsement was the result of a $500,000 contribution by the company (Barnes, 1979) to the Olympics. Similarly, Hoffman-La Roche has maintained a Vitamin Nutrition Information Service that distributes reports that quote scientific information but also exaggerate the need for vitamin supplements (Barrett & Herbert, 1981).

Some physicians, psychiatrists, and psychologists also advocate the use of megavitamin treatment, hair analysis, and other unproven methods for treating various physical and mental disorders (Jarvis, 1983). In spite of continued misuse and misrepresentation of the value of foods and nutrition, scientific information is accumulating that indicates that the food we eat has effects both on our physical and mental health, especially from studies of vitamins.

Vitamin Deficiency Diseases

Vitamin deficiency diseases have existed throughout recorded time (Darby et al., 1977). Astute observers noticed that consuming certain foods could cure the deficiency diseases long before it was ever suspected that the illnesses were caused by something missing from the diet. Explorer Jacques Cartier, for example, spent the winter of 1534 on the eastern coast of North America. During this time, almost all of his party developed scurvy. In the spring of the next year he saw one of the local Indians who had, about 10 days earlier, been afflicted with scurvy but was now healthy. When Cartier inquired as to the cure, the Indian informed him that the juice of the leaves of a specific tree cured him. Cartier treated his surviving men with this juice, and all returned to health (Carpenter, 1986). It is obvious to us now that the juice obtained from the leaves of the tree were rich in vitamin C, because scurvy is the result of a deficiency of this vitamin. In the eighteenth and nineteenth centuries, pellagra, which is caused by deficiencies of vitamin B_3 or niacin, was a common disorder among the poor. As early as 1735, Gaspar Casal not only made careful observations of the signs and symptoms of pellagra, but also emphasized that it could be treated by diet to include milk and cheese—foods that were seldom eaten by the impoverished.

Despite early recorded successes, dietary approaches to treating vitamin deficiency diseases were still not readily or widely accepted. For example, in 1753 Lind conducted one of the first controlled dietary experiments that demonstrated that scurvy could be cured with lemon juice. In spite of this clear-cut evidence, it took the British Royal Navy another fifty years to adopt the regular practice of providing a lemon or lemon juice daily for all sailors (Lowenberg, Todhunter, Wilson, Feeney, & Savage, 1968). Between 1795 and 1796, Guiseppi Cerri of Milan was convinced that a relationship existed between the food eaten by the rural people of Italy and an excessive incidence of pellagra. He conducted a rather crude but effective experiment, in which he had 10 subjects with well-developed pellagra eat the diet of the townspeople, who had never had pellagra, for two years. The untreated control subjects in the rural area continued their customary diet. Those on the townspeople diet recovered from their pellagra and did not develop it again during the two years they consumed that diet. However, after the end of the two-year period, they returned to their traditional corn diet and their pellagra returned (Todhunter, 1962). Again, despite this early evidence, pellagra was not described in the United States until 1907 (Lowenberg et al., 1968), and even when it was, its incidence increased dramatically, particularly in the south. By 1917, there were 170,000 recorded cases and many deaths.

Although the dramatic increase in the incidence of pellagra within the United States prompted several investigations into the occurrence and cause of the disease, these studies shed little light on the etiology of pellagra. In 1913 the Surgeon-General commissioned Joseph Goldberger to reevaluate the pellagra problem. Goldberger began a series of studies in 1914 that lasted until his death in 1929 (Todhunter, 1962). In this research, Goldberger demonstrated conclusively that pellagra was not contagious and that it could be corrected by changing the diet to include more milk, meat, eggs, and beans, and changing the breakfast cereal from grits to oatmeal.

Identification of the fact that the vitamin deficiency diseases could be treated by altering the diet should have suggested that something was missing in the diet of individuals afflicted with the deficiency diseases. This thought did occur to Casimir Funk, a Polish chemist whose reading of the literature and his own experimentation led him to believe that beriberi, scurvy, and rickets were caused by something missing from the diet. In a 1912 publication, he called these substances "vitamines," a name that has subsequently been changed to vitamins (Lowenberg et al., 1968).

Although the time was ripe for the concept of vitamins, it was difficult for most physicians and scientists to discard the 19th-century notion that the deficiency diseases were caused by toxins, bacteria, or invading organisms in the food, and not by something missing from the diet (Lowenberg et al., 1968). Pellagra, for example, was consistently associated with corn as a staple food. It was generally believed that pellagra was caused by some toxin in corn, particularly moldy corn. Acceptance of the vitamin theory was not delayed very long after Funk's publication. The continued attempt to identify the cause of deficiency diseases and the simultaneous attempt to identify the substances essential for life and health revealed

Table 1.1. Dates of the Discovery, Isolation, and Synthesis of the Vitamins

Vitamin	Discovery	Isolation	Synthesis
Fat-soluble			
Vitamin A	1915	1937	1946
Vitamin D	1918	1930	1936
Vitamin E	1922	1936	1937
Vitamin K	1934	1939	1939
Water-soluble			
Vitamin C	1932	1932	1933
Thiamin (B_1)	1921	1926	1936
Riboflavin (B_2)	1932	1933	1935
Niacin (B_3)	1867	1936	
Pyridoxine (B_6)	1934	1938	1939
Pantothenic Acid	1933	1938	1940
Biotin	1924	1935	1942
Folacin	1945	1945	1945
Cyanocobalamin (B_{12})	1948	1948	1973

Table 1.2. Psychological Symptoms Associated With Vitamin Deficiencies

Vitamin	Symptom
Thiamin	Anorexia, forgetfulness, difficulty in orderly thinking, ideas of persecution, headaches, insomnia.
Riboflavin	Apathy, indifference, inability to adjust to tasks such as schoolwork.
Niacin	Depression, apprehension, increased irritability, insomnia, headaches, dizziness, muscular weakness and fatigue, and anxiety. In advanced deficiency, memory loss, excitement, mania, delirium, hallucinations, dementia, tremor, and jerky movements accompanying the mental symptoms.
Pyridoxine	Weakness, insomnia, irritability.
Cyanocobalamine (B_{12})	Dullness, headache, depression, apathy and drowsiness, or excitement and loss of self-control.
Folic Acid	Depression, loss of sense of well-being.
Ascorbic Acid	Lack of energy, irritability, lack of stamina, crying, inability to adjust to new situation.

Note. Adapted from Bell (1958).

that there were minute substances in food that not only were necessary for maintaining health but also corrected deficiency diseases: vitamins. With the exception of niacin, discovered in 1867, all the vitamins were discovered between 1913 and 1948, with most being discovered in the 1920s and 1930s (see Table 1.1).

Psychological Significance of the Discovery of Vitamins

Identification of the deficiency diseases was consistently followed by a description of their symptoms and pathology. Within the medical profession, most of the descriptions focused on physical signs and symptoms (e.g., Cooper, Barber, Mitchell, & Rynbergen, 1950). The host of psychological symptoms accompanying the deficiency diseases captured the attention of the psychiatric profession, and Fritz (1933) alerted the psychological profession to the fact that a dietary deficiency could produce a host of psychological symptoms. Psychologists demonstrated little interest, however, probably because psychology was a new and developing field and psychologists were more interested in developing a theoretical base and a tradition of research than in applied problems per se.

The psychiatric and medical professions, however, were very interested in the deficiency diseases as well as the psychological and physical manifestations of the deficiency diseases. Numerous experiments were conducted in the late 1930s and in the 1940s in which both animals and humans were administered a diet deficient in one or more of the vitamins, a situation creating an experimentally induced vitamin deficiency. Sydenstricker (1941), for example, described the progression of the symptoms of pellagra from its early stages, prior to the development of the clinical manifestations of scaly, cracked, and pigmented skin rash. The early stages consisted of a host of psychological symptoms such as loss of memory, nervousness, fatigue, irritability, anxiety, apprehension, and mild delusional states.

Williams, Mason, Wilder, and Smith (1940) maintained subjects on a diet deficient in thiamin (vitamin B_1) and observed that the subjects became irritable, depressed, and weak and that several threatened suicide. Similar deficiency studies were conducted with other vitamins such as riboflavin (e.g., Horwitt, Hills, Harvey, Liebert, & Steinberg, 1949). In addition to these experimentally induced deficiency studies, there were many reports of individuals experiencing a deficiency disorder who were successfully treated with vitamin therapy. Clarke and Prescott (1943), for example, successfully treated 17 emotionally disturbed individuals with thiamin and riboflavin.

The results of the experimental deficiency studies and the psychiatric treatment studies provided a picture of the types of symptoms accompanying a deficiency in the various vitamins. In Table 1.2, it can be seen that a deficiency in most of the B vitamins and ascorbic acid produce a host of psychological symptoms. The important point to remember is that these psychological symptoms are the first indication of a vitamin deficiency and may precede the physical signs and symptoms by weeks or even months (Bell, 1958).

The 1930s, 1940s, and 1950s must have been an exciting period in diet research, because a new weapon had emerged in the treatment of a host of psychological symptoms and psychiatric disorders that previously had not been available. This newfound evidence demonstrating the devastating effects of consumption of a diet deficient in essential nutrients provided considerable support for the preaching and teaching of food and nutrition experts regarding the value of good food. In 1936 the first national food consumption survey was conducted; it supported President Franklin D. Roosevelt's concern with the nutritional status of the American people (Stare & McWilliams, 1981). One of the results of this survey and concern was the enrichment of bread and flour. The enrichment program is still in effect, and most states require the enrichment of bread and flour with thiamin, riboflavin, niacin, and iron. With this enrichment program many of the vitamin deficiency diseases, at least within developed countries such as the United States, declined dramatically. Currently, vitamin therapy for deficiency diseases is a phenomenon that exists primarily within third world countries, although occasionally a case appears in developed countries.

The enrichment of foods virtually wiped out the deficiency disorders among developed nations such as the United States. However, the scientific studies of the deficiency disorders demonstrated that food and the vitamins it contains can influence an individual's psychological and physical health. This knowledge continued to promote the belief in the restorative power of food, so that the popular press continues to promote exaggerated beliefs about the medicinal value of food (e.g., Mark & Mark, 1989). Fortunately, the scientific investigation of the behavioral effects of food and nutrients has also continued.

Conclusion

Throughout recorded time food has been used for multiple purposes, ranging from increasing the libido to curing arthritis. Most of these associations were based on speculation, and there were few, if any, scientific data to support the presumed beneficial or detrimental effects. Although there are several reports of vitamin deficiency diseases being treated effectively by altering the diet of the afflicted individuals, the discoveries suggested by these reports were not generally accepted until the early 1900s, when food was experimentally demonstrated to represent an effective treatment for deficiency disorders.

Research to identify the cause of the deficiency disorders and the nutrients essential for health and life resulted in the discovery of the vitamins. Subsequent studies of individuals being treated with vitamins for their deficiency disorder and individuals consuming an experimental diet deficient in a specific vitamin or vitamins revealed that a deficiency in many of the B vitamins produced a host of psychological symptoms. Awareness of the psychological manifestation of the deficiency disorders and treatment of them with vitamins was a significant part of medical practice in the 1930s, 1940s, and 1950s. In the 1940s, however, an enrichment program was initiated that eliminated the appearance of most of the deficiency disorders within developed countries, which resulted in a decline in emphasis on vitamin therapy in psychiatric disorders.

2

Research Strategies and Methodological Issues

Investigation of the behavioral effects of food and nutrients has increasingly attracted the attention of the scientific community. This interest seems to have been prompted by several factors (Spring, 1986). There are numerous popular beliefs about the behavioral effects of certain foods such as sugar or preservatives. Physicians, psychiatrists, psychologists, and other professionals have reported anecdotal observations of the beneficial or detrimental effects of consuming certain foods or vitamins. There has been an interest in identifying the timing and composition of meals that optimize performance. Additionally, it has been demonstrated that certain food constituents represent the precursors for neurotransmitters. Altering the diet to provide more or less of these constituents can alter the synthesis and release of specific brain neurotransmitters such as serotonin. These are the neurotransmitters that have been implicated in a variety of behaviors such as sleep and affective disorders. Some scientists have been interested in determining whether manipulation of these precursor nutrients and foods containing these nutrients could have a behavioral effect.

In order to identify the behavioral effects of a dietary variable, it is essential that internally valid experiments are conducted. Unfortunately, many of the reports claiming to have identified a relationship between diet and behavior can readily be criticized both in terms of study design and data interpretation (Anderson & Hrboticky, 1986). Each field has its own set of idiosyncratic variables that must be controlled or incorporated into the design of an experiment or study, and the investigation of the behavioral effect of dietary variables is no exception. One primary issue that must be considered is the separation of nutritional from nonnutritional factors. Although this idea may seem obvious, constructing a study that accomplishes this goal is difficult, because numerous variables can confound the results of a study and create rival hypotheses for the presumed relationship identified. There are three types of research designs that have been used in most studies of the effect of diet on behavior: correlational, experimental, and quasi-experimental. Each is best suited to answering a particular type of research question, and each is associated with particular strengths and weaknesses.

Research Designs

Correlational Design

The correlational research design is best suited to describing the degree of relationship that exists between two variables. Prinz, Roberts, and Hantman (1980), for example, used the correlational approach to determine the relation between the consumption of sugar and destructive-aggressive behavior, restlessness, and quadrant changes in hyperactive children and nonhyperactive children. Prior research and speculation had suggested that hyperactive children may be adversely affected by consumption of large amounts of sugar. In this study, the consumption of sugar products was found to be significantly correlated with destructive-aggressive behavior and restlessness in the hyperactive children but not in the nonhyperactive children.

When such a relationship is identified, it is tempting to infer a causal relationship between the food or nutrient consumed and the behavior of interest; however, correlation cannot disentangle cause from effect. For example, although it is possible that the large amounts of sugar consumed by hyperactive children cause an increase in destructive-aggressive and restless behavior, it is also possible that this behavior represents hyperactive children's increased activity level, which, in turn, requires increased energy, a need that is met by the increase in sugar consumption. The degree of relation described by a correlational design can, however, be used to generate hypotheses about causal relationships that can be investigated in experimental studies. Prinz and Riddle (1986) pointed out that correlational designs can generate hypotheses about the cumulative or chronic effects of diet that are seldom investigated.

Experimental Design

The experimental design is useful for identifying the causal links between diet and behavior by allowing the researcher to observe, under controlled conditions, the effect of systematically varying one or more variables. Christensen and Burrows (1990), for example, systematically varied the type of diet consumed by depressed individuals and observed the effect that this variation had on their level of depression, controlling for other variables that may affect level of depression. Participants were randomly assigned to two dietary treatment conditions. The experimental group eliminated any added sucrose and caffeine from their diets, and the control group eliminated any red meat and artificial sweeteners. All participants were monitored weekly and provided saliva samples that were analyzed for caffeine content. All participants remained on their diet for 3 weeks, at which time their level of depression was assessed. The results of this study revealed that elimination of added sugar and caffeine from the experimental group's diet resulted in a significant amelioration of their depression as compared to the control group who had eliminated red meat and artificial sweeteners. This amelioration in depression persisted at a 3-month follow-up.

Quasi-Experimental Design

A quasi-experimental design does not require controlling for the influence of all extraneous variables. In most cases, this design is used when random assignment of participants to groups is not feasible. Although this design has weaknesses and limitations, it is the only viable option for some kinds of investigations, as the following example will illustrate.

During the summer of 1973, ten to twenty 50-lb. bags of a fire retardant composed of polybrominated biphenyls (PBB) were accidentally mixed into cattle feed and sold to Michigan farmers. The farmers fed their cattle and poultry this feed, allowing the PBB to enter the food chain through beef, milk, and poultry. Over the next year, the farmers and purchasers of produce from these farms presented with a cluster of neurological and psychological symptoms that they attributed to PBB consumption. The symptoms included fatigue, headache, dizziness, irritability, diminished appetite, weight loss, abdominal pain, and diarrhea. That these symptoms were caused by consumption of PBB seemed plausible, because prior research had demonstrated that PBB appeared to affect neuromuscular function in rats. In the spring of 1974, those farms contaminated with PBB were quarantined and the cattle slaughtered.

Several studies were subsequently conducted to determine whether the Michigan farmers experienced any detrimental effect from their PBB exposure, and most of these studies necessarily used a quasi-experimental design, because it is not ethically justifiable to randomly assign participants to a condition that exposes them to PBB. Instead, researchers found other exposed and nonexposed participants for scientific comparison. Valcuikas, Lilis, Wolff, and Anderson (1978) identified a nonexposed group of Wisconsin farmers similar to the Michigan farmers along variables such as age and gender. Brown and Nixon (1979) used employees of a hospital as a nonexposed comparison group. In both of these studies it was found that the Michigan farmers experienced more symptoms suggestive of neurological disturbance and a greater impairment in memory, suggesting that the PBB was responsible for the symptoms and memory deficit. Brown et al. (1981) compared the Michigan farmers with chemical plant workers who had had much greater exposure to and higher body concentrations of PBB. In this study, the chemical workers showed less memory impairment than that of the Michigan farmers despite their higher bodily concentration of PBB. Such evidence seems to contradict the conclusions of Valcuikas et al. (1979) and Brown and Nixon (1979) and to suggest that the symptoms and memory deficit of the Michigan farmers may have been caused by a variable other than PBB. Spring (1986) has suggested that a confounding variable may be a degree of psychological distress experienced by the Michigan farmers, which, in turn, may have led to greater symptom reporting and poorer memory.

This example illustrates the difficulty encountered in drawing causal conclusions from quasi-experimental designs. In particular, when it is not possible to randomize participants, there is a greater likelihood that unidentified variables could influence the outcome of the study. At times, such as was the case with accidental contamination of cattle feed with PBB, there is no option but to proceed with a quasi-experimental design. When doing so it is imperative that all possible rival hypotheses are considered and that evidence is obtained to demonstrate that such rival hypotheses are not operating prior to making a causal inference.

Methodological Issues

Every research area has a unique set of methodological issues that must be considered before a researcher can design a study that minimizes the potential influence of confounding variables. One of the more prominent methodological concerns in diet and behavior research is that of separating nutritional from nonnutritional variables. We consume food to sustain health and life; however, food is consumed in the larger context of family, social relationships, religion, and culture. These contextual variables contribute to our likes, dislikes, and beliefs about the potential influence and contributions of food. These expectations and beliefs have the potential for biasing the outcome of research and need to be controlled.

Most of the discussion will be directed to issues unique to diet and behavior; general issues such as sampling and sample size will not be discussed. Some issues will be more relevant to correlational studies, whereas others apply only to experimental research. However, because a number of these issues apply to both types of research, no attempt has been made to separate the issues according to research approach.

Idiosyncratic Response

One of the first issues to be considered when designing a diet–behavior study is that an individual's reaction to a given food may be idiosyncratic.

If foods were considered to be drugs, they would be of low intrinsic pharmacological activity (Neims, 1986); drugs, in most instances, can be expected to have a much more potent effect than do foods. However, pharmacologically speaking, people's reactions to food are similar to those of drugs, even though the effects are weaker or more subtle.

For example, a diet of pure carbohydrates may increase the synthesis and release of the central neurotransmitter serotonin, an effect that can also be reduced with drugs. Caffeine, the most widely used behaviorally active drug in the world (Gilbert, 1984), produces very different reactions in different individuals as well as in different species (Christensen, 1991). Caffeine disturbs the sleep of some individuals, whereas others experience little adverse effect. In others, the effect of caffeine on sleep can even vary between occasions (Dews, 1982). Teratogenic effects observed in rats have been difficult to document in humans (Oser & Ford, 1981).

There is also some evidence suggesting that individuals may differ in their sensitivities to particular foods and nutrients. Spring, Maller, Wurtman, Digman, and Cozolino (1983) demonstrated that an individual's sensitivity to a particular food or nutrient can be affected by age and gender: In their study, women and older individuals seemed to be more sensitive to an acute carbohydrate-rich and protein-poor meal. It must be pointed out, however, that these findings are in need of replication.

A person's disease state seems to represent an important determinant of individuality in the selection of and response to foods. Depressed individuals seem to increase their preference for sweets as they become depressed. Some obese individuals have an enhanced desire for carbohydrates, as do individuals with seasonal affective disorder and premenstrual syndrome (Fernstrom, Krowinski, & Kupfer, 1987; Lieberman, Wurtman, & Chew, 1986; Rosenthal et al., 1984; Reid, 1985). One study suggested that carbohydrate consumption seems to produce mood lifts for obese people, whereas it causes increased fatigue for nonobese individuals (Lieberman et al., 1986). Some depressed individuals experience a lifting of their depression after eliminating refined sucrose and caffeine from their diet (Christensen & Burrows, 1990); others find no beneficial effect.

It may be that a psychiatric disorder creates an alteration in the metabolic response to food or that the consumption of the food contributes to both the psychiatric disorder and an alteration in metabolic response. Several studies have revealed that a depressed individual's glucose response to an insulin infusion is different from that of a nondepressed individual's (e.g., Lewis, Kathol, Sherman, Winokur, & Schlesser, 1983). Others have demonstrated that the hypothalamic-pituitary-adrenocortical axis does not operate normally in depressed individuals (Amsterdam, Maislin, Winokur, Kling, & Gold, 1987). However, these studies have not identified whether the alteration in biological response preceded or followed the psychiatric disorder.

Researchers must take into account the possibility of differential responses both when designing and interpreting a study, as both the preceding and the following examples illustrate. Caffeine has been demonstrated to have a greater effect in a fatigued and bored individual than in someone that is alert and well rested (Dews, 1982). If a study were conducted with only a nonfatigued population, caffeine might appear to have no demonstrable effect, which would be inaccurate. Similarly, one study of the effects of eliminating refined sucrose and caffeine from the diet of depressed dietary responders, nonresponders, and a mixed group of responders and nonresponders (cited in Christensen, 1991) showed significant differences (see Figure 2.1). If only nonresponders had been studied, null results would have been obtained, and it would have erroneously been concluded that the caffeine and refined sucrose diet had no effect on amelioration of depression.

Unfortunately, little data exist suggesting the individual difference variables that could moderate an individual's response to a given food or nutrient. Research investigating these variables is only beginning to de-

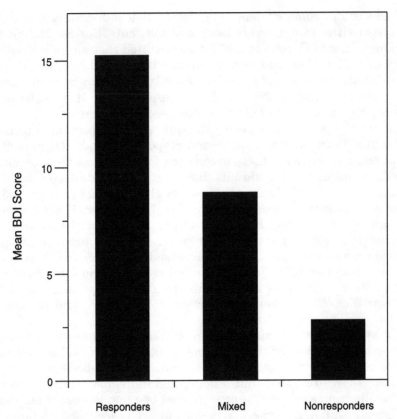

Figure 2.1. The effects of eliminating refined sucrose and caffeine from the diets of depressed participants, as expressed by a comparison of Beck Depression Inventory mean scores of participants who responded to the dietary change (responders), of participants who did not respond to the dietary change (nonresponders), and both groups together (mixed). Data are from Christensen, Krietsch, and White (1989), adapted in Christensen (1991). Copyright 1991 by the American Psychological Association.

velop. Until future studies uncover such variables one must constantly be alert to the possible differential influence that factors such as stress, type of disorder, or other variables such as cigarette smoking or phase of the menstrual cycle may have on both food consumption and reaction to the food consumed.

Expectancy

In chapter 1, attention was devoted to the beliefs surrounding the effect of different foods on not only our physical and mental health but also on our ability to perform. Certain foods, for example, were supposed to increase our sexual desire. These beliefs in the power of food have persisted over time and pervade the beliefs of a large segment of the population. The continued destruction of the rhinoceros population, for example, is traced to the medicinal value of the rhino horn. A recent news broadcast stated that an ounce of rhino horn was worth three times the price of gold in some Asian countries.

The attitudes and beliefs that individuals have about the effect of various foods can create the expectancy of a given effect following consumption. This expectation has the potential result of creating the presumed effect, although the actual effect of the food may be nonexistent. The psychological and medical literature are replete with examples of such expectancy effects. Most medical treatments prior to the turn of the century probably did more harm than good. The therapies used by the medical community during this time included delicacies such as "lizard's blood, crocodile dung, the teeth of swine, the hoof of an ass, putrid meat, and fly specks" (Honigfeld, 1964, p. 145). Nevertheless, physicians were held in high esteem probably because the treatments, although useless, created an expectancy of benefit. Most individuals ultimately recovered from their malady and probably attributed some of the recovery to the treatment prescribed rather than to nature (Ross & Olson, 1981). Similar expectancy effects have been demonstrated more recently in both pharmacological and psychological research (see Ross & Olson, 1981, for a discussion of expectancy effects).

When conducting research investigating the effect of diet on behavior, expectancy effects should be anticipated. As Sprague (1981) has pointed out, people who believe a certain nutrient or food will alter their physical or mental state will be more likely to experience that alteration following consumption than will individuals without such an expectation. Surprisingly, such expectancy effects have not been consistently demonstrated in diet–behavior research (Spring, Chiodo, & Bowen, 1987). Whereas several studies have demonstrated expectancy effects (e.g., Kirsch, 1985), others (e.g., Christensen, White, & Krietsch, 1985) have not. One explanation for the discrepancy may be that many individuals expect food to exert stronger behavioral effects on others than on themselves (Christensen et al., 1985).

Although expectancy effects may not always occur in diet–behavior research, any study design should control for their potentially confounding effect. There are two procedures that are typically recommended for handling expectancy effects: the double-blind placebo controlled experiment and the challenge experiment (Sprague, 1981). In the double-blind placebo controlled experiment, neither the subject nor the experimenter are aware of the treatment condition received. For example, to test the benefits derived from daily consumption of a vitamin supplement, the researcher might give the vitamin supplement to the experimental group and a placebo to the control group. If double-blind procedures were used, neither the experimenter nor the participants would know which group got the vitamin and which got the placebo. This double-blind condition is frequently accomplished by having the manufacturer prepare a placebo capsule that looks exactly like the vitamin supplement, perhaps by coating one in blue and the other in red or providing one box of capsules labeled A and another box labeled B. Only after completion of the experiment does the manufacturer reveal which capsule is which. In challenge experiments, a target food or nutrient is typically removed from the diet for several days or weeks. The target food is then reintroduced at periods unknown to the participant or using the double-blind procedure to eliminate the possible confounding effect of expectancy.

Placebo Identification

Identifying an appropriate placebo is relatively easy with certain nutrients such as amino acids, vitamins and minerals, or caffeine. Anhydrous caffeine can be paired with a placebo such as cellulose, because both substances are white and can be placed in gelatin capsules. Similarly, a specific amino acid such as tryptophan and a placebo containing an inert filler can be packaged in identical capsules to maintain double-blind conditions. Identifying an appropriate placebo for other nutrients, such as sucrose, represents one of the greatest challenges facing the investigator.

Sucrose has been the topic of considerable scientific and nonscientific discussion for several decades. Researchers have alleged that sucrose has detrimental effects on a range of behaviors, including hyperactivity (Kavale & Forness, 1983) and criminal behavior (Stasiak, 1982). Attempts to verify or refute the presumed effect of this nutrient have typically been conducted using a double-blind challenge experiment, but identifying an appropriate placebo to pair with sucrose has been problematic. Sucrose and an inert substance such as cellulose can be placed in gelatin capsules; however, the number of capsules required to produce a behavioral effect would be prohibitive.

To overcome this difficulty, investigators have typically used a beverage such as Kool-Aid (Christensen & Burrows, 1990; Milich & Pelham, 1986), because it can be sweetened with sucrose or one of the available artificial sweeteners. Aspartame is most frequently selected (e.g., Christensen & Burrows, 1990), because, unlike saccharin, it cannot be distinguished from sucrose (Schiffman, Crofton, & Beeker, 1985) by taste at comparable sweetness levels (Christensen & Archer, 1990). Aspartame does not seem to meet the criteria for being a placebo, however, because it has the potential for producing adverse behavioral reactions (Centers for Disease Control, 1984), possibly because it can alter the amino acid profile and, in turn, the synthesis of central neurotransmitters (Wurtman, 1983). Nonetheless, in spite of its potential reactive effect, aspartame may be the best choice at present because of its similarity to sucrose in taste and because well-controlled double-blind studies (Schiffman et al., 1987) have not verified its presumed detrimental behavioral effect.

Selection of an appropriate placebo is equally troublesome when attempting to test the behavioral effect of foods as opposed to single nutrients. For example, protein foods have frequently been used as a control for carbohydrate foods (Spring, 1986); however, protein lowers the plasma ratio of tryptophan, whereas carbohydrates can elevate it (Lieberman, Spring, & Garfield, 1986). This alteration in plasma tryptophan ratios has been demonstrated to alter central neurotransmitter levels in rats (Wurtman, Hefti, & Melamed, 1981) as well as certain behaviors (see Spring et al., 1987, for a review).

As an alternative, most studies have focused on testing the behavioral effect of meals containing different amounts of certain foods. For example, Christensen and Redig (1993) investigated the mood-altering effects of three midday meal conditions: a high-carbohydrate and low-protein meal, a high-protein and low-carbohydrate meal, and no midday meal. In designing such studies an attempt is made to make the meals isocaloric, because meals of differing calorie content may alter behavior. One of the primary mechanisms for creating isocaloric meals is to alter the fat content. Consequently, high-protein meals typically contain greater amounts of fat than do high-carbohydrate meals. However, the fat content of the meal not only affects texture but also increases the palatability of food, which may have a subtle influence on behavior. Kanarek, Glick, and Marks-Kaufman (1991) for example, have found that the fat content of a meal can affect food selection. Consequently, there does not seem to be an appropriate placebo or control meal condition that can be used to assess the effects of consuming various amounts of specific foods such as carbohydrates. This means that research designs must include various food combinations and test the interactive effects of these combinations.

Prior Nutritional Status

In most cultures the traditional pattern is to consume three meals a day consisting of breakfast, lunch, and dinner. There is, however, considerable variation within this general theme. Some individuals skip breakfast, eat a light lunch, and then consume a large evening meal. Others consume a light breakfast, lunch, and dinner but snack between meals. Yet other individuals follow one of the numerous weight-reduction plans that range from restricting calorie intake to a combination of calorie restriction and consumption of specific foods. This variation in the pattern of food intake means that different individuals vary not only in their nutrient intake but also in the quality and quantity of food ingested.

The prior nutritional status of participants must be considered when designing a study, because the type and amount of food previously consumed can affect not only the metabolism of the food or nutrient being tested but also its potential behavioral effect. This variable is particularly important when testing the short-term effect of a food or nutrient on behavior. For example, the metabolic response to breakfast should be different from that of lunch or dinner. Breakfast is typically consumed following an overnight fast, whereas a meal or snack typically precedes lunch or dinner. The insulin response and performance following breakfast may, therefore, be different from that following lunch or dinner. Studies have even demonstrated that the behavioral effect of consuming lunch differs from that of consuming breakfast. Whereas a performance deficit is a consistent behavioral response to consumption of lunch, some studies have shown superior performance in response to consumption of breakfast (see Craig, 1986, for a review). Kanarek and Swinney (1990) revealed that the ability of participants to pay attention to relevant stimuli improved following consumption of a late afternoon snack (a candy bar or yogurt) but not when the snack was eaten in the late morning.

The easiest way to control the prior nutritional status of the individual is to follow some procedure that will ensure that all individuals consume about the same quality and quantity of food. This is typically accomplished by having participants consume a standard meal prior to the experiment. Christensen and Redig (1993), for example, had all subjects consume a standard breakfast between 8:00 and 9:00 a.m. and avoid consumption of any food prior to consuming the test lunch between 1:00 and 1:15 p.m. This technique controls only for the immediately prior nutritional status, however, not for the long-term prior nutritional status.

Whole Foods Versus Single Nutrients

When designing a study to investigate the behavioral effect of nutrition, one of the first decisions that must be made is whether the focus of the study is to be on single nutrients (e.g., a specific amino acid such as tryptophan) or on whole foods (e.g., carbohydrates). This decision is critical and really relates to the research question. For example, some researchers (e.g., Young, 1986b) have investigated the role that the central neurotransmitter serotonin may play in aggression. One way of manipulating central serotonin is to alter the consumption of the amino acid tryptophan. Christensen and Burrows (1990) investigated the effect that consumption of refined sucrose had on depression; this study required manipulation of this macronutrient within the context of the consumption of whole meals.

Selection of single nutrients as the focus of the study has the advantage of experimental control. Investigation of the behavioral effect of single amino acids, such as tryptophan, valine, or tyrosine, or single vitamins, such as vitamin C or vitamin B_6, has the advantage of being analogous to psychopharmacological studies. Single nutrients can typically be packaged so that they are indistinguishable from a placebo, and they can be administered under double-blind conditions. The dose of the nutrient administered can be controlled tightly, and the effect of varying the dose can be incorporated into the research design. It is also typically possible to biochemically monitor the consumption of the nutrient. Blood samples can be taken and analyzed for the various amino acids, and plasma levels of various vitamins can be monitored. Consequently, the research protocol used in single-nutrient studies can be powerful and elegant.

The primary disadvantage of single-nutrient studies is that they are not representative of how people eat. This does not mean that they are not meaningful; these studies provide considerable information on the behavioral effects of nutrients. Considerable attention has been devoted to the effect that the amino acid tryptophan has on sleep and depression (e.g., Hartmann, 1986). These studies convinced many individuals to ingest significant amounts of this amino acid in an attempt to treat their depression or insomnia (tryptophan was taken off the shelf several years ago because of an outbreak of a flu-like affliction among individuals who consumed it). Studies of single nutrients have, therefore, provided evidence of their psychopharmacological effects and indicated how they may be used in a manner analogous to drugs.

Studies of whole foods have high face validity and have the advantage of providing an answer to the question of how the consumption of ordinary meals affects behavior. Although such studies are targeted at the heart of the problem, they are, as Spring (1986) has pointed out, rife with design problems. The behavioral effect of whole foods consumed within the context of a meal seems to have smaller effects and, therefore, require large samples and very tight methodology to identify behavioral effects. Dose–response parameters are not known, therefore, at the present time, it is not possible to identify the portion size that must be used to obtain a behavioral effect.

This difficulty is compounded because the behavioral effects of whole foods do not operate in isolation. The behavioral effect of carbohydrates is, for example, influenced by the amount of protein in the diet (Fernstrom, 1986). With little protein in the diet, a greater proportion of the available tryptophan crosses the blood–brain barrier to be converted to the neurotransmitter serotonin. This effect is blocked as the amount of protein in the diet reaches a critical point (Wurtman et al., 1981). Consequently, most studies (e.g., Christensen & Redig, 1993) have compared the behavioral effect of meals consisting of primarily carbohydrates with balanced meals or meals containing mostly protein. The problem with this procedure is that this also does not mirror the typical pattern of meal consumption: Most individuals do not ordinarily consume predominately carbohydrates or proteins in a single meal.

It is also difficult to maintain double-blind test conditions in studies investigating whole foods, because foods differ in appearance, texture, and taste and produce different feelings of satiety. Ideally, investigators would equate such factors, but it is difficult to accomplish, and investigators must focus instead on the variables that seem to be most crucial or would have the most effect on the behavior under study. For example, one investigator may match on calorie content of the test meals and another may match on taste or volume of the meal consumed, depending on which effect is targeted for study and which variables can be controlled.

Time Course of the Behavioral Effect

Studies should be conducted for a time period long enough for the target nutrient to reveal its behavioral effects. For some nutrients, behavioral effects should occur quite rapidly, whereas others may not manifest themselves for weeks or even months. Knowledge of the time course of biochemical changes is important because it determines how long the experimental conditions must be maintained and when the expected behaviors should be measured. Unfortunately, such knowledge does not always exist, and time course may be affected by variables such as the characteristics of participants, the environment in which they live, and which nutrient is being investigated (Sprague, 1981).

Most of the recent studies seem to have assumed that foods and specific nutrients exert acute effects, probably because a large portion of these studies have been focused on the behavioral influence of protein and carbohydrate meals. Prior research (see Wurtman, Hefti, & Melamed, 1981, for a review) had revealed that a pure carbohydrate meal leads to an increase in the levels of central serotonin, whereas adding protein to a meal counteracts this effect. The carbohydrate–serotonin effect occurs within the first two hours following meal consumption and persists for about five hours (Lieberman, Spring, & Garfield, 1986). This finding may have led researchers to assume that any behavioral effect should occur within two hours of meal consumption. Carbohydrate-induced behavioral changes have not been identified in all studies, however. Spring et al. (1989), for example, found that a carbohydrate meal increased participants' fatigue level two hours later. Milich and Pelham (1986), however, could not document the presumed acute detrimental effect of sucrose on hyperactivity.

Although recent studies have focused on the acute effects of nutrition, there are times and research questions that can be answered only through investigation of the chronic ingestion or elimination of a nutrient. Vitamin deficiency studies (e.g., Williams et al., 1940) have lasted for weeks and even months, because vitamin stores had to be depleted before the manifestations of the deficiency state would become apparent. In sucrose-sensitive people, sucrose has to be ingested for up to a week or longer to manifest its effects (Christensen, 1991). Harley used a four-week time interval to assess the effect of the Feingold diet program (Feingold, 1975b) on hyperactive children, because Feingold had stated that an improvement in behavior required adhering to his diet for up to three weeks, depending on the age of the child (Harley, 1981).

If the behavioral effect is not based on a known metabolic alteration or a previous empirically determined time interval, identification of the appropriate time interval is difficult and must be empirically based. Harley and his colleagues, for example, had to rely on Feingold's assessment of the appropriate time interval, because the pharmacokinetic information required to determine the duration of the study was not available (Harley, 1981). Similar information was not available when my colleagues and I began our studies investigating the detrimental effect of refined sucrose and caffeine consumption. To identify the appropriate temporal duration, we first began with a 45-minute temporal duration (Christensen, Krietsch, et al., 1985) and then extended it to 24 hours and finally to 6 days (Christensen & Burrows, 1990). Selecting less than the 6-day study duration would not have allowed sufficient time to demonstrate the behavioral effect. Figure 2.2 reveals that participants' mean Beck Depression Inventory (BDI; Beck, Ward, Mendelson, Mock, & Erbaugh, 1961) score at baseline was less than 5, indicating an absence of depression. During the 6-day challenge with refined sucrose, the BDI score gradually increased. If the

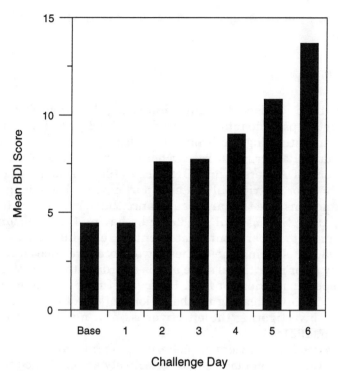

Figure 2.2. [Mean Beck Depression Inventory scores across a 6-day challenge with the substance, sucrose or caffeine, to which participants were sensitive.] Data are from Christensen and Burrows (1990), adapted in Christensen (1991). Copyright 1991 by the American Psychological Association.

duration had been less than the allotted 6 days, a significant change may not have been observed in mood, and the inappropriate conclusion may have been drawn that refined sucrose or caffeine has little effect on mood.

A complication that must also be considered in identifying the appropriate time interval for identifying the effect of a specific nutrient or food is that the sensitivity to a food may decline when the food is avoided for a period of time (Christensen, 1991; Egger, Carter, Graham, Gumley, & Soothill, 1985). This decline could signify an actual reduction in sensitivity to the target food, and it may be that a certain threshold must be crossed prior to revealing an effect. If this is the case, the study must be continued until this threshold is crossed in order to demonstrate the behavioral effect.

It is also possible that an alteration in food intake could contribute to a reduced sensitivity to the target food. As one food is eliminated from the diet, the calorie value derived from it is typically obtained from another food. If refined sucrose, for example, is eliminated from the diet there may be a decline in carbohydrate intake with an accompanying increase in protein intake (Christensen, Krietsch, et al., 1985). The added protein could blunt the effect of the carbohydrate because it alters serotonin synthesis (Fernstrom, 1986). This possibility underscores the fact that dietary substances act in concert and, as was discussed earlier, that the prior nutritional state of the subject must be considered when assessing behavioral effects.

Washout Phase

A washout phase consists of totally eliminating the target food or nutrient from the diet of participants for a predetermined period of time. Most of the studies investigating the behavioral effect of diet have not included a washout phase. Rather, most researchers seem to have followed the recommendations of Anderson and Hrboticky (1986), that is, to control the immediately prior nutritional state of participants by having them fast overnight and consume the target substance the next morning (e.g., Milich & Pelham, 1986; Spring et al., 1989) or by having them consume a standard meal prior to experimental intervention (e.g., Lieberman, Wurtman, & Chew, 1986). Following one of these two procedures does control for the immediately prior nutritional state and is appropriate for testing the acute effect of a specific nutrient or food. However, it may not be the most effective method for investigating the behavioral effect of a target food or nutrient or for investigating the effectiveness of a nutritional intervention (Christensen, 1991).

When a food or nutrient is believed to create an adverse effect on individuals, verification may be most effectively accomplished by including a washout phase followed by a dietary challenge of the suspected offending food. This procedure has been followed in the field of allergies for some time (Lessof & Brueton, 1984). It has, however, been absent from most psychological research. For example, most studies investigating the relation between sugar and hyperactivity have either not incorporated a washout phase (e.g., Gross, 1984) or have included only an overnight fast (e.g., Rosen et al., 1988) or a 1-day washout phase (e.g., Wolraich, Milich, Stumbo, & Schultz, 1985). In the field of allergies, the typical washout phase lasts 2 weeks (Lessof & Brueton, 1984), the amount of time assumed to be needed to eliminate any adverse influence of the target substance.

Including a 2- to 3-week washout phase seems essential, because it provides an opportunity to obtain a baseline measurement void of the influence of the food suspected of influencing behavior. If the washout phase is not included, a ceiling effect may mask the full range of effects. A washout phase increases the likelihood of detecting an effect and rejecting the null hypothesis, thereby revealing the true influence of the target food (Christensen, 1991).

Figure 2.3 illustrates the rather significant behavioral influence that a washout phase can have. This figure shows that, prior to a 2-week washout period in which refined sucrose and caffeine were eliminated from participants' diets, the mean BDI score was 25.6. After washout, the mean BDI declined to 8.7 (in the nondepressed range), providing a greater opportunity to demonstrate an effect during a challenge phase with the suspect food. Thus, inclusion of a washout phase enhances the probability of demonstrating not only the detrimental influence following consumption

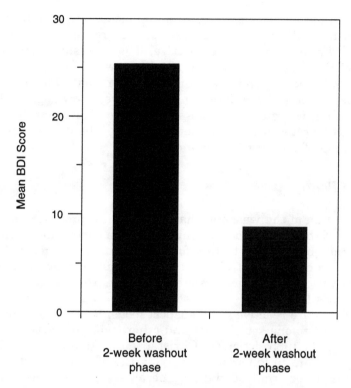

Figure 2.3. Beck Depression Inventory scores of participants before and after a 2-week withdrawal of caffeine and refined sucrose. From Christensen (1991). Copyright 1991 by the American Psychological Association.

of a suspect food, but also the beneficial effect derived from avoiding consumption of that food.

Withdrawal Effect

Whenever a food is removed from the diet, the possibility arises that withdrawal effects may occur, and researchers have an ethical obligation to inform participants of this possibility. Caffeine withdrawal, for example, can produce a variety of symptoms, ranging from headaches to fatigue and irritability (Griffiths & Woodson, 1988), and ranging in severity from a total absence of signs and symptoms to total incapacitation (Dreisbach & Pfeiffer, 1943; Griffiths & Woodson, 1988). Those experiencing severe withdrawal effects should follow a structured behavioral dose-tapering program (James, Stirling, & Hampton, 1985) to reduce the severity of the effects and, thereby, enhance the probability of continuing to avoid caffeine consumption.

Some seem to experience withdrawal effects when eliminating refined sucrose from their diet (Christensen, 1991)—internal nervousness, weakness, and shakiness is typical in the afternoon during the first few days following elimination. Participants who experience such effects should be instructed to eat something such as a complex carbohydrate when this occurs and then attempt to anticipate its occurrence and eat something beforehand. From an ethical perspective, it is necessary to instruct participants of the possible occurrence of withdrawal effects, their expected duration, and severity, and the course of action that should be taken if they are experienced. From a design perspective, knowledge of the possibility of withdrawal effects should seldom pose a problem, because this phase is incorporated prior to implementation of the double-blind experimental testing of the target substance.

Challenge Phase

After completion of the washout phase, the typical procedure is to experimentally test the target food by challenging the participant with the suspect food and observing or testing for any detrimental effect. This procedure must incorporate controls for the potentially confounding effects of extraneous variables such as expectancy effects. This is particularly true if several foods have been eliminated during the washout phase, because few individuals are reactive to all suspect foods. Rather, some individuals will be reactive to one set of foods and others will be reactive to another set (Egger et al., 1985; Krietsch, Christensen, & White, 1988). The most effective procedure to follow in identifying the offending food is to use a double-blind placebo controlled design because this design has the advantage of ruling out expectancy effects.

When testing the potential detrimental influence of several foods, each food must be tested individually with its appropriate placebo. If a behavioral reaction is not obtained to the target food, then a second food can be tested immediately. However, if a reaction is found, a washout period must proceed the assessment of the next food.

Once the double-blind challenge is initiated, close contact must be maintained with each individual. Some individuals are so sensitive to a target food that a behavioral change occurs within a matter of hours, and the symptoms can range from mild to severe. If severe symptoms occur, the challenge should, ethically, be discontinued. Emphasis is placed on severe symptoms before considering terminating the challenge, because expectancy can operate and create the temporary appearance of a return of symptoms. If symptoms are not severe, the subjects should be encouraged to continue the challenge for the predetermined time interval to maximize the probability of detecting a true behavioral reaction. However, judgment must be exercised in deciding when to terminate a challenge (Christensen, 1991).

Dose Level

In any study of the effects of a food or nutrient on behavior, a decision must be made regarding the dose of the food or nutrient to be examined. For example, if a researcher is investigating the effect of tryptophan on sleep, he or she must decide whether to use 1, 2, or 3 grams or more, depending on what dose would be expected to produce a reaction. Unfortunately, this information is not always available. For example, most studies of the effect of food dyes on the behavior of hyperkinetic children have used a daily dosage of 1 to 26 mg (Feingold, 1981) and have failed to identify any significant behavioral effect. However, in a study by the U.S. Food and Drug Administration (reported in Feingold, 1981) children's mean daily dose of synthetic dyes was 57.5 mg, and the 90th percentile was between 100 and 300 mg. Clearly, most studies investigating the effect had used a low-end dose. When a dose of up to 150 mg was used, an impairment in performance was detected (Swanson & Kinsbourne, 1980).

Making use of several different doses in a research design will demonstrate a dose–response curve that will define the different response rates for low versus high doses. Using a dose–response procedure would also help researchers determine whether there was a systematic relationship between the dietary variable and behavior. There is, however, a major difficulty encountered in using this design procedure. There is little evidence to suggest that increasing amounts of a dietary variable will produce increasing changes in behavior. For example, a high-carbohydrate and low-protein meal consisting of 4 g of fat and 57 g of carbohydrate has been demonstrated to increase sleepiness in women (Spring, Lieberman, Swope, & Garfield, 1986). However, no evidence exists indicating that increasing the carbohydrate content of the meal would produce a greater effect or that consuming half that amount would produce less of an effect. Instead, the crucial element seems to be that very little protein and sufficient carbohydrate has to be consumed to elevate the ratio of the amino acid tryptophan to the other large amino acids. This, rather than the absolute amount of carbohydrate consumed, seems to be a key factor in generating a carbohydrate-induced change in behavior.

The conclusion to be drawn is that a dose–response curve should not be expected; rather, the dose–response procedure should be used to maximize the probability of including the dose that may produce a change in behavior.

Cyclical Changes

One of the more consistent facts about food consumption is that people do not eat the same foods throughout the day. The traditional and culturally accepted foods that are typically consumed at breakfast differ from those that are consumed at lunch and dinner. Frequently, the largest meal of the day is consumed at dinner. Such information suggests that both our pattern of meal consumption and the quantity of various nutrients consumed may have a cyclical pattern that may confound or influence a behavioral manifestation of a dietary variable.

DeCastro (1987) revealed clear gender differences in the pattern of macronutrient consumption, showing that male college students consumed much more than female students in the morning, especially carbohydrates

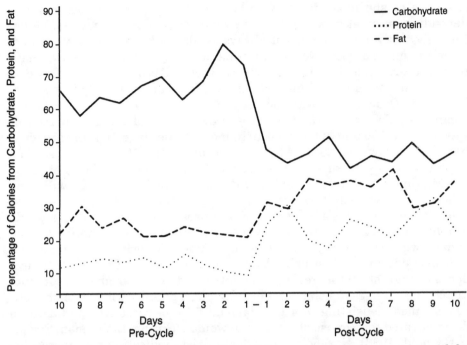

Figure 2.4. Percentage of calories derived from carbohydrate, protein, and fat for eight female participants for 10 days pre- and postmenstrual period. Daily carbohydrate, protein, and fat were first converted to calories and then expressed as a percentage of each participant's total daily caloric intake for each of the 10 days prior to and after menstruation. Each point represents a composite average for carbohydrate, protein, and fat for all eight participants on a given day of the cycle for both cycles, an average of 16 numbers. Reprinted from *Physiology & Behavior, 31,* S. P. Dalvit-McPhillips, "The Effect of the Human Menstrual Cycle on Nutrient Intake," p. 211. Copyright 1983, with kind permission from Elsevier Science Ltd., The Boulevard, Langford Lane, Kidlington OX5 1GB, U.K.

and fat. The female students ate relatively little in the morning; most of their calories came from carbohydrates, and they increased their consumption of food as the day progressed. DeCastro (1987) also revealed a clear circadian variation in meal size with, as might be expected, peak calorie consumption at noontime and early evening. Interestingly, the circadian variation occurred for fat and protein but not carbohydrate consumption.

For women, monthly cyclical variations must also be considered. Many studies (e.g., Dalvit-McPhillips, 1983; Lissner, Stevens, Levitsky, Rasmussen, & Strupp, 1988) have documented that women consume more calories during the luteal phase of their menstrual cycle than during the follicular phase. This increase in energy consumption is not equally distributed across the three macronutrients. As Figure 2.4 reveals, most of the dietary alteration comes from an increase in carbohydrate consumption during the luteal phase or the period of time just preceding menstruation. Any study of the effect of a dietary variable on behavior must take into account this cyclical variation in the food preferences of women.

Assessment of Dietary Intake

Frequently, when conducting a diet–behavior study, there is a need to assess the dietary intake of the participants. Studies to determine whether women select different macronutrients at different stages of the menstrual cycle (e.g., Dalvit-McPhillips, 1983), studies aimed at determining whether different groups of individuals select foods comprised of different nutrients, and studies comparing the diets of depressed and nondepressed individuals (e.g., Christensen & Somers (in press) are examples of research in which assessment of dietary intake is necessary. There are three basic methodologies that can be used: 24-hour recall, dietary records, and food-frequency questionnaires.

The 24-hour recall, the most widely used assessment method, consists of an interview with a participant who is asked to recall the specific foods consumed and the quantity consumed. The interview is conducted by trained nutritionists who use standardized forms and food models to maximize the probability of obtaining an accurate recall. The interview usually lasts 10 to 20 minutes and, therefore, is an economical method (Witschi, 1990). Discussion may center around the main dish in a meal, or on nonmeal eating such as snacking while watching television.

The most serious limitation in the use of the 24-hour recall is the day-to-day variation in nutrient intake: People eat different foods on different days and eat much larger meals on some days and a greater variety of foods on other days. Intra-individual variation can be even greater than inter-individual variation. Table 2.1 illustrates the degree of daily variation that can occur for intakes of different nutrients.

Because of its limitations, the 24-hour recall should be confined to assessing the average intake of large groups of individuals. For example, the 24-hour recall would be appropriate for calculating the mean nutrient

Table 2.1. Estimated Coefficients of Variation (CV) for Total, Inter-Individual, and Intra-Individual Variability of One-Day Food Intakes

Nutrient Vector (units/day)	Mean Intake	CV		
		Total (%)	Inter (%)	Intra (%)
Energy (kcal)	2637	35.5	24.5	25.7
Total carbohydrate (g)	264	37.4	23.0	29.5
Starch (g)	120	51.1	26.1	43.9
Other carbohydrate (g)	140	43.2	25.1	35.2
Vitamin C (mg)	112	76.6	35.9	67.0
Calcium (mg)	902	49.6	27.9	41.0
Caffeine (mg)	557	61.2	43.7	41.1

Note. From Beaton, Milner, McQuire, Feather, & Little (1983). Copyright 1983 by *American Journal of Clinical Nutrition.* Adapted with permission.

intake of the American public. It would also be appropriate to use if the goal was to compare the mean nutrient intake of culturally different groups or variation in the mean nutrient intake of a large group of individuals over time (Witschi, 1990). It would not be useful in assessing the standard deviation of usual intakes within a population, which would be smaller than the standard deviation estimated from a one-day-intake (Anderson & Hrboticky, 1986).

A dietary record is a detailed description of the types and amount of foods and beverages consumed over a specified period of time, typically 3 to 7 days. Participants are given a booklet or group of pages with detailed instructions on how to describe and record everything they consume. In some instances participants are required to weigh or measure the foods and beverages; in other instances they are asked to estimate amounts consumed.

Use of dietary records can provide a reasonably accurate account of nutrients consumed, but the procedure does place a substantial burden on the participant. Accuracy is attained only when literate and motivated participants are used and the diary is completed soon after a food or beverage is consumed. Before making use of dietary records to measure nutrient intake, consideration should be given to the fact that the act of recording may have a reactive effect of heightening awareness of foods eaten, which could alter the foods or beverages selected. This reactive effect is undesirable if the purpose of the study is to identify a person's usual dietary intake. If dietary records are used to monitor an intervention program, however, heightened awareness could be an advantage and increase compliance with the intervention program (Witschi, 1990).

Although the dietary record is a useful tool for identifying food intake, the exact number of days and the specific days during the week for which a diet record should be maintained is unclear. Stuff, Garza, Smith, Nichols, and Montandon (1983) found that a 3-day diet record produced results similar to that of a 7-day diet record, suggesting that the 3-day diet record is sufficient. Houser and Bebb (1981) evaluated the variation in 3-day food records collected at monthly intervals for 12 months and concluded that both weekend days and weekdays must be included to have a representative sample of food intake.

The food-frequency questionnaire consists of a list of foods and a frequency response section. A person completing the questionnaire is to read through the list of foods and check the food consumed. Then they are to identify the frequency with which they consume the food (e.g., number of times during the day, week, or month). The food-frequency questionnaire is currently viewed as the dietary assessment method that is best suited for epidemiologic studies (Willett, 1990), because these questionnaires are conducive to attaining information about average dietary intake over an extended period of time, they are easy to complete, and processing can be done inexpensively by computer.

Several cautions should be taken with questionnaires. They should not be used to provide an assessment of nutrient intake of an individual. Users should be aware that data collection is dependent on the respondent's ability to recall and report his or her usual food intake accurately. Construction of the food-frequency questionnaire should be given careful thought, and attention should be given to the choice of foods and the format of the frequency response section. Willett (1990) provides an excellent discussion of the issues that should be considered in developing such a questionnaire.

Analysis of Dietary Intake

The data on dietary intake, obtained through use of 24-hour recall, dietary records, or a food-frequency questionnaire, can be used for a variety of purposes. Knowledge of the types of food consumed is intrinsically useful in some instances, but most researchers are interested in nutrient intake and not the specific foods providing the nutrients. To compute nutrient intake, a nutrient database must be used. The standard source is the U.S. Department of Agriculture (USDA) food composition tables, although some cookbooks have them as well (see USDA, 1981, 1988).

A number of microcomputer dietary analysis systems, such as those listed in Table 2.2, have been developed to simplify analysis of the nutrient content of foods. To ensure the validity and reliability of any nutrient analysis system, however, users should be aware of two potential problems. One is that the portion size of a food that is used to compute nutrient content is often an estimate. If a portion size is not specific, the nutrient content for a typical or average portion should be used (Willett, 1990), which obviously introduces error in individual nutrient assessment. A second problem is that it is not uncommon to encounter a food from a food record or 24-hour recall that is not contained in the database. Furthermore, only scant data exist for some nutrients of particular interest to behavioral researchers. Simple sugars, for example, have been implicated in a variety of behavioral disorders ranging from hyperactivity (e.g., Prinz et al., 1980) to depression (Christensen & Burrows, 1990); however, as Table 2.3 reveals, knowledge of the quantity of simple sugars contained in

Table 2.2. A Selected List of Microcomputer Dietary Analysis Systems

System	Address
DINE Windows	DINE Systems, Amerst, NY
Food Processor	ESHA Research, Salem, OR
Minnesota Nutrition	Nutrition Coordinating Center, University of Minnesota Data System
Nutri-Calc HD	CAMDE, Tempe, AZ
Nutritionists IV	First Data Bank, San Bruno, CA
Professional Dietitian	Wellsource, Clackamas, OR

Table 2.3.   Food Composition Knowledge as a Percent of
Applicable Food Categories Containing Substantial Data

Nutrient	Percent of food categories with substantial data[a]
Total protein	82
Total fat	54
Niacin	53
Riboflavin (vitamin B_2)	53
Thiamin (vitamin B_1)	53
Calcium	46
Iron	44
Phosphorus	44
Sodium	44
Potassium	44
Cholesterol	42
Magnesium	40
Zinc	40
Copper	37
Fatty acids	34
Vitamin A	27
Vitamin B_6	20
Simple sugars	10

Note. Reprinted with permission from *National Survey Data on Food Consumption: Uses and Recommendations.* Copyright 1984 by the National
Academy of Sciences. Courtesy of the National Academy Press, Washington, DC.
[a]USDA has divided the food supply into 42 broad categories. Because
some nutrients are known to be absent from some foods and food categories, not all nutrient analyses are desired or needed for all 42 categories. Percent of food categories with substantial data is calculated
only for categories in which the nutrient is suspected to be present in
an important amount. "Substantial data" means sufficient information
to establish normal amounts of nutrient in most foods in category.

foods exists only for a small percentage of food categories. Such difficulties
limit the accuracy of the nutrient analysis obtained from any database,
nonetheless, databases such as those contained in the microcomputer
analysis systems currently seem to provide the most accurate means of
obtaining a nutrient analysis. It must be remembered that an analysis
derived from use of these databases provides only an estimate.

Conclusion

Scientific investigation of the effect of dietary variables on behavior has
made use of correlational, experimental and quasi-experimental design.
Regardless of the type of design used, attention must be given to a number
of methodological issues, some of which are unique to the diet–behavior
area of investigation. Because foods can be viewed as pharmacological
agents with low intrinsic value, it is understandable that individuals may

respond differently to foods. People's beliefs can also create expectancy effects that are best controlled by use of a double-blind procedure.

Investigators must also consider the prior nutritional state of the individual, whether a food or nutrient is to be investigated, dose level, expected time course of the behavioral effect, and whether a washout or challenge phase is to be incorporated. In addition to considering these design and methodological issues, investigators must decide whether to assess dietary intake and how this assessment will be conducted. Only through consideration of these design issues can a valid study be conducted that will contribute to our knowledge of the behavioral effects of dietary variables.

Part II

Theoretical Bases of Diet–Behavior Relationships

3 ──────────────────────

Metabolic Mechanisms Underlying the Effects of Carbohydrates on Behavior

The scientific community has been very reluctant to accept the notion that food influences the way in which we act and think. One reason for this professional skepticism is that many of the alleged effects of food have been refuted when they are subjected to rigorous scientific investigation. For example, one of the most widely publicized associations between food and behavior was made by Feingold. Feingold asserted that hyperactivity in children was caused by the ingestion of additives and preservatives incorporated in our food supply (Feingold, 1981). According to Feingold (1975a), this disorder could be treated by placing these children on a diet that eliminated these substances and that between 50% and 70% of children placed on the diet he prepared would experience a remission of their disorder (see Chapter 9 for a more detailed discussion). In a more rigorous scientific investigation, Lipton and Wheless (1980) found that only about 2% to 3% of hyperactive children benefited from the diet.

A second reason for the professional skepticism is that there has been a general ignorance regarding the existence of a plausible metabolic or psychological mechanism whereby foods could influence behavior (Spring et al., 1987). It has been known for decades that deficiencies of essential nutrients, such as vitamins, could profoundly impair the function and development of the central nervous system and result in severe behavioral disturbances, but similar information has not existed regarding the potential influence of specific foods.

In this chapter and the one that follows, I present several possible mechanisms that may explain the basis for a carbohydrate-induced effect on behavior. I focus on carbohydrates because they seem to have the most dominant potential influence. I also focus on depression because it is the behavioral effect most frequently associated with carbohydrate consumption.

Dietary Control of Neurotransmitters: General Principles

Work conducted within the past 20 years has dramatically changed perceptions of the metabolic effects of food. Information has accumulated to indicate that consumption of certain types and amounts of food can affect the chemical composition of the brain, and altered chemicals in the brain have been linked to specific behaviors. For example, alterations in the diet can influence the activity of neurons containing serotonin, which is involved in a variety of behaviors such as mood and sleep.

The idea that foods can alter the production of neurotransmitters in the brain has suggested that foods may in some way be operating like low-potency drugs. If they do, it may be possible to treat some neurological and psychological disorders with specific diets or nutrients rather than drugs and potentially avoid the side effects of drugs. Depression, for example, has been treated with the nutrient L-tryptophan. It has also been suggested that food may have an effect on the potency of specific drugs. Wurtman (1987), for example, revealed that consumption of a high-protein diet could reduce the potential benefit that patients with Parkinson's disease may derive from the drug L-dopa.

Currently, there are several dozen substances that are believed to act as neurotransmitters in the mammalian central nervous system. These substances fall into the following three chemical groups:

1. Monoamines, which include substances such as serotonin, the catecholamines, dopamine and norepinephrine, and acetylcholine.
2. Peptides, which include substances such as thyrotropin-releasing hormone, somatostatin, endorphins, and substance P.
3. Nonessential amino acids, such as glutamine, aspartate, and glycine.

Evidence exists that most of these neurotransmitters are under precursor control: their availability is controlled by the presence of a precursor or the substance from which they are synthesized. These precursors are substances that must be obtained in whole or in part from our diet. For example, serotonin is synthesized from tryptophan, which cannot be produced by the cells of the body; an individual must consume a diet that contains a sufficient amount of the precursor material tryptophan. Choline, on the other hand, can be formed in the liver and brain, but the major portion comes from dietary lecithin (Hirsch, Growdon, & Wurtman, 1978). Because choline is the precursor for acetylcholine, this neurotransmitter is partially dependent on diet. The influence of diet on the monoamines, the neurotransmitters that seem to have the most pronounced behavioral effects, has been most thoroughly investigated. I will focus on serotonin and the catecholamines, dopamine and norepinephrine, because they seem to have the most effect on behavior and have been the most frequently investigated from the dietary perspective.

Before discussing the way in which diet influences neurotransmitters, it is important to identify the conditions that must be met for diet to affect the synthesis of a neurotransmitter. The research demonstrating that diet can alter the rate at which neurons synthesize a given neurotransmitter suggests that this relationship will exist only when five specific conditions exist (Wurtman, Hefti, & Melamed, 1981):

1. The plasma levels of a precursor such as tryptophan must be al-

lowed to fluctuate with dietary intake and not be kept within a narrow range by a physiological mechanism.

2. The brain level of the precursor must be dependent on its plasma level. There cannot be an absolute blood–brain barrier. A mechanism has to be available to transport the precursor material from plasma into the brain's extracellular space, and it must be one that increases the transport of the precursor as plasma levels increase.

3. The transport mechanism must not be saturated at normal plasma concentrations so that precursor levels in the brain can fluctuate with fluctuations in the plasma concentrations. If the transport mechanism were fully saturated with its precursor substance, then further increases in plasma levels of the precursor would have no effect on the amount transported into the brain.

4. The enzyme transforming the precursor into the neurotransmitter must not be saturated. If the enzyme is unsaturated, the synthesis of the neurotransmitter will accelerate when additional precursor material becomes available. If the enzyme is saturated, no amount of additional precursor material will increase the synthesis of neurotransmitter material.

5. The enzyme that catalyzes the synthesis of the neurotransmitter must not be subject to feedback inhibition. If feedback inhibition exists then the synthesis of an additional amount of neurotransmitter substance will be dampened after the transmitter levels have increased.

Synthesis of the neurotransmitter serotonin seems to meet all these conditions, and synthesis of the catecholamines seems to meet these conditions under specific circumstances.

Dietary Control of Serotonin

Tryptophan Availability and Serotonin Synthesis

The biosynthesis of central serotonin, also called 5-hydroxytryptamine or 5-HT, is accomplished within the serotonergic neurons located in the brain. As can be seen in Figure 3.1, tryptophan is first converted to 5-hydroxytryptophan or 5-HTP by the reaction of the enzyme tryptophan hydroxylase. 5-HTP is then converted to serotonin by the enzyme 5-HTP decarboxylase. Tryptophan is an amino acid, and amino acids are the building blocks of protein; therefore, it should be easy to see that serotonin is related to diet. If a diet contains little tryptophan, the essential precursor for synthesis of serotonin will not be available, the synthesis of serotonin would decline. Fernstrom and Wurtman (1971b) demonstrated this effect by feeding rats a corn diet for 5 weeks. Because corn has very little tryptophan, the rats were deprived of this essential amino acid. These rats demonstrated not only a reduction in the plasma levels of tryptophan but also reduced levels of brain tryptophan and brain serotonin levels.

That serotonin levels depend on the dietary intake of tryptophan and that serotonin synthesis should increase as tryptophan levels increase

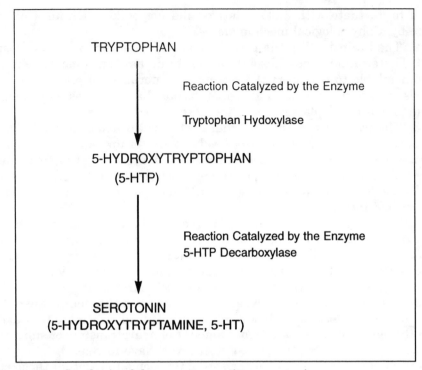

Figure 3.1. Synthesis of the neurotransmitter serotonin.

seems obvious. However, the synthesis of serotonin, as well as other monoamines such as the catecholamines, also involves the action of several enzymes, vitamins, and minerals (Lovenberg, 1986). A dietary deficiency in any of the necessary vitamins or minerals or the lack of availability of the enzyme to catalyze the reaction would preclude the synthesis of serotonin, even if additional tryptophan were available.

It is generally acknowledged that the primary factor limiting the synthesis of serotonin is the hydroxylation of tryptophan to 5-HTP, the reaction catalyzed by the enzyme tryptophan hydroxylase. For additional tryptophan to increase the rate of serotonin synthesis, the enzyme tryptophan hydroxylase must not be saturated with tryptophan. If it were, then no matter how much additional tryptophan were available, tryptophan could not be converted to 5-HTP, the intermediate step in the synthesis of serotonin. The availability of tryptophan hydroxylase, therefore, is the rate-limiting step in the synthesis of serotonin.

Investigations of tryptophan hydroxylase have revealed that this enzyme is only half saturated at the concentrations of tryptophan normally found in the rat brain (Sved, 1983), which suggests that increasing the availability of tryptophan could double the rate of serotonin synthesis. Several studies have indicated that serotonin synthesis increases as the supply of tryptophan increases. For example, Fernstrom and Wurtman (1971b) revealed that rats injected with small doses of tryptophan demonstrated an increase in both brain tryptophan and serotonin levels. As

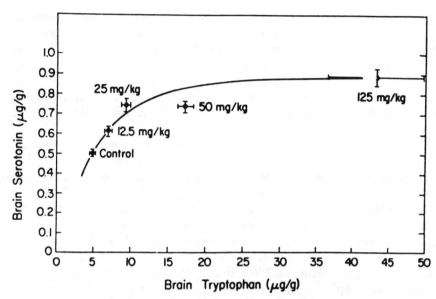

Figure 3.2. Dose–response relationship of brain tryptophan and serotonin. Groups of 10 rats received injections of L-tryptophan (0, 12.5, 25, 50, or 125 mg/kg i.p.) at noon and were killed 1 hour later. Brains were removed and assayed for tryptophan and serotonin. Horizontal bars represent SEM for brain tryptophan, and vertical bars represent SEM for brain serotonin. All brain tryptophan and serotonin levels were significantly higher than those of controls, $p < .01$. Reprinted with permission from "Brain Serotonin Content: Physiological Dependence on Plasma Tryptophan Levels," by J. D. Fernstrom & R. J. Wurtman, 1971, *Science, 173*, p. 150. Copyright 1971 American Association for the Advancement of Science.

brain tryptophan levels decrease, serotonin synthesis demonstrates a corresponding decline. Brain serotonin levels are, therefore, sensitive to changes in brain tryptophan levels and, as is illustrated in Figure 3.2, even small changes in brain tryptophan levels produce significant effects on serotonin levels. Figure 3.2 also shows that when tryptophan levels have increased to the point that the enzyme tryptophan hydroxylase is saturated, synthesis of additional serotonin begins to be limited. Similar findings have been obtained for humans (Young, 1986a). A sixfold elevation in cortical tryptophan levels was revealed in excised brain tissue obtained from neurosurgical patients following an infusion of tryptophan (Gillman et al., 1981). Additionally, cerebral spinal fluid 5-HIAA (the principal metabolite of serotonin) has been shown to increase following a tryptophan load (Ashcroft et al., 1973).

Influence of Meal Composition on Brain Serotonin

Studies conducted with rats at The Massachusetts Institute of Technology in the early 1970s consistently demonstrated that brain tryptophan levels and the synthesis of serotonin varied as a function of plasma levels of tryptophan. In these experiments, the dose of tryptophan given was much larger than that typically received from any given meal. In one experiment, for example, a supply of tryptophan equal to half of that which would be received in a day's food ration was administered (Fernstrom & Wurtman, 1974). Such a strategy is appropriate when the goal is to determine whether tryptophan influences central serotonin, but it can reveal little about the influence that tryptophan obtained from a single meal may have on serotonin levels.

Interest in the influence of a meal composed of a single nutrient on brain serotonin levels was prompted by studies indicating that both insulin and a carbohydrate meal produce an increase in plasma tryptophan levels while decreasing all other amino acids (Fernstrom & Wurtman, 1972a, 1972b) and that large doses of insulin increase the synthesis of central serotonin (Gordon & Meldrum, 1970). To determine whether the changes in brain tryptophan and serotonin occurred as a result of the fall in blood glucose levels following insulin injection or as a result of the insulin itself, Fernstrom and Wurtman (1971a) gave rats an injection of insulin or fed them a carbohydrate diet. Both groups of rats demonstrated an increase in plasma tryptophan levels and an increase in brain tryptophan and serotonin levels. Surprisingly, the same results occurred: Both brain tryptophan and serotonin levels increased.

It was now established that insulin, whether it was administered exogenously or secreted endogenously, resulted in an increase in both plasma tryptophan and brain tryptophan and serotonin levels. However, the cause of the rise in plasma tryptophan levels was unclear. Why should insulin increase plasma tryptophan levels but decrease the plasma level of other amino acids? Subsequent research (e.g., Madras, Cohen, Messing, Munro, & Wurtman, 1974) has revealed that plasma tryptophan has the unusual characteristic of binding loosely to circulating albumin. When insulin is secreted, non-esterified fatty acid molecules, which are typically bound to albumin, dissociate themselves and enter adipocytes. This dissociation permits tryptophan to be loosely bound to albumin and protects it from being taken up by peripheral cells. The net effect of this action is that there is little change in total plasma tryptophan levels following insulin secretion, although the plasma levels of many of the other amino acids decrease. Because the bound tryptophan is almost as accessible to being taken up into the brain as is unbound tryptophan (Yuwiler, Oldendorf, Geller, & Braun, 1977), insulin spares plasma tryptophan levels and has no effect on the amount transported into the brain.

The results of studies conducted up to this point clearly suggested that consumption of food could have a substantial influence on the concentration of brain serotonin. Apparently, anything that increased plasma tryptophan levels, such as consumption of a tryptophan supplement, would also increase brain tryptophan and serotonin levels. A diet consisting of both carbohydrate and protein should, therefore, provide an even greater increase in plasma tryptophan as well as brain tryptophan and serotonin levels, because the protein should increase the supply of tryptophan. However, experimental results did not support such an assumption (Fernstrom

& Faller, 1978). Whenever protein is introduced into the diet, the plasma levels of tryptophan do increase, but the brain levels of tryptophan and serotonin decrease.

Blood–Brain Barrier

Why is it that a carbohydrate diet increases brain tryptophan and serotonin levels but that a protein diet does not, even though a protein meal increases plasma tryptophan levels? Fortunately, the answer for this paradox is straightforward. Prior research has demonstrated that amino acids are transported into a variety of tissues, including the brain, by carrier-mediated transport systems.

For tryptophan to enter the brain, it must cross the blood–brain barrier. As Figure 3.3 reveals, the endothelial cells that line the capillaries of the central nervous system have tight junctures that preclude the movement of nutrients between the blood and the brain's extracellular space (Pardridge, 1977). However, the endothelial cells contain a variety of macromolecules or transport systems that shuttle specific nutrients across this blood–brain barrier.

Circulating amino acids are transported across the blood–brain barrier by one of three transport systems (Pardridge, 1977). Each transport system is specific and transports either the basic, acidic, or large neutral amino acids (LNAAs), which include tryptophan, tyrosine, phenylalanine, valine, leucine, isoleucine, and methionine. The system transporting the LNAAs has the important characteristic of being relatively unsaturated at normal plasma LNAA concentrations. Therefore, if plasma levels of the LNAAs rise, as would happen following consumption of a protein-rich meal, the saturation of the transport system would increase and thereby increase the transport of LNAAs into the brain.

A second important feature of the transport system is that it is competitive. In other words, the amount of a given amino acid that is transported into the brain is dependent on the level of that amino acid in the blood relative to the other amino acids (Sved, 1983). The LNAA carrier system transports several amino acids in addition to tryptophan. Consequently, anything that increases the plasma levels of tryptophan relative to the other LNAAs would increase the amount of tryptophan transported into the brain.

Tryptophan typically comprises only 1.0% to 1.5% of most dietary proteins. Consequently, plasma tryptophan levels would increase slower than other amino acids following consumption of virtually any type of protein, which would cause a decline in the ratio of tryptophan to the other LNAAs and decrease the transport of tryptophan into the brain. Because of the small relative amount of tryptophan contributed by dietary protein, other approaches have to be used to increase the ratio of tryptophan to the other LNAAs.

One such approach is consumption of a carbohydrate-rich and protein-poor meal, because the lack of protein would preclude any increase in

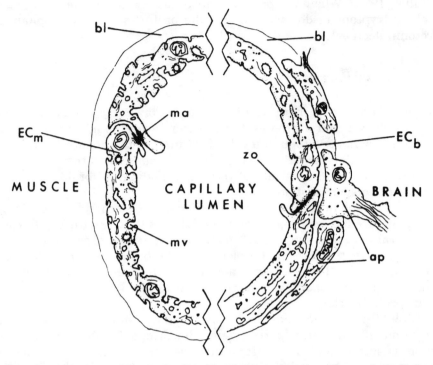

Figure 3.3. Structural basis for the blood–brain barrier. The endothelial cells of capillaries in the brain (EC_b) differ ultrastructurally from those in muscle (EC_m) in that those in the brain have tight junctions or zona occludens (zo) rather than macula adherens (ma), and there is a sparcity of micropinocytotic vesicles (mv) in cerebral endothelium. Although a basement lamina (bl) occupies the immediate precapillary space in both brain and muscle, the cerebral capillary is further enveloped by a discontinuous sheath of astrocytic foot processes (ap), which are interposed between blood vessels and neurons. The plasma membranes of cerebral endothelial cells provide a continuous lipid barrier between blood and brain, and are the anatomical basis of the barrier. Reprinted with permission from "Permeability Changes in the Blood–Brain Barrier: Causes and Consequences," by W. M. Pardridge, J. D. Connor, & I. L. Crawford, 1975, *CRC Critical Reviews of Toxicology, 3,* p. 162. Copyright CRC Press, Boca Raton, Florida.

plasma levels of amino acids. However, the carbohydrate component stimulates the secretion of insulin, which, as was indicated earlier, causes plasma amino acids to be taken up by the peripheral cells. It also causes non-esterified fatty acid molecules to enter adipocytes, leaving albumin in an unbound state. The unbound albumin binds loosely to tryptophan and spares it from entering peripheral cells, which increases the ratio of plasma tryptophan to the other LNAAs. Because bound and unbound tryptophan are available for transport across the blood–brain barrier, this increase in the total tryptophan/LNAA ratio results in an increase in the amount of tryptophan that enters the brain's extracellular space.

Model of the Dietary Control of Brain Serotonin

The results of many experiments, such as those just discussed, have led to the development of a model predicting how the composition of a single meal would alter brain serotonin levels. This model, presented in Figure 3.4, postulates that consumption of a carbohydrate-rich and protein-poor meal causes an increased uptake of tryptophan by the brain by changing

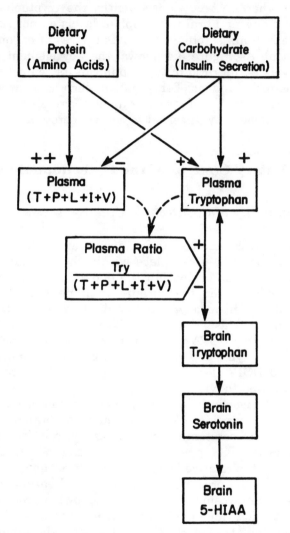

Figure 3.4. Hypothesized model to describe diet-induced changes in brain serotonin synthesis. The ratio of tryptophan to the sum of the other large neutral amino acids (Tyrosine [T] + phenylalanine [P] + leucine [L] + isoleucine [I] + valine [V] in the blood is thought to control tryptophan uptake into the brain and brain tryptophan concentration. Reprinted with permission from "Brain Serotonin Content: Physiological Regulation by Plasma Neutral Amino Acids," by J. D. Fernstrom & R. J. Wurtman, 1972, *Science, 178,* pp. 414–416. Copyright 1972 American Association for the Advancement of Science.

the tryptophan/LNAA ratio and thereby changing competition for transport across the blood–brain barrier in tryptophan's favor. The increased transport of tryptophan provides an added supply of the precursor for synthesis to serotonin, which occurs because tryptophan hydroxylase is unsaturated. Consequently, the increased supply of tryptophan increases the saturation of tryptophan hydroxylase and the synthesis of serotonin.

When a protein-rich meal is consumed, plasma tryptophan levels rise, but so do the other LNAAs. Consequently, the tryptophan/LNAA ratio changes little, if any, and brain tryptophan levels do not rise. Thus there is little change in brain serotonin levels as the result of consumption of a protein-rich meal. As Figure 3.4 shows, the key element altering brain tryptophan levels is the ratio of tryptophan to its competitors. Anything that alters this ratio in favor of tryptophan, such as a carbohydrate meal or pure tryptophan, will increase the amount crossing the blood–brain barrier and the amount synthesized to central serotonin.

Dietary Control of the Catecholamines

Tyrosine Availability and Catecholamine Synthesis

The biosynthesis of the catecholamine neurotransmitters dopamine (DA) and norepinephrine (NE) takes place within the catecholaminergic neurons: Synthesis of DA occurs within the dopaminergic neurons, and synthesis of NE occurs within the noradrenergic neurons. Tyrosine is first converted to DOPA (dihydroxyphenylalanine) by the reaction of the enzyme tyrosine hydroxylase, then DOPA is synthesized to dopamine by the reaction of the enzyme DOPA decarboxylase. Noradrenergic neurons, however, contain the enzyme dopamine B-hydroxylase in addition to tyrosine hydroxylase and DOPA decarboxylase; dopamine B-hydroxylase permits DA to be synthesized to NE.

As Figure 3.5 clearly illustrates, the catecholamines are synthesized from tyrosine, and tyrosine, like tryptophan, is obtained from the diet. Because synthesis of serotonin increases as the relative level of plasma tryptophan increases, it appears that synthesis of the catecholamines should increase as the relative level of plasma tyrosine increases. Tyrosine also meets most of the precursor conditions cited earlier in this chapter. The plasma level of tyrosine does increase following protein intake or tyrosine administration (Melamed, Glaeser, Growdon, & Wurtman, 1980), and the system that transports tryptophan and the other LNAAs does exist for ferrying tyrosine across the blood–brain barrier (Pardridge, 1977). Tyrosine hydroxylase, the rate-limiting enzyme involved in the synthesis of the catecholamines, is unsaturated (Sved, 1983). Most of the evidence suggests that tyrosine hydroxylase is 70% to 80% saturated under normal plasma concentrations. The maximum increase in catecholamine synthesis resulting from increased tyrosine availability would, therefore, be limited to 20% to 30% of the normal rate. A reduction in brain tyrosine

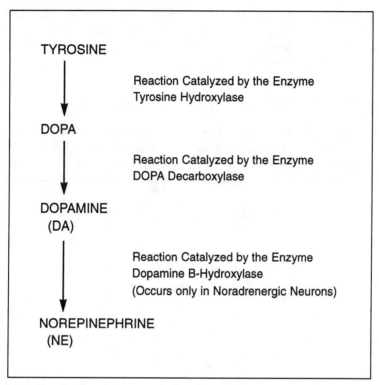

Figure 3.5. Synthesis of the catecholamines.

availability could have a more profound effect on catecholamine synthesis than an increase in tyrosine levels.

Although most of the conditions required for tyrosine to increase the synthesis of its neurotransmitter product are met, the majority of studies have revealed that tyrosine administration has no effect on catecholamines synthesis. Most studies have indicated that tyrosine administration not only does not increase DOPA, it also does not increase brain levels of the metabolites of the catecholamines (Sved, 1983). Conversely, reductions in brain tyrosine levels produced by injections of the other LNAAs clearly reduced the level of catecholamine synthesis (Wurtman, Larin, Mostafapour, & Fernstrom, 1974).

There are, however, many experimental situations in which tyrosine administration was shown to enhance catecholamine synthesis. When animals were given an experimental treatment that accelerated the firing of the dopaminergic (Scally, Ulus, & Wurtman, 1977) or noradrenergic (Gibson & Wurtman, 1978) neurons (e.g., when given dopamine receptor blockers, reserpine, cold exposure, or partial lesions of dopaminergic tracts), tyrosine administration resulted in marked increases in catecholamine synthesis, ranging from 15% to 70% (Sved, 1983). Thus the increase in catecholamine synthesis is frequently greater after experimental treatments than that which would occur from saturating tyrosine hydroxylase with tyrosine. These observations suggest that the catecholaminergic neurons are responsive to additional tyrosine only when these neurons are firing. When they are quiescent, tyrosine has little, if any, influence on catecholamine synthesis, indicating that the enzyme tyrosine hydroxylase is subject to end-product inhibition.

Model of the Dietary Control of the Catecholamines

Developing a model to explain the effect of dietary carbohydrates on serotonin was somewhat complicated, because carbohydrates influence plasma tryptophan levels indirectly through the effect that their con-

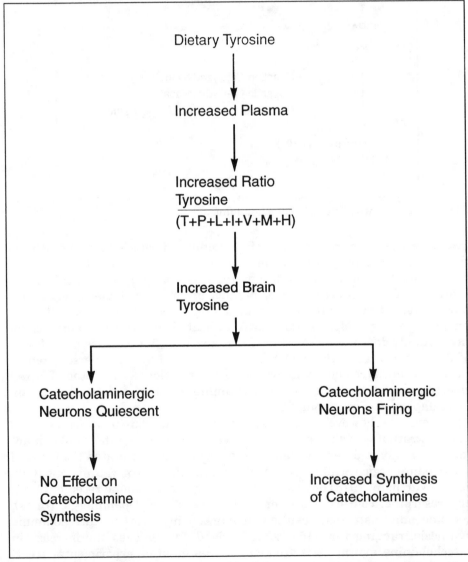

Figure 3.6. A model describing the effect of dietary tyrosine on catecholamine synthesis.

sumption has on the availability of the albumin to which tryptophan is bound. The dietary control of the catecholamines is a more straightforward process that is linked directly to the consumption of protein or the administration of tyrosine. When protein is consumed, plasma tyrosine levels increase, providing a larger pool of available tyrosine for transport across the blood–brain barrier. Because the carrier system is competitive (that is, it transports all of the LNAAs, including tyrosine), the relative and not the absolute level of a given amino acid is the important characteristic determining the amount that will be transported to the brain's extracellular space.

The most efficient way of increasing the tyrosine/LNAA ratio is to administer tyrosine. In this way, plasma tyrosine levels will increase relative to the other LNAAs, and more tyrosine will cross the blood–brain barrier. The increase in brain tyrosine levels stimulates an increase in catecholamine synthesis, but only if the catecholaminergic neurons are firing. Figure 3.6 depicts this model.

Factors Influencing Interpretation of Carbohydrate-Induced Effects on Behavior

Research Design

It has been well established that specific diets or administration of specific nutrients can alter the synthesis of serotonin and of the catecholamines under certain conditions. The importance of this finding hinges on whether this effect has any influence on other important processes such as various behaviors, physiological processes, or responses to drugs. Research has shown that administration of tryptophan or tyrosine affects not only neurotransmitters but other processes as well. Sved (1983) has summarized much of this work, which illustrates that tryptophan influences processes such as food selection, pain, aggression, sleep, blood pressure, and certain drugs. Tyrosine has been demonstrated to have an effect on the influence of various drugs and blood pressure. It must be remembered, however, that most of the research on the effects of diet on neurotransmission is based on experimentation with rats and not humans. Although some data exist to indicate that findings for humans mirror findings for rats, controversy remains, particularly about the postulated effects of a carbohydrate meal on the synthesis and release of serotonin.

Fernstrom (1988a) has pointed out that, although a carbohydrate-rich and protein-poor meal may stimulate serotonin synthesis, this effect is limited to the specific condition in which a fasting animal consumes a single carbohydrate-rich meal, and the condition would not persist over time. Neither rats nor humans would consume a diet containing virtually no protein for any extended period of time, because they would become malnourished and seek to increase their protein consumption. Furthermore, the chronic ingestion of a low-protein diet, such as would exist with the carbohydrate-rich diet, would lead to a decrease in brain tryptophan levels and serotonin synthesis, because plasma tryptophan levels would decrease and not increase over time.

Of greater concern is the evidence indicating that the effects of carbohydrates on behavior do not seem to be mediated by their effects on serotonin levels. It has generally been assumed that a carbohydrate-rich and protein-poor meal increases the synthesis of serotonin in humans just as it does in rats. Lieberman, Spring, and Garfield (1986) bolstered this assumption by demonstrating that a carbohydrate-rich meal increased the plasma ratio of tryptophan to the other LNAAs in humans just as it did in rats. Young (1991a), however, pointed out that this evidence is circumstantial and indirect, and other evidence suggests that the effect may not be as robust in humans as in other animals. For example, Ashley, Liardon, and Leathwood (1985) demonstrated that the changes in plasma tryptophan ratios that occur in humans are much smaller than those that occur in rats and suggested that the changes in human plasma ratios may be too small to influence brain serotonin significantly. Other researchers found that as little as 4% protein in a carbohydrate meal can block the rise in plasma tryptophan ratio (Teff, Young, & Blundell, 1989). Seldom will a meal eaten by humans contain as little as 4% protein: A meal containing only rice contains 11% protein (Christensen & Redig, 1993). These findings suggest that no carbohydrate-rich meal typically eaten by humans will be likely to mediate a change in central serotonin.

Teff, Young, Marchand, and Botez (1989) conducted a study to investigate the effect of a carbohydrate meal on the cerebral spinal fluid levels of 5-HIAA, the major metabolite of serotonin. This study revealed that a 100 g carbohydrate meal failed to significantly elevate cerebral spinal fluid tryptophan levels or 5-HIAA levels. A 45 g protein meal did elevate cerebral spinal fluid tyrosine levels, but not the major metabolites of the catecholamines. Although cerebral spinal fluid concentrations represent an indirect measure of brain levels of the amino acid or its neurotransmitter product, this study does suggest that any carbohydrate-induced increase in central serotonin that does occur is small.

Hypoglycemia

Hypoglycemia is a metabolic disturbance characterized by a low blood glucose level. Most individuals maintain a constant blood glucose level through a complex homeostatic process. Following carbohydrate consumption, plasma glucose levels rise, triggering a release of insulin from the pancreas resulting in a return to pre-meal baseline glucose levels over a four- to six-hour interval. If glucose levels continue to decline below baseline level, counterregulatory hormones (adrenaline, glucagon, cortisol, and growth hormone) are released to stop further decline. These hormones, particularly adrenaline, can trigger a variety of symptoms such as palpitation, hunger, nervousness, and tremulousness. If the hypoglycemic episode is prolonged, depriving the brain of the required amount of glucose, neuroglycopenic symptoms, such as headache, confusion, impaired concentration, and bizarre behavior, may occur (Messer, Morris, & Gross, 1990).

The diversity of symptoms and bizarre behavior that can be experienced by individuals with hypoglycemia has led some to suggest that hypoglycemia may be the cause of a variety of psychopathological symptoms or disorders. For example, it has been suggested that the restlessness characteristic of hyperactive children could be associated with the increased production of epinephrine during hypoglycemia. Langseth and Dowd (1978) claimed that 75% of 265 hyperactive 7- to 9-year old children had abnormal glucose tolerance curves. Schoenthaler (1982) based his initial study of juvenile delinquents on the presumption that their antisocial behavior was precipitated, at least in part, by hypoglycemia as a result of the ingestion of sugar. Virkkunen (1986) administered an oral glucose tolerance test, the primary diagnostic test for hypoglycemia, to habitually violent offenders, based on prior reports that hypoglycemic tendencies may be connected with violent and impulsive behavior.

Messer et al. (1990) extensively reviewed the literature relating hypoglycemia to a variety of psychopathological conditions including anxiety disorder, affective disorder, somatization and neurotic personality traits, and antisocial and aggressive behavior. Messer et al. (1990) concluded that there was little evidence to support the proposition that hypoglycemia was a covariate of more persistent and pervasive psychopathology, although it can induce a variety of transient psychological symptoms. Consequently, hypoglycemia does not seem to represent a viable explanation for a carbohydrate-induced effect on behavior.

Chromium

Chromium is an essential trace element that functions in carbohydrate and lipid metabolism. Although the role of chromium in the metabolism of carbohydrates and lipids has been known since the 1950s, the importance of its role in the disease process was not conclusively demonstrated for several decades (Anderson, 1986). Its importance became apparent when Jeejeebhoy, Chu, Marliss, Greenberg, and Bruce-Robertson (1977) reported on a female patient who received total parenteral nutrition and developed diabetic symptoms. She had glucose intolerance, unexpected weight loss, and impaired nerve conduction, none of which responded to 45 units of insulin per day. Following two weeks of chromium supplementation, these symptoms disappeared, and no exogenous insulin was needed to maintain normal blood glucose levels.

In sedentary individuals, a chromium deficiency manifests itself in the form of impaired glucose tolerance, decreased number of insulin receptors, elevated serum cholesterol and triglyceride levels, decreased HDL cholesterol level, and increased incidence of aortic plaques (Anderson & Guttman, 1988). Numerous studies (summarized by Anderson, 1986) have demonstrated the beneficial effects of chromium on individuals with varying degrees of glucose intolerance. Because of its glucose regulating effect, chromium appeared to have potential behavioral implications, particularly with respect to depression.

It has been well documented that individuals with major depression also exhibit altered glucose tolerance (Heninger, Mueller, & Davis, 1975; Wilkinson, 1981). Winokur, Maislin, Phillips, and Amsterdam (1988) revealed that patients meeting *Diagnostic and Statistical Manual of Mental Disorders* (*DSM-III-R*; American Psychiatric Association, 1987) criteria for major depression exhibited significantly higher basal glucose levels, greater cumulative glucose responses, and larger cumulative insulin responses during a glucose tolerance test. Serum glucose concentrations remained elevated longer in the depressed patients, and the mean glucose response of the depressed patients was twice that of a control group. Such studies indicate that severely depressed individuals manifest glucose intolerance and suggest that the intolerance may be, at least in part, a function of a chromium deficiency.

The existence of a chromium deficiency in individuals with major depression is also suggested by studies (e.g., Christensen & Somers, 1994; Fernstrom et al., 1987) that have demonstrated that depressed individuals increase their consumption of sucrose. A diet high in simple sugar consumption stimulates chromium losses (Kozlovsky, Moser, Reiser, & Anderson, 1986). Furthermore, the dietary intake of chromium of individuals in the United States is suboptimal (Gibson & Seythes, 1984; Kumpulainen, Wolf, Veillon, & Mertz, 1979), and depressed individuals frequently consume a diet supplying less than the recommended dietary allowance of energy (Christensen & Somers, 1994). Thus it seems very probable that individuals with major depression could have a marginal chromium deficiency.

The significance of a chromium deficiency for depression is not at all clear, however. Chromium may correct the glucose intolerance of the depressed, but will it ameliorate depression or any of its symptoms? Anderson, Polansky, Bryden, Bhathena, and Canary (1987) have demonstrated that chromium supplementation (200 μg/day) alleviated a number of hypoglycemic symptoms such as trembling, sweating, and blurred vision, as well as normalizing oral glucose tolerance test blood glucose values, following a 6- and 12-week supplementation trial. This study suggests that chromium supplementation can have an effect on subjective symptom reporting and could influence symptoms characteristic of depression.

Although scant data exist on which to base the proposition that a chromium deficiency could contribute to the depression of some individuals through its effect on carbohydrate metabolism, it is an idea worthy of investigation because it would begin to explain some previously puzzling results. Christensen and Burrows (1990) demonstrated that elimination of simple sugars such as sucrose from the diet was effective in eliminating depression in some individuals, but they did not restrict complex carbohydrates. Kozlovsky et al. (1986) found that the simple sugars that stimulated chromium losses and complex carbohydrates did not. It may be that simple sugars stimulate chromium loss to an extent that is not matched by complex carbohydrates.

Variables such as psychosocial stressors have also been shown to be related to depression. Brown and Harris (1978) found, however, that a stressful episode provoked a depressive episode in only one person in five in a nonpatient sample. Stressors tend to increase glucose utilization; as glucose utilization increases, chromium excretion is also increased (see Anderson, 1986, for a review); therefore, when placed under stress, the person with inadequate chromium stores would experience a chromium deficiency more rapidly than would an individual with more adequate stores of chromium. It would seem, then, that the person with more adequate chromium stores would survive stressors and be less likely to become depressed than would the person with fewer chromium stores, assuming, of course, that chromium and its effect on glucose tolerance is an important contributor to depression.

Conclusion

In the past 20 years research has shown that diet influences neurotransmitter synthesis, but only under a set of specific conditions. Synthesis of serotonin seems to meet all these conditions, and synthesis of the catecholamines does so when the catecholaminergic neurons are firing. The synthesis of serotonin increases under any condition that increases the brain levels of its precursor tryptophan, because the enzyme that catalyzes the initial reaction, tryptophan hydroxylase, is unsaturated under normal physiological conditions. Consequently, tryptophan administration results in an increase in brain serotonin levels. Surprisingly, a carbohydrate-rich and protein-poor meal also increases brain serotonin levels, because the carbohydrate meal increases the ratio of plasma tryptophan to the other large neutral amino acids that are transported into the brain by a common carrier mechanism. When more tryptophan is transported into the brain's extracellular space, more tryptophan becomes available for synthesis into serotonin. An increase in the available supply of brain tyrosine, the precursor for the catecholamines, does not automatically result in an increase in a catecholamine synthesis because of feedback inhibition. However, if the catecholaminergic neurons are firing, this feedback inhibition does not operate, and tyrosine administration increases the synthesis of the catecholamines.

Tryptophan and tyrosine have both been demonstrated to increase their neurotransmitter products and to have behavioral effects. This finding suggests that the behavioral effect is a result of the increased synthesis and release of the neurotransmitter. A carbohydrate load has also been demonstrated to have a behavioral effect; however, an increasing body of evidence suggests that the behavioral effect of carbohydrates may not be mediated by an increased synthesis of serotonin.

Hypoglycemia has frequently been mentioned as the causal variable contributing to a variety of psychopathological conditions; however, data indicate that it is not a viable explanation for the effect that carbohydrates seem to have on some individuals. Chromium operates in carbohydrate metabolism by contributing to the regulation of glucose tolerance. It has been suggested that because depressed people consume more simple carbohydrates when they are depressed, and because simple carbohydrate consumption stimulates the loss of chromium, they may have a chromium deficiency. Additionally, severely depressed individuals tend to show glucose intolerance, which is one of the first signs of chromium deficiency. When these factors are coupled with the fact that the typical American diet is deficient in chromium, it seems probable that correcting the chromium deficiency of depressed individuals would correct their glucose intolerance and, perhaps, ameliorate their depression.

4

Psychological Mechanisms Underlying the Effects of Carbohydrates on Depression

In chapter 3, I discussed several possible metabolic mechanisms that could influence the effects of carbohydrates on behavior. It seems only logical that any effect arising from the consumption of food would be mediated metabolically or biochemically. There are, however, several psychological mechanisms that could also provide some explanation for food-induced effects.

Expectancies

In a survey of teachers in Kentucky, McLoughlin and Nall (1988) demonstrated that more than 90% of these teachers believed that sugar-containing foods can have adverse effects on the classroom behavior and academic performance of children. That such beliefs can have a powerful influence on behavior has been demonstrated in the classroom by Rosenthal and Jacobson (1968). Although the effects of food-related beliefs on behavior have not been demonstrated, it is possible that expectancies can produce a behavioral change that is then attributed to the food.

The potentially powerful influence that expectancies can have on evaluating the effect of diet on behavior has been discussed repeatedly (e.g., Christensen, 1991; Sprague, 1981), and it has been agreed that researchers should design studies in such a way that expectancies are controlled. Spring et al. (1987) have suggested that expectancies may not represent a powerful influence in diet–behavior research. Christensen, White, and Krietsch (1985) found that neither preexisting nor experimentally induced expectancies about the behavioral effects of sugar created the expected symptoms following sugar or placebo ingestion, perhaps because the participants did not hold personal expectations about the effects of foods such as sugar and caffeine on their behavior but expected the presumed effects to occur in others.

If expectancies do exert a powerful influence in diet–behavior research, Spring et al. (1987) pointed out that major research findings should parallel popular stereotypes about sugar's effect on behavior, but the available data do not support such parallels. Although depression does seem to be related to sugar ingestion, it occurs only in some individuals. Little data exist to support the belief that attention deficit hyperactivity disorder (ADHD) results from sugar ingestion; in fact, the data indicate that children with ADHD may experience a calming effect following sugar ingestion. Expectancies, therefore, do not seem to represent a major contribution to exploring the influence of diet on behavior, and they do not seem to represent a reasonable explanation for carbohydrate-induced effects.

Fatigue

Transient fatigue is a phenomenon that is experienced by most individuals and accepted as a normal part of everyday life. However, a substantial number of individuals complain of persistent tiredness or listlessness. According to the National Ambulatory Medical Care Survey (National Center for Health Statistics, 1978), fatigue is the seventh most frequent initial complaint in U.S. medical offices. Epidemiological studies conducted in the United States have revealed that between 21% and 41% of adults report fatigue (Manu et al., 1989).

Although persistent fatigue is a common complaint, it has attracted little attention until recently, and most of this attention has been directed toward chronic fatigue syndrome. Laboratory tests have been notably uninformative (Kroenke, Wood, Mangelsdorff, Meier, & Powell, 1988) in identifying its cause, although physical causes have been found (Morrison, 1980). The most frequent finding is that fatigue is associated with measures of psychopathology, with depression being the most frequently occurring association (Kroenke et al., 1988; Manu et al., 1989).

Throughout this book I discuss studies that demonstrate a relationship between carbohydrates, particularly simple carbohydrates, and depression. Imbedded in many of these studies is the fact that fatigue seems to be related to both depression and consumption of simple carbohydrates. For example, individuals develop an added preference for junk food and simple carbohydrates when they become depressed (e.g., Christensen & Somers, in press). Nondepressed individuals (e.g., Spring et al., 1983) and some depressed individuals (Christensen, Krietsch, White, & Stagner, 1985) develop feelings of fatigue and a lack of vigor following consumption of foods high in simple carbohydrates. Although the exact relationship between fatigue, depression, and simple carbohydrates is not known, the data seem to suggest that simple carbohydrate consumption can induce fatigue and that persistent fatigue may contribute to the development or maintenance of the symptoms of depression. It is this postulated path from simple carbohydrate consumption to fatigue to depression that I focus on.

In postulating this causal path, it must be acknowledged at the outset that carbohydrate consumption does not lead to feelings of fatigue in everyone. Moreover, carbohydrate consumption is not the only variable that can lead to feelings of fatigue, and fatigue is not the only variable that may contribute to depression. In some instances, feelings of fatigue might follow the onset of a depressive episode (Manu et al., 1989). Similarly, a depressive episode might induce an increase in carbohydrate consumption

(Fernstrom et al., 1987). In such instances, carbohydrate consumption and fatigue would probably contribute to the maintenance of the depression. No single pathway can be expected to contribute to or maintain all cases of depression. Depression is a polydimensional phenomenon with a heterogeneity of causes (Craighead, 1980; Lewinsohn, Hoberman, Teri, & Hautzinger, 1985), and the postulated carbohydrate–fatigue–depression pathway is to be viewed as only one possible path.

Simple Carbohydrates and Fatigue

Studies have demonstrated that carbohydrate consumption, in normal subjects, may increase feelings of sleepiness or fatigue (Spring et al., 1983, 1989). In some depressed individuals, elimination of simple carbohydrate consumption results in an increase in feelings of vigor, a decline in feelings of fatigue, and an amelioration of depression. Reintroduction of the simple carbohydrates is accompanied by a return of the depression and its accompanying feelings of fatigue and lack of vigor (e.g., Christensen & Burrows, 1990; Christensen, Krietsch, White, & Stagner, 1985).

In contrast, other studies (e.g., Lieberman, Wurtman, & Chew, 1986) have demonstrated that consumption of carbohydrates ameliorates depression by increasing feelings of vigor. This apparent contradiction may be explained by the fact that the immediate reaction of increased vigor and slightly enhanced mood is short lived and that increased fatigue is a longer term effect (Christensen, 1991). This suggested curvilinear reaction to simple carbohydrates was demonstrated by Thayer (1987). As Figure 4.1 reveals, participants first experienced increased energy, but energy then declined, particularly in the afternoon.

Fatigue and psychomotor retardation are dominant characteristics of depression and represent diagnostic criteria; however, these factors are typically seen as symptoms of, rather than contributors to, depression. Little, if any, consideration has been given to the role that fatigue or a decline in energy level may play in depression. When fatigue and depression are associated, the most frequently suggested causal path is that depression causes the experience of fatigue (e.g., Wessely & Powell, 1989). Such an assumption is probably bolstered by the fact that fatigue is listed as a criterion for depression in the DSM-III-R (American Psychiatric Association, 1987). If depression is a principal cause of fatigue, it is possible that a large portion of the self-report of persistent tiredness or listlessness is due to the actual presence of depression or to a low level of dysphoria, in which case the fatigue could be viewed as a mood-congruent response. When viewed from this perspective, the self-reports of fatigue represent a manifestation of depression.

It is also possible that fatigue contributes to the onset and maintenance of depression. Beck (1967) stated that tiredness could influence the negative mental set so prevalent in depression. Thayer (1989) suggested that the state of very low arousal among depressed people is due primarily to low energy levels. Manu et al. (1989) and Wessely and Powell (1989)

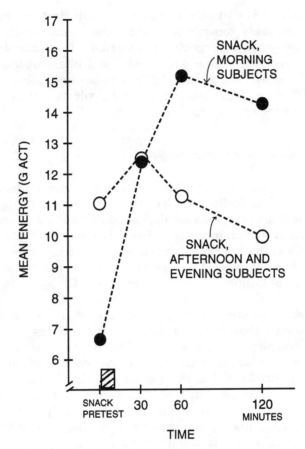

Figure 4.1. Self-ratings of energy (means for 6 days) over 2 hr as a function of a sugar snack. From Thayer (1987). Copyright 1987 by the American Psychological Association. Adapted with permission of the author.

have revealed that fatigue is strongly associated with the onset of the first episode of depression, and about 50% of individuals experiencing chronic fatigue meet criteria for major depression. These findings are consistent with the evidence revealing that more than 75% of depressed patients experience fatigue (Beck, 1967). Hickie, Lloyd, Wakefield, and Parker (1990) have demonstrated that the pre-morbid prevalence rate of depression among patients with chronic fatigue syndrome was no greater than that among the general population, suggesting that the chronic fatigue experienced by these individuals contributes to their experience of depression and that chronic fatigue may be producing the depression.

During the past several decades it has become increasingly evident that depression occurs in a significant portion of patients with physical illness (see Whitlock, 1982, for a comprehensive review of this literature). Although the direction of causality has remained unclear, because most of the literature has demonstrated only a covariation between depression and physical disease, there are indications that chronic depression may be a result of physical illness. Several studies (e.g., Nielsen & Williams,

1980) have demonstrated that depression increases as physical illness gets worse and that a dramatic recovery is accompanied by an equally dramatic lifting of the depressed mood (Moffic & Paykel, 1975).

Cassileth et al. (1984) found that the degree of depression expressed in physically ill patients is independent of their diagnostic classification. Depression has been documented in disorders ranging from viral infections such as influenza to more life-threatening disorders such as cancer (Whitlock, 1982). However, bacterial infections are seldom associated with depression (Whitlock, 1982). It may be, then, that a common factor and not a specific type of illness contributes to depression, and the common factor seems to be the symptom of fatigue or lack of energy. I do not mean to imply that other factors do not contribute to depression or that factors related to illness, that influence depression such as helplessness and hopelessness, do not operate in physical disorders, because they obviously do. With viral infections, major depression does not seem to exist without the coexistence of low energetic arousal. For example, in viral infections such as acquired immunodeficiency syndrome (AIDS), the most common psychiatric diagnosis in the asymptomatic individual is adjustment disorder with anxiety or depressive features. Major affective disorder is uncommon (O'Dowd & Zofnass, 1991), and depression does not become a serious issue until the latter symptomatic stage, when the individual experiences anergy and apathy.

Watson, Clark, and Carey (1988); Watson and Pennebaker (1989); and Clark and Watson (1991) have demonstrated that low positive affect, or a loss of pleasurable engagement (Clark & Watson, 1988), is uniquely related to depression. Low positive affect has even been demonstrated (Clark & Watson, 1991) to represent the specific factor in depression that differentiates it from anxiety and phobias. Clark and Watson (1991) have conceptualized low positive affect as a relative absence of positive affective arousal. However, low positive affect "is best defined by descriptors reflecting lethargy and fatigue" (Watson, Clark, & Carey, 1988, p. 347).

Characterization of Fatigue Among Depressed Individuals

To characterize the fatigue experienced by depressed people, it may be instructive to begin by considering how fatigue is experienced by nondepressed people. When nondepressed people engage in physical exertion or do not sleep for an extended period of time, they begin to tire and experience fatigue, feelings that may be accompanied by a lack of pep, excitement, alertness, enthusiasm, and vigor or a decline in energy and a desire to rest. Rest typically restores feelings of vigor, and energy returns; feelings of fatigue and tiredness arising from physical exertion are not necessarily related to negative affect and depression. To the extent that the physical exhaustion is eliminated with rest, any negative affect would be minimal and transitory in nature. Similarly, about 2 hours after consuming simple carbohydrates, some nondepressed individuals experience an increase in fatigue and a decline in energy (e.g., Spring et al., 1989), but the increase is mild and temporary, which means that the effect on mood would also be minimal and temporary.

Depressed people have similar but more exaggerated and persistent feelings. They also generally feel tired and experience a lack of excitement, alertness, and enthusiasm, a state that has been characterized as a state of low positive arousal (Clark & Watson, 1988). But for these individuals, rest does not seem to restore feelings of vigor. Depressed people tend to experience feelings of fatigue persistently over time. This more exaggerated and persistent feeling of fatigue that is experienced by depressed people can be produced by simple carbohydrate consumption in individuals sensitive to this nutrient (Christensen, Krietsch, et al., 1985). As was pointed out earlier, depressed individuals tend to exhibit increased preference and consumption of simple carbohydrates; it may be that increased consumption creates a persistent state of fatigue which, over time, leads to exaggerated feelings of fatigue, and, finally, to depression. This process is described in detail in the next section. First, however, it is necessary to clarify the connotations of the term *fatigue* as it pertains to depressed people. Fatigue is typically understood as being a state arising from exertion or sleep deprivation; however, the concept of low energetic arousal, originally advanced by Thayer (1989), seems to more accurately describe the nature of the energy decline or fatigue state related to depression. Thayer's concept includes subjective feelings of little energy, vigor, and peppiness, and I would extend this definition to include the additional subjective feelings, such as sensations of being weighted down, of having heavy limbs, and feeling as if the body has been sapped of all energy.

Energetic Arousal

The idea that a lack of energy may represent an important variable in the depression equation has received very little attention in spite of the fact that fatigue is a frequent covariate of depression and a diagnostic criterion. Most depressed individuals report increased tiredness (Beck, 1967), and individuals experiencing chronic fatigue score higher on measures of depression than do their nondepressed counterparts (Montgomery, 1983). However, depression is not an inevitable consequence of low energetic arousal (Wessely & Powell, 1989). For depression to emerge or to be maintained as a result of low energy levels, the symptoms and covariates of depression must emerge. I argue that these symptoms and covariates can arise at least in part from the existence of a *persistent* level of low energetic arousal and that the persistence, therefore, is the crucial factor in the development and maintenance of depression.

When nondepressed individuals experience fatigue as a result of exertion or sleep deprivation, self-awareness theory (Duval & Wicklund, 1972) predicts that individuals will initiate an evaluation to identify the cause of the lack of energy in an attempt to eliminate the discrepancy between the standard state of vigor and vitality and the current state of fatigue and lethargy (Duval & Wicklund, 1972; Pyszcynski, Holt, & Greenberg, 1987). The self-focus caused by the discrepancy also increases the tendency to make an internal attribution (Fenigstein & Levine, 1984), that is, an individual may attribute the fatigue to an event such as lack of sleep, effort expended, or a stressful experience. An outcome expectancy (Bandura, 1977) is then established, whereby the individual expects rest to eliminate the state of low energy and restore feelings of vigor. For most individuals, the rest accomplishes this goal and merely represents an additional verification of the fact that energy levels fluctuate with variables such as rest and effort expended. In those for whom low energy levels persist following adequate rest, however, several psychological mechanisms may underlie the appearance of negative affect and symptoms characteristic of depression: Self-focus of attention, self-efficacy, and dysfunctional cognitions.

Self-Focus of Attention

There are a number of studies (e.g., Ingram, Lumry, Cruet, & Sieber, 1987) demonstrating that depressed people are chronically high in self-focus of attention. As was stated in the previous section, this self-focus and the negative discrepancy motivates an individual to engage in behaviors such as resting, with the accompanying outcome expectancy that rest will ameliorate this low energy state. However, in the depressed person, added rest does not accomplish the desired result of restoring energy levels, motivating the individual to search for other causes of the discrepancy. Initially the search probably focuses on an organic cause. It is well documented (e.g., Brown & Harris, 1978; Weissman & Myers, 1978) that most psychiatric patients seek assistance in nonpsychiatric settings, especially from general practitioners. This is a logical and appropriate approach because a number of organic disorders, such as viral infections, autoimmune diseases, and endocrine disorders, induce a state of energy decline as one of their symptoms (Kennedy, 1988).

Although seeking medical attention is probably the most prevalent and initial response to obtaining an explanation and treatment for low energy levels, in most instances laboratory tests are uninformative (Kroenke et al., 1988). Therefore, most individuals receive no organic explanation for the cause of their fatigue, and it may even be recommended that the fatigue is of psychogenic origin. It is well documented (e.g., Brown & Harris, 1978) that depressed people experience more stressful life experiences during the six months preceding a depressive episode than do their nondepressed counterparts. Depressed people also generate some of the stress that befalls them (Hammen, 1991). Consequently, because depressed people typically can find no organic reason for their distressing symptoms, they frequently attribute them to the repeated occurrence of stressful life events (Ginsberg & Brown, 1982), which can delay treatment (Monroe, Simons, & Thase, 1991).

Over time, this combination of events would seem to negate the depressed person's motivation to work at discrepancy reduction. It is known, for example, that depressed people tend to engage in characterological self-blame (Peterson, Schwartz, & Seligman, 1981). This tendency to attribute blame to ones character would seem to be a logical sequelae to a failure to identify and to eliminate the cause of one's symptoms because it resolves the tendency to feel guilty over events about which a person is helpless (Janoff-Buhman, 1979). Characterological self-blame, once established, would also seem to negate the motivation for discrepancy reduction because, although bad character is blamable, it is also uncontrollable.

Although characterological self-blame may negate the motivation toward discrepancy reduction, it does not diminish the degree of self-focusing. As long as low energy levels persist, self-focusing will be maintained. This continued self-focusing contributes to the negative affect experienced by the depressed. However, it does not contribute to the attributions or self-esteem deficits seen in depression (see Ingram, 1990, for a review).

Self-Efficacy Expectations

Being hedonistic individuals, we tend to engage in behaviors that help us obtain what we want and that we believe we can do. These behaviors are typically oriented toward goals that we value highly and will lead to desired outcomes (Maddux, 1991). Bandura (1977) has postulated that one of the prime determinants of our choice of behaviors is self-efficacy judgments or a judgment of the ability to successfully execute a behavior that will produce a desired outcome. Most studies (e.g., Condiotte & Lichtenstein, 1981) have demonstrated that self-efficacy judgments are good predictors of behavior and that they directly influence behavioral intentions as well as behavior (Maddux, Norton, & Stoltenberg, 1986).

Self-efficacy has also been viewed as contributing to problems of psychological adjustment (Maddux, 1991). According to this approach, adjustment problems arise when behavioral expectations are unrealistic or inaccurate, when behavioral outcomes are undervalued or overvalued, or when it is perceived that a desired behavior cannot be accomplished, not because of a lack of skill, but because of a lack of capability to perform the behavior. There are a number of both correlational and experimental studies (see Maddux, 1991, for a review) that have demonstrated that low self-efficacy expectations are a dominant feature in depression and may be causally related.

One source of information that influences self-efficacy expectations is a person's physiological state (Bandura, 1982). In arriving at an assessment of capabilities, a person makes use of factors such as energy levels, particularly when physical exertion is required. One of the primary symptoms of depression is low energetic arousal, and depressed individuals exhibit a preference for sedentary activities, a lack of motivation, and various levels of fatigue. In the extreme, even small activities such as brushing teeth are viewed as monumental (Beck, 1967). Maddux (1991) has suggested that the low self-efficacy expectations held by depressed people are due to a skills deficit. However, self-efficacy is not concerned "with the skills one has but with judgments of what one can do with the skills one possesses" (Bandura, 1977). Lewinsohn and Larson (1982) found that depressed people have negative expectancies for events pertaining to the self but not for events that affect others, suggesting that the depressed have low self-efficacy expectations or low expectations of their ability to perform behaviors (Maddux, 1991).

This decline in self-efficacy or the perceived ability to perform given tasks can reasonably be attributed to the low energetic arousal experienced by the depressed person, because a physiological state of low energy levels represents a dominant factor in judging one's capabilities and personal resources (Thayer, 1989). Low energy levels cause people to perceive themselves as having fewer resources for performing a behavior, particularly ones that require an expenditure of energy. As a result, depressed people may resist initiating and persisting in adaptive behaviors.

Dysfunctional Cognitions

One of the most consistently identified covariates of depression is that depressed people are self-deprecating and extremely pessimistic in their outlook. This finding has suggested to several researchers (e.g., Beck, Rush, Shaw, & Emery, 1979) that depressed people suffer from a distorted cognitive process that contributes significantly to the onset and maintenance of depression. There are even a number of theories of depression and treatment programs (e.g., Abramson, Seligman, & Teasdale, 1978; Beck et al., 1979) based on a cognitive model that incorporates the characteristic negativism of depressed people. Although the treatment-based programs have been shown to be effective in ameliorating depression (Robinson, Berman, & Neimeyer, 1990), the postulated role of dysfunctional cognitions in the onset of depression has received little support (Barnett & Gotlib, 1988b). The support that does exist (e.g., Cutrona, 1983; Riskind, Rholes, Brannon, & Burdick, 1987) has been obtained most frequently from studies of individuals who are already depressed or of a sample of people with various levels of depression. Studies that have undertaken to determine whether dysfunctional cognitions predict subsequent depression in nondepressed people (e.g., Rhode, Lewinsohn, & Seeley, 1990) have indicated an absence of a predictive or causal role of cognitions in depression.

Studies in which experimental manipulation of cognitions by means of success/failure, autobiographical recall, and Velten statements (see Thayer, 1989, for a review of these techniques) altered mood may be seen as supporting the idea that dysfunctional cognitions play a role in the onset of depression. However, there is evidence that even such manipulations have an effect on arousal levels and that mood is altered by this effect. Frost, Graf, and Becker (1979), for example, divided the Velten statements into those dealing with somatic suggestions (fatigue and exhaustion) and those relating to self-evaluations (e.g., low self-worth). Use of the regular induction procedure resulted in greater self-reported depression with the somatic statements than with the self-devaluations ones, an effect that was replicated by Kirchenbaum, Tomarken, and Humphrey (1985).

The finding that dysfunctional cognitions are a reliable covariate of depression (Hammen, Marks, deMayo, & Mayol, 1985) has led to a search for factors triggering the onset of these cognitions. Miranda and Persons (1988) have demonstrated that dysfunctional attitudes appear when people are in a negative mood state, which indicates that they are mood-state dependent. It has been suggested that induction of this negative mood-state is precipitated by events such as major stressors (e.g., marital discord, or death of a loved one) that prime the dysfunctional cognitions (Riskind & Rholes, 1984). However, Reda, Carpiniello, Secchiaroli, and Blanco (1985) found that some negative cognitions remained elevated among people who recovered from depression, and Barnett and Gotlib (1988a) found that the interaction between dysfunctional attitudes and stress did not predict subsequent depression, suggesting that dysfunctional cognitions are not primed by stressors. These findings are consistent with research indicating that even major life events have only a temporary effect on mood (Stone & Neale, 1984) and that major stressors are not predictive of new cases of depression (Rhode et al., 1990).

If environmental stressors do not reliably contribute to the development of the persistent negative mood-state and the accompanying dysfunctional attitudes characteristic of depression, the search for the priming function must shift to another arena, most likely, low energetic arousal. In a series of studies by Thayer (1987) and Thayer, Takahashe, and Pauli (1988), participants rated pessimism and personal problems as being most serious during periods of low energetic arousal and indicated that, as energetic arousal increased, so did feelings of optimism. Such research suggests that energetic arousal has a cognitive influence that is probably mediated by a person's perception of personal resources (Thayer, 1989) and by the implications that this perception has for self-efficacy expectations.

When energetic arousal is low, available resources requiring energy are also perceived as being low, and self-efficacy expectations are low. In this state, a person may experience enhanced feelings of helplessness and hopelessness about altering and resolving some stressor, focusing instead on interpreting the causes and consequences of the low energy and attributing the cause of the distress and feelings of low self-efficacy to the stressor itself (Ginsberg & Brown, 1982). Although stressors can and do promote dysfunctional cognitions, low energetic arousal can enhance feelings of pessimism (e.g., Thayer et al., 1988) and thereby exacerbate the dysfunctional cognitions. However, in the absence of a maintaining variable such as persistent low energy level, the effect of the stressor on dysfunctional cognitions would be temporary (Blaney, 1986; Stone & Neale, 1984). In contrast, high energetic arousal induces feelings of optimism and an ability to meet and solve daily issues and hassles. Although low energetic arousal can enhance feelings of pessimism, the degree of pessimism and the speed with which it develops varies. Obviously, every person who experiences a persistent level of low energetic arousal does not become clinically depressed. It may be that people who are more prone to low energetic arousal and misattribute the cause of low energy are more vulnerable to depression.

Beck (1967) and Beck et al. (1979) have postulated a cognitive triad consisting of a negative view of the self, the world, and the future as central to the development and maintenance of depression. According to this triad, depressed people perceive themselves as being inadequate, defective, and lacking the attributes to attain happiness. They view the world as presenting unreasonable demands and obstacles to reaching desired goals, and they believe that these difficulties will persist indefinitely.

Given the persistence of low energy levels and its negative effects on personal resources, these cognitions are understandable. A person who has little energy, who feels as though even the slightest tasks require excessive effort and taxes their personal resources may naturally feel inadequate and defective. And a person who experiences a state of low energetic arousal for an extended time without being able to explain it or see any possibility for amelioration would naturally have a negative view of the future.

Low energetic arousal does, therefore, have the potential for specifying or pinpointing a domain of maladaptive content about the self that is particularly important for depression. To the extent that low energy levels persist over time, the depressed individual would be expected to attribute the lack of energy to some stable, global cause, and such an attribution could fuel additional feelings of hopelessness and lead to even greater depression. Cutrona (1983), for example, demonstrated that one's attributional style influences subsequent depression, which suggests that low energy levels combined with the expectation of the persistence of low energy sets the stage for the emergence or maintenance of depression.

The evidence (e.g., Thayer, 1987; Thayer et al., 1988) suggesting that low energetic arousal levels are causally related to dysfunctional cognitions is, at best, preliminary. However, this construct represents a logical and parsimonious explanation for the existence of negative cognitions, not only in depressed people but also in nondepressed people who experience transient negative cognitions. The construct also represents a readily testable hypothesis.

Negative Affect

Beck (1967) has presented one of the more complete descriptions of the symptoms of depression. Although he identified five categories of symptoms including emotional, cognitive, motivational, vegetative, and physical manifestations, these symptoms could just as easily be categorized into psychological and somatic symptoms. When viewed in either manner, the symptoms of depression are characteristic of a general state of negative affect. Watson and Pennebaker (1989) have argued convincingly that negative affect represents a state of somatopsychic distress rather than just emotional distress, a state that describes the combination of distress-related symptoms experienced by the depressed person.

Negative affect represents a subjective distress state (Watson, Clark, & Tellegen, 1988) that is described by terms such as *anxiety, worthlessness, dissatisfaction, sadness, irritability*, and *depression*. The term describes the distress experienced by both depressed and nondepressed people; however, the precipitating factors and the duration of the negative affect seem to differ dramatically in these two populations. For nondepressed people, negative affect is precipitated by both chronic and acute stressors (e.g., Eckenrode, 1984), and nondepressed individuals recover rapidly from even intense mood states (Blaney, 1986; Eckenrode, 1984) with little enduring effect (Stone & Neale, 1984).

In stark contrast, the literature suggests that depressed people experience extreme negative affect and an inability to experience positive affect relatively persistently (Beck, 1967; Watson, Clark, & Carey, 1988). Watson and Clark's (1984) extensive review of the literature on negative affect showed that individuals who are persistently high in negative affect experience distress in both stressful and nonstressful situations, suggesting that these individuals have a biological propensity toward having high basal distress.

As was stated earlier in this chapter, low energetic arousal is a dominant characteristic of depression (Beck, 1967), although many depressed individuals also experience heightened arousal. Thayer (1989) has taken the position that depression includes a strong component of "tense-tiredness," or high tense arousal, as well as low energetic arousal. Watson, Clark, and Carey (1988) demonstrated that depressed subjects exhibit high negative affective arousal. Low positive affect (Watson, Clark, & Carey, 1988), conceptualized as low energetic arousal, however, is the unique characteristic of depression that distinguishes it from other disorders such as anxiety, phobias, and obsessive-compulsive symptoms (Watson, Clark, & Carey, 1988). Thus, persistently low energetic arousal plays a key role in producing negative affect, just as it does in enhancing self-focus of attention and low self-efficacy expectations. Both of these phenomena contribute to feelings of negative affect.

Self-focus of attention produces negative affect because people become aware of the existence of the negative discrepancy (Duval & Wicklund, 1972) and because the persistence of low energy levels leads people to believe that the probability of discrepancy reduction is low (Carver & Scheier, 1981). Low energy levels also contribute to low self-efficacy expectations because personal resources are perceived as being less when energy levels are low (Thayer, 1989). And when people perceive themselves as not being capable of performing activities leading to desired outcomes, self-devaluation (Bandura, 1982) and subjective distress (Maddux, 1991) or negative affect can result.

Fatigue or low energetic arousal can also suggest to an individual that something is physically wrong, and this perception of failing health seems to promote negative affect. Buchwald, Sullivan, and Komaroff (1987) reported that 37% of their patients experienced tiredness and fatigue prior to their illness. Feelings of fatigue have been found to be one of the best predictors of migraine headache (Harrigan, Kues, Ricks, & Smith, 1984).

People tend not only to sense the signs of impending illness but also to interpret them and respond emotionally to them (Lundh, 1987). Westbrook and Viney (1982) and others (e.g., Abram, 1972) demonstrated that the onset of disease is associated with the experience of uncertainty, anxiety, and depression. Watson and Pennebaker (1989) have demonstrated that health complaints are correlated with negative affect. Eckenrode (1984) has revealed that physical symptoms show a greater relationship with mood than do stressors.

In addition to contributing to negative affect, the suggestion of an impending decline in physical health and the introspective and ruminative nature of individuals who experience high negative affect (Watson & Clark, 1984) should result in increased physical symptom reporting. Watson and Pennebaker (1989) recently summarized the research demonstrating that negative affect is related to perceived health complaints but not with actual health status. This finding is consistent with the evidence indicating that the physical complaints of the depressed can seldom be traced to a physical abnormality (Beck, 1967). Apparently the self-focusing and the suggestion of an impending illness resulting from the low energy levels produces hypervigilant individuals who scan for bodily sensations and minor discomforts and interpret them as painful or pathological (see Watson & Pennebaker, 1989, for a brief review of this literature).

The Relationship of Carbohydrate Consumption, Energetic Arousal, and Depression

As the foregoing discussion shows, the negative affect that is characteristic of the depressed person can be viewed as arising from at least three sources: (a) low energy levels and their implications for physical health, (b) enhanced self-focusing, and (c) low self-efficacy expectations. Low energy levels may also contribute to somatic complaints by creating a hypervigilant individual who is overly sensitive to bodily sensations and discomfort. Thus, persistent low energy levels are postulated as being capable of producing the psychological, cognitive, and somatic symptoms characteristic of and indicative of depression.

The relationship between carbohydrate consumption, energetic arousal, and depression is depicted in Figure 4.2. From this figure, it can be seen that a variety of factors are capable of inducing low energetic arousal. One of these factors is simple carbohydrate consumption. Once the low energetic arousal is induced and persists over time, the psychological, cognitive, and somatic symptoms characteristic of depression emerge.

This schematic representation takes a unidirectional approach indicating that environmental factors such as simple carbohydrate consumption can produce low energetic arousal which in turn produces the covariates of depression, which result in the manifestation of depression. It should not be assumed, however, that a bidirectional effect cannot or does not exist in some instances. For example, Figure 4.2 also indicates that

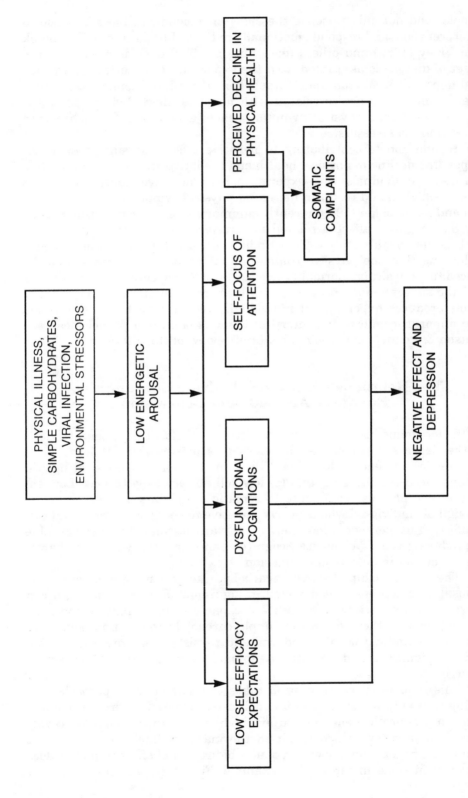

Figure 4.2. Schematic representation of the relationship of simple carbohydrate consumption, energy level, and depression.

feelings of low energetic arousal produce dysfunctional cognitions, which does not preclude an effect of cognitions on perceived energy levels or depression. Changing cognitions from negative to positive seems to have an energy-arousing effect (Thayer, 1989). Similarly, negative cognitions result in diminished feelings of energetic arousal and a depressed mood (Velten, 1968). The expression of negative cognitions have consistently been demonstrated to enhance feelings of depression through techniques such as the Velten (1968) procedure. Similarly, feelings of depression and low energetic arousal can stimulate simple carbohydrate consumption. The important point is that the generation of low energetic arousal and negative cognitions will have only a transitory effect in the absence of maintaining conditions. A persistent level of depression is postulated as existing only to the extent that some maintaining variable, such as continuous consumption of simple carbohydrates, persist and produce a continuous low energy level. This hypothesis would explain why mood induction procedures, such as the Velten (1968) procedure, can induce a depressed state, but the induced state is short lived.

Conclusion

Expectancy is one psychological factor that has been suggested as an explanation for the effect that dietary variables such as carbohydrates may have on depression. However, well-designed studies control for such extraneous variables. Furthermore, some studies have not shown expectancy to be a strong influential variable. Therefore, expectancy probably does not provide a good explanation for the effect that carbohydrates may have on depression.

Studies have indicated that simple carbohydrates may generate feelings of fatigue or a state of low energetic arousal in some individuals. If this state of low energetic arousal persists, it is postulated that the covariates of depression such as dysfunctional cognitions and low self-efficacy expectations, which are symptoms of depression, emerge. Studies also suggest that the covariates of depression can emerge once fatigue or low energetic arousal is induced. Consequently, it is assumed that simple carbohydrate consumption can induce depression but that its effect is mediated by the generation of fatigue or low energetic arousal.

Part III

Behavioral Effects of Food

5

The Effects of Diet on Mood and Task Performance

Food is one of those commodities that everyone must consume to survive and lead an active and productive life. If we deprive ourselves of food we experience stomach contractions and perhaps some degree of tension or anxiety characteristic of hunger. Once food is consumed, these symptoms disappear. If we overeat, as may occur on special occasions, we may feel unpleasantly overstuffed, lethargic, and unmotivated and are likely to attribute these feelings to the meal that has been eaten.

Although food consumption has been associated with many different feeling states and emotions, only recently have investigators systematically and scientifically attempted to determine the psychological and behavioral effects of food consumption, both on so-called normal individuals and individuals who have various types of disorders. As I discussed in chapter 3, a lot of the research has been focused on the amino acids that act as precursors for neurotransmitters and on specific foods, particularly carbohydrates, which can alter the synthesis of neurotransmitters such as serotonin. In this chapter I focus on the mood- and performance-altering effects of several amino acids, of carbohydrates, and of other dietary factors (i.e., meal size and type). Most of the research I review was conducted with people not known to be suffering from any disorder.

Dietary Factors Influencing Mood

Tryptophan Administration

The data demonstrating the mood-altering effects of tryptophan come from a variety of studies. The primary purpose of most of these studies was not to investigate tryptophan's effect on mood; however, they all included an assessment of the mood-altering effect of tryptophan. For example, Greenwood, Friedel, Bond, Curzon, and Lader (1974) found that an intravenous L-tryptophan infusion of 75 and 100 mg/kg of body weight increased people's feelings of drowsiness, clumsiness, lethargy, and of being mentally slow, dreamy, incompetent, and bored (see Table 5.1). As Table 5.1 reveals, there was no difference in subjective feelings between the 75 and 100 mg/ kg infusion, suggesting that the effect of tryptophan plateaus after a sufficiently large dose is received. While investigating the neuroendocrine effects of tryptophan Delgado, Charney, Price, Landis, and Heninger

Table 5.1. Effects of Tryptophan on Mood Ratings

	Placebo: tryptophan (75 mg/kg)		Placebo: tryptophan (100 mg/kg)		Tryptophan (75 mg/kg: 100 mg/kg)	
	t	p	t	p	t	p
Drowsy—alert	5.23	<0.001	6.22	<0.001	0.98	N.S.
Clumsy—well coordinated	5.91	<0.001	4.05	<0.01	1.86	N.S.
Lethargic—energetic	3.91	<0.01	3.94	<0.01	0.3	N.S.
Mentally slow—quick witted	2.73	<0.05	3.4	<0.01	0.12	N.S.
Dreamy—attentive	3.47	<0.01	3.53	<0.01	0.06	N.S.
Incompetent—proficient	3.67	<0.01	2.7	<0.05	0.96	N.S.
Bored—interested	3.14	<0.01	1.2	N.S.	1.14	N.S.
Factor I	5.93	<0.001	5.08	<0.001	0.8	N.S.
Relaxed—tense	2.06	N.S.	4.08	<0.01	2.02	N.S.
Calm—excited	1.6	N.S.	4.75	<0.01	3.64	0.01
Factor III	1.35	N.S.	4.9	<0.01	3.17	<0.05

Note. Change in each dimension occurs in the direction of the first adjective of each pair. N.S. = not significant. From "The Acute Effects of Intravenous Infusion of L-Tryptophan in Normal Subjects," by M. H. Greenwood, J. Friedel, A. J. Bond, G. Curzon, & M. H. Lader, 1974, *Clinical Pharmacology and Therapeutics, 16*, p. 458. Copyright 1974 by Mosby Year Book, Inc. Reprinted with permission.

(1975) demonstrated that after an infusion of 7 gm of tryptophan, participants rated themselves lower on measures of talkativeness, happiness, and energy and higher on drowsiness. Both studies suggest that an intravenous infusion of a relatively large dose of tryptophan depresses energy levels and induces feelings of fatigue and lethargy.

Because tryptophan is seldom injected intravenously, it was important to determine whether a similar effect occurs following oral consumption. Several studies (Greenwood, Lader, Kantameneni, & Curzon, 1975; Smith & Prockop, 1962; Yuwiler et al., 1981) confirmed that consumption of tryptophan (30 to 100 mg/kg of body weight) results in increased feelings of drowsiness, fatigue, and lethargy. These findings have also been supported by electroencephalographic data. Several studies (e.g., Greenwood et al., 1974, 1975) have demonstrated an increase in the theta waveband (4.0 to 7.5 Hz) following tryptophan consumption. Theta waves are characteristic of the drowsy state a person experiences as they are falling asleep (Tizard, 1966).

It is important to note that, although these studies demonstrated consistent dietary effects for tryptophan administered orally or by injection, rather large doses were administered to obtain these effects: the minimum dose was 30 mg/kg, and all but one of the studies administered at least 50 mg/kg of tryptophan. Other studies suggest that dose is a significant point. Leathwood and Pollet (1983) found only a nonsignificant trend toward fatigue and lethargy following a 500-mg dose of tryptophan, suggesting that the mood-altering effect of tryptophan is dose related. Both Smith and Prockop (1962) and Yuwiler et al. (1981) revealed that stronger

Table 5.2. Composition of an Amino Acid Drink Void of Tryptophan

Amino acid	Amount (g)
L-Alanine	5.5
L-Arginine	4.9
L-Cysteine	2.7
Glycine	3.2
L-Histidine	3.2
L-Isoleucine	8.0
L-Leucine	13.5
L-Lysine monohydrochloride	11.0
L-Methionine	3.0
L-Phenylalanine	5.7
L-Proline	12.2
L-Serine	6.9
L-Threonine	6.9
L-Tyrosine	6.9
L-Valine	8.9

Note. A balanced amino acid drink would contain 2.3 g tryptophan.

effects occurred with larger doses of tryptophan. Given the nonsignificant effect demonstrated by Leathwood and Pollet (1983), it seems as though a dose greater than 500 mg is needed to induce a significant effect.

Tryptophan Depletion

If tryptophan administration has the effect of increasing fatigue and lethargy and decreasing energy, the logical assumption seems to be that depleting tryptophan would have an energy-enhancing effect. However, because tryptophan is the precursor of serotonin, depleting tryptophan would also result in a decline in serotonin, which is correlated with depression (Van Praag, 1980). A more logical hypothesis is that a depletion of tryptophan would induce a depressed mood. Several studies have addressed this issue and revealed that tryptophan depletion does in fact induce a state of mild depression in nondepressed individuals.

Conducting a tryptophan depletion study requires implementing one of two procedures that deplete tryptophan from plasma. The most obvious procedure is to administer a diet that contains little tryptophan. Administering diets including low-tryptophan foods such as puffed rice, peaches, salad, potatoes, and carrots, Delgado et al. (1989) demonstrated a 16% decline in plasma tryptophan levels over the nine days in which this diet was followed. Although a special diet, such as that used by Delgado et al. (1989), does result in a decline in plasma tryptophan levels, this is not the most efficient way of depleting plasma tryptophan levels because any diet containing whole foods will contain some tryptophan. The lowest tryptophan diet Delgado et al. (1989) prepared still contained 200 mg of tryptophan. The best and fastest way to deplete plasma tryptophan levels is to prepare an amino acid cocktail, which is a beverage containing all amino acids except tryptophan. Young, Smith, Pihl, and Ervin (1985), for example, prepared a 100-g mixture containing amino acids in an amount approximately equal to that contained in a 500-g steak. As Table 5.2 reveals, this mixture contans 15 amino acids other than tryptophan. A balanced amino acid mixture that can be used as a control drink can be made by adding 2.3 g of tryptophan. Similarly, additional tryptophan can be added to the drink to test the effect of tryptophan supplementation.

The amino acids are mixed in 300 ml of water with 10 ml of chocolate syrup, and a small packet of saccharin or some peppermint extract are added to increase palatability. Delgado et al. (1990) have recommended administering methionine, cysteine, and arginine in capsule form to mask their unpleasant taste and to administer the remaining amino acids in a beverage flavored with chocolate. Even with this alteration, some people experience nausea following consumption and dislike the taste.

A more palatable mixture (Abbott et al., 1992) consists of 189 g of gelatin dissolved in 450 ml of hot water. After cooling, 180 ml of a 50% w/v homogenate of fresh pineapple is added. Just prior to serving, 0.5 g L-histidine, 1.4 g L-isoleucine, 1.35 g L-leucine, 2.9 g L tyrosine, 0.45 g l-valine, 0.2 g saccharine, and 75 g chocolate syrup are added. This mixture is stirred and served with capsules of 1.35 g L-cysteine, which has an unpalatable taste. To obtain a nutritionally balanced mixture, 1.15 g of tryptophan would be added. This 50-g mixture results in a depletion of plasma tryptophan similar to that of the 100-g mixture previously described.

Several studies have used either the dietary approach or the amino acid mixture to investigate the effect of depleting plasma tryptophan on mood. Young et al. (1985) assessed the mood-altering effect of tryptophan depletion by comparing the affective responses of men who were given a tryptophan-depleted amino acid mixture with those given a balanced or tryptophan-supplemented mixture. Increased depression was obtained for the tryptophan depletion group. Smith, Phil, Young, and Ervin (1987) replicated this effect and also demonstrated that the mood-lowering effect of the tryptophan depletion mixture was not altered by informing participants of the probable cause of their shift in mood or by placing them in a pleasant or unpleasant environment. This finding suggests that the mood-altering effect of lowering plasma tryptophan levels is endogenously produced and can probably be attributed to a decline in brain serotonin levels.

It is important to realize that the level of depression experienced by the participants was in the range of mild depression; these studies provide no evidence that participants would have experienced more severe depression if the tryptophan depletion had persisted over time. Delgado et al. (1989) did provide some insight into this issue when they had subjects adhere to a 700- or 200-mg tryptophan diet over a 9 day period. Because a normal diet contains approximately 1200 mg of tryptophan, participants were consuming a tryptophan-reduced rather than a tryptophan-depleted diet. Sixty percent of the participants experienced a decline in energy after nine days, but a specific measure of depression was not included, so it is not known whether depression would have been affected. However, because energy decline is one of the major symptoms of depression, it is reasonable to conclude that they may have experienced some alteration in mood.

The Delgado et al. (1989) study suggests that reducing tryptophan consumption over a relatively short period of time may have a very mild mood-altering effect. An acute depletion of tryptophan from the diet, however, has the effect of inducing a state of mild depression (e.g., Smith et al., 1987), probably because of the relative reduction in plasma tryptophan levels. The dietary manipulation used by Delgado et al. (1989) resulted in a 16% decline in plasma tryptophan level after nine days on the tryptophan-restricted diet. However, consumption of an amino acid beverage, which totally excludes tryptophan, results in a 76% (Young et al., 1985) to an 82% (Smith et al., 1987) reduction in plasma tryptophan levels. A similar decline in plasma tryptophan levels in rats results in a decrease in brain serotonin levels of about 50% (Biggio, Fadda, Fanni, Tagliamonte, & Gessa, 1974). These findings suggest that the dietary alteration used by Delgado et al. (1989) did not affect plasma tryptophan levels sufficiently to significantly alter the synthesis of brain serotonin.

The tryptophan-depletion approach, in contrast, reduced plasma tryptophan levels by more than 75%. Data obtained with rats suggest that such a reduction results in an alteration in brain serotonin levels by as much as 50%. With such a dramatic alteration in brain serotonin levels, an alteration in mood would be expected, and this alteration would be in the direction of increased depression. This is exactly what Young et al. (1985) and Smith et al. (1987) found. However, it must be remembered that Young et al. (1985) and Smith et al. (1987) studied male participants and that depression occurs about twice as frequently in women (Georgotas & Cancro, 1988). Delgado et al. (1989) found that women manifested an 80% greater reduction in plasma tryptophan levels than did men following the tryptophan-reduced diet, suggesting that women may be more sensitive to alterations in the tryptophan content of a meal and more susceptible to experiencing depression following chronic reduction in tryptophan intake.

It is also possible that there is a subpopulation of individuals whose plasma tryptophan levels are less stable and more sensitive to dietary alteration. Delgado et al. (1990) revealed that both male and female patients on psychotropic medication whose depression was in remission experienced a return of their clinical depression following consumption of an amino acid beverage void of tryptophan. However, all previously depressed subjects did not experience a relapse of depression following the tryptophan depletion. Melancholic patients and patients who failed to respond to more than one prior antidepressant trial were more likely to relapse. It may be that the more chronically depressed individuals or individuals who are more susceptible to depression may also be more likely to respond to tryptophan depletion and its subsequent reduction in serotonin synthesis.

Abbott et al. (1991) provided support for this hypothesis: Their participants consumed a tryptophan-depleted amino acid beverage but experienced no decline in depression. One of the key characteristics in this study was that participants were carefully screened to ensure that they had very low baseline levels of depression. Consequently, it appears as if tryptophan depletion will increase feelings of depression in previously non-depressed subjects, but its effect occurs primarily in individuals who have some degree of susceptibility to depression. It would be important to identify the variables increasing a person's susceptibility to depression from tryptophan depletion.

Tyrosine Administration

There are several studies that have investigated the potential effect that tyrosine may have on mood. The basis for these studies is that tyrosine is the precursor of the catecholamines, dopamine and norepinephrine. Ingestion of tyrosine can, under certain circumstances, modify the neurotransmission of these amines (Wurtman, Hefti, & Melamed, 1981). Because both dopamine and norepinephrine deficiencies have been implicated in depression (van Praag, 1985), it is reasonable to assume that they may have an impact on mood.

Leathwood and Pollet (1983) administered 500 mg tyrosine along with a high-carbohydrate, low-protein meal and detected no significant effect on mood. The meal may have had a confounding effect in this study, because this meal pattern should enhance plasma tryptophan levels and, therefore potentially counteract the effect of the tyrosine supplement. However, in a subsequent study, Lieberman, Corkin, Spring, Growdon, and Wurtman (1983) administered 100 mg/kg tyrosine in the morning following an overnight fast and also found no mood-altering effect of tyrosine.

These two studies suggest that tyrosine has little effect on mood, perhaps because tyrosine hydroxylase is subject to end-product inhibition when the catecholaminergic neurons are quiescent. This lack of effect should exist in participants whose only activity is to consume tyrosine and then complete a series of behavioral tests including an assessment of mood. To detect a tyrosine-induced effect, it would be necessary to have participants engage in some activity that would activate the catecholaminergic neurons. In support of this assumption, Banderet and Lieberman (1989) found that individuals subjected to altitude and cold stress experienced fewer psychological symptoms, such as dizziness and fatigue, when taking a 100 mg/kg tyrosine supplement.

Aspartame

When the two amino acids aspartate and phenylalanine are combined, the result is an exceptionally sweet dipeptide called aspartame. Tests have shown that aspartame is 180 to 200 times sweeter than sugar. Because aspartame is a very low-calorie sweetener and does not have the bitter aftertaste frequently associated with other artificial sweeteners such as saccharin, its use in products ranging from beverages to puddings has increased exponentially since the FDA approved its use in 1981.

Since its introduction into the food supply, aspartame, marketed under the trade name of Nutrasweet, has come under repeated attack. Probably the most frequent and persistent complaint related to the use of aspartame is that some individuals have experienced adverse behavioral reactions following its use. At the request of the FDA, the Centers for Disease Control in Atlanta investigated 517 complaints associated with the consumption of aspartame. Sixty-seven percent of these individuals complained of a variety of neurological or behavioral symptoms following aspartame ingestion, including headache; a variety of mood alterations such as anxiety, agitation, and irritability; and depression, insomnia, dizziness, and fatigue. Less frequently reported were gastrointestinal, allergic, and menstrual symptoms.

Reports by physicians of symptoms provoked by aspartame consumption also appeared in medical journals, which further bolstered the belief that aspartame consumption could cause a series of physical disorders, such as seizures (Wurtman, 1985), and mental disorders, such as panic attack (Drake, 1986). These reports occurred in conjunction with research revealing that aspartame ingestion increased both the plasma and brain levels of phenylalanine in rats. If aspartame is consumed in conjunction with carbohydrates, the elevation in plasma and brain phenylalanine is even greater (Yokogoshi, Roberts, Caballero, & Wurtman, 1984).

This concern over the behavioral and medical effects of aspartame consumption has resulted in the publication of a book titled *Aspartame (Nutrasweet*): Is it Safe?* (Roberts, 1990a) which attempts to alert the public to the dangers of this sweetener. It has also prompted the scientific community to conduct studies, mostly behavioral studies, to investigate the consequences of aspartame consumption.

Schiffman et al. (1987) recruited 40 people who believed that they had a history of experiencing headache and other neurologic symptoms within 24 hours of consuming products containing aspartame. To determine whether there was any validity to the allegations of these individuals, Schiffman and her associates administered a 10 mg/kg dose of aspartame or placebo at 8:00 a.m., 10:00 a.m., and 12:00 noon in a double-blind format. Interestingly, people taking the placebo reported about as many headaches as did subjects taking the aspartame, which suggested that something other than aspartame had caused the headaches. Participants also experienced a variety of other symptoms such as dizziness, fatigue, nausea, and anxiety as frequently when taking the placebo as when taking the aspartame.

Although this study demonstrated that aspartame does not seem to have an acute effect on behavioral symptoms, it did not reveal whether there are long-term or cumulative effects. Leon, Hunninghake, Bell, Rassin, and Tephly (1989) provided an answer to that question by having participants take either a placebo or 200 mg/kg of aspartame a day for 24 weeks. In this double-blind study no differences were found between the two groups in terms of the number of headaches or other symptoms they experienced.

None of these studies address whether aspartame alters mood. Yokogoshi et al. (1984) demonstrated that aspartame, by itself or with carbo-hydrates, elevated the plasma and brain levels of tyrosine and phenylal-anine. Because these are the substrates of the catecholamines, it is possible that they could have a mood-altering effect. Steglink, Filer, and Baker (1988) had healthy adults fast for 12 hours and then consume three 12-ounce beverages, each providing 10 mg/kg of aspartame, at 2-hour in-tervals. A person would have to drink seven-and-a-half 12-ounce servings of a commercially prepared aspartame drink over a 4-hour period to obtain the amount of aspartame supplied by this formula. Plasma aspartate lev-els were not significantly affected, but plasma phenylalanine concentra-tions rose 25%. These levels are considered to be within the normal post-prandial range, which suggests that aspartame should have little behavioral effect.

In addition to studies such as those conducted by Steglink et al. (1988), several more recent studies have focused directly on the effects of aspar-tame on mood. Pivonka and Grunewald (1990) and Lapierre, Greenblatt, Goddard, Harmatz, and Shader (1990) investigated the mood-altering ef-fect of a single dose of aspartame; neither of these studies showed an effect. Ryan-Harshman, Leiter, and Anderson (1987) extended these find-ings by demonstrating that neither a large dose of aspartame (10.08 gm) consumed over time nor a large single dose of phenylalanine (10.08 gm) had any effect on mood or the types of symptoms such as stomachache, dizziness, and nausea associated with aspartame consumption. These studies support rather strongly the conclusion that aspartame is safe for most individuals and that it should be expected to have little if any effect on a person's mood.

Carbohydrates

In chapter 3, I presented evidence suggesting that a carbohydrate-rich meal may increase brain serotonin synthesis in humans as it does in rats. When these data are coupled with the evidence demonstrating that tryp-tophan supplementation can alter behavior, the logical suggestion is that a carbohydrate-rich meal may have the same effect as tryptophan supple-mentation does. The studies investigating the influence of carbohydrates on mood have assessed this effect following breakfast and lunch. Both time periods have been the focus of attention because a period of fasting prior to carbohydrate ingestion is necessary to get the rise in the plasma tryp-tophan/LNAA ratio. If a test animal or human has not fasted for a suffi-cient period of time, the effect of the carbohydrate-rich meal on tryptophan ratios will be blunted, and the possibility of finding an effect may be precluded.

There are only a few studies focusing on the effect of breakfast meal composition on mood in adults. Brody and Wolitzky (1983) found that a 100-gm sucrose drink, consumed between 8:00 and 8:30 a.m., had no effect on mood 20 minutes or 4 hours later. Spring et al. (1983), however, found that the effect of a carbohydrate-rich meal did alter mood, but the effect depended on the sex and age of the participant and the time in which the meal was consumed. These investigators had men and women between the ages of 18 and 65 consume either a high-carbohydrate or a high-protein breakfast or a high-carbohydrate or high-protein lunch to enable them to assess the effect of meal composition at both time periods. This study revealed that women reported more sleepiness after eating the carbohydrate meal, collapsing across meal time. Older men reported less tension and greater feelings of calmness after the carbohydrate breakfast.

Little can be concluded from these two studies other than that any mood-altering effect of a carbohydrate-rich breakfast is, at best, a weak effect. Both studies included measures of a variety of moods and either found no effect or a marginal effect, and this effect was demonstrated only among a restricted sample consisting of older men. There was little consistency between the studies; therefore, it is difficult to draw any firm conclusion from them.

Findings from studies investigating the effect of a carbohydrate-rich diet on mood consumed at lunch time have been similarly weak. Spring et al. (1989) assessed mood at five different times following either a carbohydrate-rich, protein-rich, balanced, or no-lunch condition and found only one mood-altering effect: an increase in fatigue when the carbohydrate-rich condition was compared with the no-meal condition. However, when Lieberman, Spring, and Garfield (1986) compared the mood-altering effect of a lunch-time meal consisting predominately of carbohydrates or protein, the strongest effect they could find was a nonsignificant trend toward a decline in vigor and an increase in sleepiness following carbohydrate consumption. Smith, Leekam, Ralph, and McNeill (1988) compared the mood-altering effect of a high-protein versus a high-starch or high-sugar meal and found no differences in mood before or after consumption. Similarly, Christensen and Redig (1993) found no mood-altering effect of a lunch-time carbohydrate-rich meal when compared to a protein-rich or a no-meal condition. The primary effect identified was a consistent alteration in mood over time and across all meal conditions.

These results clearly indicate that the mood-altering effects of carbohydrates are either very weak or nonexistent. There were slight differences in the three studies that could have accounted for the different results, but even in the study that identified a fatigue-producing effect following a lunch time carbohydrate load (i.e., Spring et al., 1989) this effect was not part of a significant main or interaction effect. Consequently, this effect should also be viewed as weak or nonexistent. It also seems improbable that a carbohydrate-rich meal consumed in the evening would affect mood because such a meal does not elevate the plasma tryptophan/LNAA ratio (Ashley, Barclay, Chauffard, Moennoz, & Leathwood, 1982). The inability to consistently demonstrate a mood-altering effect of a carbohydrate-rich meal is somewhat surprising given the data indicating that carbohydrates elevate the plasma tryptophan/LNAA ratio and that tryptophan supplementation consistently induces an alteration in mood. There are some data, however, that seem to provide a reasonable explanation.

Ashley, Liardon, and Leathwood (1985) reanalyzed Fernstrom and

Wurtman's (1972) data obtained from fasted rats and, using the sum of 5-HT + 5-HIAA as the measure of synthesis, identified that the tryptophan/LNAA ratio must at least double before reliable increases in 5-HT synthesis can occur. Curzon and Sarna (1984) suggested that a 50% rise in the tryptophan/LNAA ratio must occur to produce significant increases in 5-HIAA levels. From these two studies, we can assume that a 50% to 100% increase in the tryptophan/LNAA ratio is needed to produce a significant change in brain 5-HT synthesis. Several studies indicate that a change of this magnitude is very difficult to obtain in humans, and it does not occur following a carbohydrate-rich diet composed of whole foods.

Ashley, Fleury, Golay, Maeder, & Leathwood (1985) revealed that a high-carbohydrate drink containing only 1.6% protein raised the plasma tryptophan/LNAA ratio only 16%, whereas a 400 mg addition of tryptophan to the high-carbohydrate drink increased the ratio by 180%. Teff, Young, and Blundell (1989) revealed that a high-carbohydrate pudding containing 0% protein resulted in a significant rise in the tryptophan/LNAA ratio, whereas as little as 4% protein blocked this rise. More significant is the fact that even the high-carbohydrate pudding containing 0% protein produced only a 26% rise in the tryptophan/LNAA ratio.

These two studies suggest that even a pure carbohydrate meal containing absolutely no protein does not alter the tryptophan/LNAA ratio sufficiently to cause an appreciable change in brain 5-HT. This is supported by Teff, Young, Marchand, and Botez's (1989) demonstration that a 100 gm carbohydrate drink did not affect CSF tryptophan levels or its metabolite 5-HIAA. When these findings are coupled with the fact that as little as 4% protein can block the rise in the plasma tryptophan/LNAA ratio and that virtually anything we consume contains at least this much protein, the logical conclusion is that any change in mood or behavior resulting from a carbohydrate load is almost certainly not due to an alteration in brain 5-HT. A danish, for example, contains 5 gm protein, which is about 10% of total calories. Pure rice contains about 10% protein. Consequently, the only way to obtain a pure carbohydrate load is to consume a pure carbohydrate such as sucrose, and this is seldom done in an ad lib environment.

Findings that a carbohydrate-rich meal has little effect on mood do not mean, however, that meal consumption has no effect on mood. The lethargy and lack of motivation that can follow the consumption of a large meal prompted some researchers to investigate whether meal size may affect mood. Michaud, Musse, Nicolas, and Mejean (1991) compared the mood-altering effect of consuming an average of 389 calories at breakfast with consuming an average of 634 calories. Participants showed no difference in feelings of tranquility or alertness. A no-difference effect was also found by Smith, Ralph, and McNeill (1991) when they compared participants who consumed 206 calories and 78% of their normal lunch intake with those who consumed their typical intake. Smith et al.'s (1991) participants, however, felt more feeble, dreamy, and bored and less alert, excited, clear-headed, energetic, quick-witted, friendly, sociable, and elated following lunch consumption, suggesting that consuming any lunch may make a person less active and alert.

Dietary Factors Influencing Performance

In addition to focusing attention on the mood-altering effect of food intake, increasing effort is being directed toward identifying the potential effect that meal consumption may have on performance of a specific task. Figure 5.1 summarizes the results of several studies revealing that reaction time (Voigt, Engel, & Klein, 1968), frequency of errors made by shiftworkers reading meters (Bjerner & Swensson, 1953), falling asleep while driving (Prokop & Prokop, 1955), and lapses of attention resulting in compulsive brakings by locomotive drivers (Hildebrandt, Rohmert, & Rutenfranz, 1974) tend to occur with greater frequency at about 2:00 p.m. These studies suggest that performance on tasks that require alertness and efficiency declines in mid-afternoon. This phenomenon is also found in laboratory studies as well as real-life tasks. As Figure 5.2 reveals, Blake (1971) found

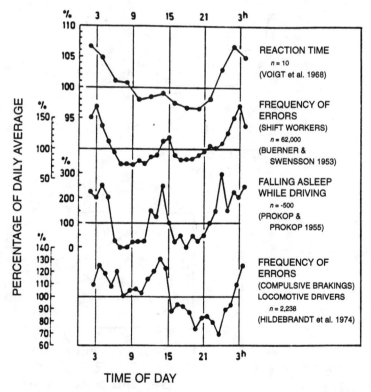

Figure 5.1. Mean daily course of auditory reaction time, error frequency in shift workers, relative frequency of car drivers falling asleep, and relative frequency of compulsive brakings caused by errors of omission by locomotive drivers. From Craig (1986). Copyright 1986 International Life Sciences Institute. Reprinted with permission.

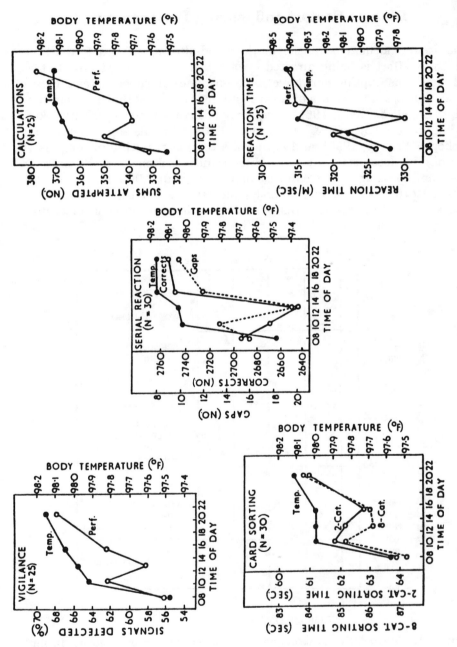

Figure 5.2. Diurnal variations in mean temperature and in mean performance scores on a range of tasks. From Craig (1986). Copyright 1986 International Life Sciences Institute. Reprinted with permission.

performance declines in studies measuring the proportion of signals detected in a task requiring vigilance for infrequent auditory signals, in the number of calculations of simple arithmetic sums in a given period of time, in the speed and accuracy of serial reactions to light flashes emanating from one of several sources, in the time to sort a deck of cards into several specified categories, and in reaction time to extinction of a bright light.

This early afternoon dip in performance is obviously undesirable and could lead to serious consequences in jobs such as air traffic control; therefore, it is important to identify the cause of the performance dip so that corrective measures can be employed. The performance dip could represent a natural decline in alertness and efficiency arising from an underlying circadian rhythm (Craig, 1986). If this were the cause of the decline in efficiency, it may be difficult to design a program that would counteract the effect. A rival hypothesis is that consumption of lunch could cause a decrement in performance.

Tryptophan

The evidence demonstrating that tryptophan reliably induces a state of drowsiness and feelings of lethargy would seem to suggest that tryptophan would also impair performance. Several studies have investigated the effect of tryptophan supplementation on a variety of tasks ranging from reaction time tasks to the digit symbol substitution test of the Wechsler Adult Intelligence Scale. These studies (Greenwood et al., 1974, 1975; Lieberman et al., 1983) have not been able to identify an alteration in performance as a result of tryptophan ingestion. The only performance effect identified in these studies was a reduction in number of taps made in a 60-second period after 3 hours of continuous tryptophan infusion (Greenwood et al., 1974). When the tryptophan infusion ceased, the effect disappeared.

It is possible that the failure to find a performance altering effect from tryptophan consumption is due to the selection of tasks that are insensitive to its effect (Spring et al., 1987). However, given the variety of tasks that have been investigated and the difficulty in identifying an effect, it is more likely that any performance effect that exists is very small and of little importance.

Although tryptophan may have little effect on performance, it is possible that another amino acid, such as tyrosine, does. Based on the biochemical and physiological role of tyrosine in normal and stressful situations, it would appear to be useful in counteracting stress-related performance deficits. In the absence of stress, a performance deficit would not seem to exist (Owasoyo, Neri, & Lamberth, 1992). Lieberman et al. (1983) administered 100 mg/kg of tyrosine to nonstressed healthy men and found that it did not affect their performance. When subjects were subjected to a combination of altitude and cold stressors, tyrosine supplementation counteracted the detrimental effects of the environmental stressors and improved the men's ability to engage in a variety of cognitive abilities such as coding, mathematics, and correctly completing pattern recognition problems (Banderet & Lieberman, 1989). Although this study suggests that tyrosine may be beneficial when subjects are stressed, it is the only study of its kind and must be replicated before confidence can be placed in the results.

Lunch

A phenomenon that most individuals can relate to is the dip in performance that occurs in early afternoon. Typically, people feel less energetic and more lethargic at about 2:00 p.m. Hildebrandt, Rohmert, and Rutenfranz (cited in Craig, 1986) have attributed this dip to an underlying circadian rhythm. Several researchers have challenged this interpretation and presented evidence indicating that this dip may be due in part to the consumption of lunch. Studies have revealed that perceptual sensitivity (Craig, Baer, & Diekmann, 1984), the ability to detect and respond quickly to sensory signals (Smith & Miles, 1986c), and the ability to engage in a cognitive vigilance task requiring discrimination between successive events (Smith & Miles, 1986a, 1986b) are impaired when lunch is consumed, although the ability to perform a letter cancellation task is not (Blake, cited in Craig, 1986; Christie & McBrearty, 1979). These findings suggest that those tasks that require vigilance and sustained attention are most vulnerable to the lunch effect.

In several studies researchers have also attempted to determine whether the timing of lunch is a variable. Some found that it seems to make no difference whether lunch is eaten between 12:00 noon and 1:00 p.m. or is delayed until 1:15 p.m. to 2:30 p.m. (Craig et al., 1981; Smith & Miles, 1986b, 1986c). Smith and Miles (1986a) revealed that a dip also occurs among individuals working a night shift after a meal consumed between 1:30 and 2:30 a.m., the night shift equivalent of lunch. These findings seem to provide further evidence that consumption of a meal eaten in the middle of the waking cycle is at least a partial cause of the dip in performance.

Smith et al. (1991) and Craig and Richardson (1989), in an attempt to further define the factors responsible for the post-lunch dip in performance, investigated the effect of size of lunch on performance. They found that consuming a large lunch increased the number of errors made on a task requiring participants to rapidly search and identify a target stimuli. The detrimental effect of a large lunch may, however, be partially dependent upon an individual's typical eating habits, because individuals who normally consume a light lunch experience the most detrimental effect from consumption of a large lunch (Craig & Richardson, 1989).

The literature seems to rather reliably demonstrate that consumption of the lunch meal results in a decrement in performance on tasks requiring vigilance and sustained attention. Given such knowledge, it would be important to try to determine whether there is any way of counteracting such an effect. Kanarek and Swinney (1990) found that administering a calorie-rich snack about 3 hours after lunch improved cognitive performance on tasks requiring sustained attention. The interesting point is that a snack can increase performance in mid-afternoon on the same type of tasks that the noon meal adversely affected. One of the key factors is that the adverse affect of the noon meal occurs 1 to 2 hours after meal consumption, whereas the positive effect of the snack was demonstrated within the first hour following snack consumption and during the time corresponding to the greatest dip in performance. It may be that the positive effect of the snacks occur rapidly and only when performance has deteriorated, suggesting that there may be an interaction between the effect of a meal and the time of testing.

Carbohydrates

The suggestion that consumption of carbohydrates may have an influence on performance can, in recent studies, be traced to the literature suggesting that this macronutrient may increase the tryptophan/LNAA ratio and result in an increase in the synthesis of serotonin. Administration of tryptophan, as I discussed in an earlier part of this chapter, induces a state of drowsiness and lethargy. If consumption of a carbohydrate-rich meal were to produce the same effect, it would seem to have a detrimental effect on tasks requiring sustained attention.

The literature on the effects of a carbohydrate-rich meal on performance is somewhat inconsistent. Simonson, Brozek, and Keys (1948) found that accuracy on a high-paced letter-cancellation task was impaired following a carbohydrate-rich lunch. This is consistent with Spring et al.'s (1983) results revealing that accuracy on a dichotic shadowing task declined following a carbohydrate-rich meal. However, the adverse effect was apparent only in individuals over 40, and a reaction-time task was not sensitive to the carbohydrate consumption.

In contrast, Spring et al. (1989) found that a high-carbohydrate lunch had no effect on a digit symbol substitution test, a letter cancellation test, or an addition task. King et al. (1945) even found that a high-carbohydrate lunch improved performance on a psychomotor task and decreased the area of scotoma or the visual blind spot over a no-lunch condition. In this study the participants had consumed breakfast between 4:30 and 5:30 a.m., ate lunch at 1:30 p.m., and then ascended to 17,000 feet where they completed the performance tests. Because participants in the no-lunch condition had not eaten for 8 to 10 hours, it does not seem surprising that those who had eaten lunch performed better.

Conclusion

Research on the effects of diet on the mood and performance has produced an interesting mix of results. Tryptophan administration either by intravenous injection or oral consumption reliably increases feelings of drowsiness and lethargy but seems to have little, if any, effect on performance. It seems as though people feel more lethargic following tryptophan consumption but if asked to perform can overcome these feelings of drowsiness and still engage in effective task performance.

Tryptophan depletion seems to reliably increase feelings of depression, although not to clinical levels. This finding is consistent with those demonstrating that depressed individuals have a deficit in central serotonin. Individuals who experience a complete absence of depression do not experience an increase in depression following an acute depletion of tryptophan, which suggests that those most susceptible to depression are affected most by tryptophan depletion.

Whereas tryptophan reliably alters mood, tyrosine seems to do so only when an individual is placed in a situation in which the catecholaminergic neurons are active. Aspartame does not have a mood-altering effect, although many individuals have attributed their physical and psychological symptoms to consumption of this sweetener.

Most studies have demonstrated that consumption of a carbohydrate-rich meal has little, if any, effect on mood, probably because a carbohydrate-rich meal does not alter the plasma tryptophan/LNAA ratio sufficiently to increase the synthesis of central serotonin. Similarly, carbohydrates seem to have little effect on performance. Other studies have demonstrated, however, that consumption of the lunch meal, regardless of composition, contributes to the dip in performance on a variety of tasks. This dip may be partially dependent on the size of the lunch consumed and whether a person normally consumes a light or heavy lunch, and it may be counteracted by a carbohydrate-rich snack consumed at the time of the dip in performance.

6 _____

Nutrition and Depression

Recently, a freelance writer contacted me and asked me to give her an update on the effect that food has on mood. She was writing an article for one of the popular magazines and wanted to include any current research that had been conducted that might provide the readership of this magazine with clues as to how their mood might be affected by the food which they eat. Telephone calls such as this one are relatively common and indicate the general public's interest in this topic. This interest has been fueled for decades by the publication of books (e.g., Cheraskin & Ringsdorf, 1976) and articles (e.g., Gelman, King, Hager, Raine, & Pratt, 1985) enthusiastically claiming that people's psychological well-being can be enhanced if they would only eat or avoid eating certain foods. This general interest in the psychological effect of foods is also clearly shared by mental health professionals. Most psychotherapists believe they should disseminate health education (Royak-Schaler & Feldman, 1984). According to Burks and Keeley (1989), 68% have recommended that a client follow a specific diet or have referred a client to someone to suggest a specific diet.

Despite widespread interest in this topic, the field of psychiatric nutrition has generally been neglected. For example, only one study (Christensen & Somers, 1994) has been conducted assessing the nutrient intake of a group of depressed women. Table 6.1, which summarizes the results of this study, reveals that, although the average nutrient intake exceeded the recommended daily allowance (RDA), many depressed patients consumed a diet that supplies less than the RDA of essential nutrients. Further analysis of these data revealed that insufficient intakes of a nutrient were due to intake of insufficient calories rather than selection of foods that do not supply the essential nutrients. The failure to ingest an adequate energy supply could lead, over time, to nutrient deficiencies that could exacerbate or maintain a psychiatric disorder.

Although the field of psychiatric nutrition has received inadequate attention (Ryan, Rao, & Rekers, 1990), interest in this area is growing and has yielded some interesting findings. The available research suggests that nutrition may play a role in the development or maintenance of depression. In this chapter, I discuss the knowledge base that has accumulated regarding the relationship between depression and several nutrients.

Carbohydrates

In a study of people's food preferences during different emotional states, Lyman (1982) asked participants questions such as the following. Think

Table 6.1. Mean Nutrient Intake of Depressed Females Compared With 1989 Recommended Dietary Allowance

| | Intake | | M % | % of RDA | |
Nutrient	M	SD	RDA	<2/3 RDA	<1/3 RDA
Energy (kcal)	2445	1036	111	—	25
Protein (g)	80	54	160	—	20
Vit A (RE)	941	596	117	10	20
Vit E (mg)	19	11	237	—	5
Vit C (mg)	108	84	180	10	10
Thiamin (mg)	1.8	2.2	164	—	20
Riboflavin (mg)	2.6	4.6	200	—	10
Niacin (mg)	20	11	133	—	20
Vit B_6 (mg)	1.6	1.0	100	—	45
Folate (μg)	266	167	148	5	5
Vit B_{12} (μg)	3.8	3.2	190	15	15
Calcium (mg)	864	387	108	10	20
Phosphorous (mg)	1481	1478	185	—	15
Iron (mg)	25	52	167	5	30
Selenium (μg)	53	33	96	27	18
Zinc (mg)	16	19	133	20	30

Note. From Christensen and Somers (1994a). Copyright 1994 by Journal of the American College of Nutrition. Reprinted with permission.

about a time in which you were feeling excited, happy and self-confident. Now think about the type of food you would like to eat and contrast that with the type of food you would like to eat when you are feeling sad, depressed, frustrated, and worried. Would you tend to prefer foods such as meat, vegetable, fruits, and breads when happy and more of a junk-food diet such as ice cream, cakes, cola drinks, or sweets when depressed and worried? The results of this study, shown in Table 6.2 reveal that individuals tend to prefer healthy foods when experiencing positive emotions and junk food when experiencing negative emotions such as depression.

Because Lyman did not assess participants' food intake while they were actually experiencing the emotions, this study is far from conclusive. These results, however, are mirrored in several other studies. Fernstrom et al. (1987) found that depressed subjects report an increase in their preference for sweets (high-carbohydrate/high-fat foods) when depressed compared to when they are not depressed. Leibenluft, Fiero, Bartko, Moul, and Rosenthal (1993) reported that individuals with a psychiatric diagnosis of major depression, seasonal affective disorder, alcohol dependence, and comorbid primary depression and secondary alcohol dependence all reported greater consumption of carbohydrates and caffeine when experiencing depressive symptoms.

These retrospective studies clearly indicate that depressed subjects believe that their food selection changes when they become depressed, but they do not reveal whether depressed subjects actually do consume more sweets than do the nondepressed. Christensen and Somers (in press) con-

Table 6.2. Ordered Frequencies of Individuals Preferring Foods With Healthful, Junk, and Half-and-half Nutritional Values During Emotions

Healthful		Junk		Half-and-half	
Emotion	f	Emotion	f	Emotion	f
Self-confidence	62	Joy	23	Boredom	48
Friendliness	53	Boredom	21	Relaxation	38
Happiness	53	Frustration	18	Happiness	32
Solemness	46	Amusement	17	Amusement	31
Relaxation	39	Depression	17	Friendliness	31
Excitement	37	Guilt	17	Depression	30
Joy	36	Anxiety	16	Love	30
Love	35	Worry	16	Anxiety	28
Anxiety	33	Loneliness	15	Loneliness	28
Frustration	33	Jealousy	13	Frustration	24
Loneliness	33	Embarrassment	12	Sadness	24
Amusement	31	Fear	12	Excitement	23
Anger	29	Anger	11	Worry	23
Depression	29	Happiness	11	Joy	22
Guilt	28	Friendliness	9	Self-confidence	22
Sadness	26	Excitement	8	Anger	21
Jealousy	25	Sadness	8	Solemness	17
Worry	25	Hostility	6	Fear	16
Boredom	23	Love	6	Hostility	13
Embarrassment	23	Relaxation	6	Jealousy	13
Hostility	23	Solemness	3	Embarrassment	11
Fear	21	Self-confidence	1	Guilt	9

Note. From *Journal of Psychology, 112,* p. 125, 1982. Reprinted with permission of the Helen Dwight Reid Educational Foundation. Published by Heldref Publications, 1319 Eighteenth Street, NW, Washington, DC 20036-1802. Copyright 1982.

ducted a prospective study of the dietary intake of depressed and nondepressed individuals and found that depressed participants consumed a diet that was different from that consumed by those who were nondepressed. An analysis of the diet records of depressed participants and a matched sample of nondepressed participants showed that the depressed consumed significantly more carbohydrates than the nondepressed, a finding that seems to verify the data obtained from the retrospective studies (see Table 6.3). Interestingly this increase in carbohydrates came primarily from an increase in simple carbohydrates but not fat, although many of the foods that participants were ingesting were high in both carbohydrate and fat. Apparently, the fat in the carbohydrate-rich foods consumed by the depressed was replaced by an equivalent amount of fat in foods consumed by nondepressed participants.

The retrospective and prospective studies conducted to date are very consistent in demonstrating that depressed subjects consume more carbohydrates than do the nondepressed. It seems as though this increase comes primarily from an increase in simple carbohydrate consumption. For such an alteration in preference for a specific type of food to occur

Table 6.3. Carbohydrate Intake for Depressed and Nondepressed Individuals

	Depressed		Nondepressed			Difference
	M	SD	M	SD	T-ratio	in intake
Carbohydrate (g)	330	140	232	118	2.86*	98
Sugars (g)	169	165	89	63	2.43*	80
Sucrose (g)	91	150	29	25	2.19*	62
Maltose (g)	0.06	0.8	0.4	0.5	1.15	0.2
Lactose (g)	5.6	5.2	6	7	0.29	0.4
Glucose (g)	11	28	8	16	0.4	3
Galactose (g)	0.08	0.13	0.01	0.04	2.98*	0.07
Fructose (g)	4.2	4.2	7	14	0.86	2.8

Note. From "Effects of Eating Behavior on Mood: A Review of the Literature," by L. Christensen, 1993, *International Journal of Eating Disorders, 14*, pp. 173–183. Copyright 1993 by John Wiley & Sons, Inc. Reprinted with permission.
*p < .05.

when experiencing an emotion such as depression, the food consumption must be serving some type of function. Leibenluft et al. (1993) and others have speculated that the carbohydrate and caffeine consumption characteristic of depressed patients is a form of self-medication. Depressed subjects ingest carbohydrates to obtain some relief from their depressive symptoms. The self-medication hypothesis is interesting and one that would explain the enhanced preference for carbohydrates; however, most of the support for this intriguing hypothesis comes primarily from studies conducted with participants who experience carbohydrate cravings and have a diagnosis of seasonal affective disorder, premenstrual syndrome, or obesity with depressive symptoms. These studies, which will be discussed in the next chapter, reveal that consumption of carbohydrates, as well as caffeine, reduces feelings of fatigue and anergy. Because feelings of fatigue and anergy are dominant characteristics of depression, anything that would ameliorate these feelings would reinforce the probability of repeating this behavior, which supports the idea of self-medication.

All studies conducted to date have shown the mood-altering effects of carbohydrate consumption to be temporary or acute. Given that individuals experiencing depressive symptoms, such as those with seasonal affective disorder, crave and increase consumption of carbohydrates during a depressive episode, and given that the carbohydrate consumption of depressed individuals seems to be significantly greater than that of nondepressed individuals, this finding seems logical. If carbohydrate consumption produced a long-term enhancement in mood, the depressed individual would consume this macronutrient only infrequently to achieve the beneficial effect. However, foods such as carbohydrates are used rapidly by the body and need to be replenished frequently, indicating that the mood-altering effect of carbohydrates would naturally be acute.

Several studies have suggested that, for some depressed individuals, carbohydrate consumption may actually be contributing to the development and maintenance of depression. My colleagues and I (Christensen,

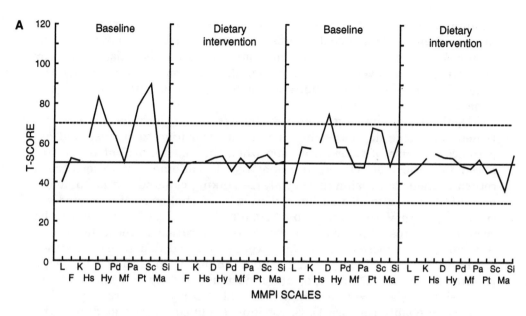

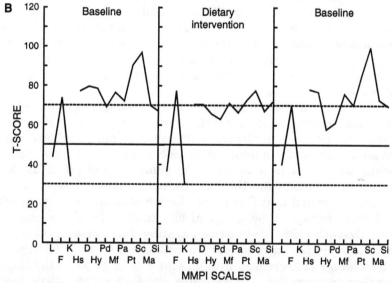

Figure 6.1. MMPI scores of two depressed individuals before and after a dietary intervention to eliminate caffeine and refined sucrose. Hs = Hypochondriasis; D = Depression; Hy = Hysteria; Pd = Psychopathic Deviate; Mf = Masculinity-Femininity; Pa = Paranoia; Pt = Psychasthenia; Sc = Schizophrenia; Ma = Hypomania; Si = Social Introversion. From Christensen, White, & Krietsch (1985). Copyright 1985 by the American Psychological Association.

White, & Krietsch, 1985; Christensen et al., 1988, 1989) demonstrated that a subsample of depressed individuals experienced an amelioration of their symptoms following the elimination of caffeine and refined sucrose from their diet. Figure 6.1 presents the results of the MMPI scale scores of two individuals before and after a dietary intervention consisting of the elimination of caffeine and refined sucrose. In both instances, the predietary intervention MMPI scale scores revealed a distressed individual. Following dietary intervention, the emotional distress either disappeared or dramatically improved. The emotional distress returned following the reintroduction of baseline conditions consisting of the consumption of caffeine and refined sucrose.

Double-blind challenges with caffeine, sucrose, and placebo have revealed that some depressed individuals are sensitive to sucrose and experience a return of their symptoms when this macronutrient is reintroduced into the diet. Others are sensitive to caffeine and experience a return of their depression as they start drinking caffeine again. Table 6.4 presents the results of a 24-hour, double-blind challenge of a refined sucrose responder with a female participant identified as "D. S." As can be seen, only sucrose resulted in a significant alteration in mood (a decline in vigor and an increase in fatigue, confusion, and depression). Neither saccharin, Equal, or lactose had any effect on mood. The caffeine challenge resulted in an increase in vigor and a decrease in fatigue, confusion, and depression. It shold be noted, however, that these scores were elevated at baseline, probably because D. S. consumed refined sucrose at dinner the evening prior to the caffeine challenge. Because she was very sensitive to sucrose, D. S. experienced a deteriorated mood state that was evident at baseline measurement. The improvement in mood during the caffeine challenge was confounded by the fact that the mood improvement could have been due more to abstinence from sucrose than from caffeine consumption.

Some studies have demonstrated that consumption of carbohydrates results in an improvement in mood, whereas others have demonstrated that elimination of carbohydrates, particularly simple carbohydrates, results in an amelioration in depression. Because it would seem difficult for the consumption of a food to have the same type of effect as does the elimination of the food from the diet, these findings may seem contradictory. I have suggested that this contradiction may be more apparent than real and that there may be a logical explanation for these dual effects. Based on Thayer's (1987) data demonstrating that consumption of refined carbohydrates produce a temporary increase in energy levels that is followed by feelings of increased fatigue and Blouin et al.'s (1991) data indicating that cravings for carbohydrates and feelings of fatigue increased in bulimics following a 25-gm glucose load, I postulated (Christensen, 1993) that carbohydrate consumption may create a vicious cycle in depressed individuals. Simple carbohydrates may be consumed to provide a temporary relief from feelings of dysphoria and fatigue. Following this temporary relief, feelings of dysphoria and fatigue increase, contributing to the development and maintenance of negative affect characteristic of depression, an effect similar to that noted following consumption of alcohol among alcoholics. Alcoholics remember the more immediate mood-elevating and energy-enhancing effect of alcohol consumption and not the negative effects that occur much later (Tamerin & Mendelson, 1969). A similar phenomenon may exist with carbohydrate consumption in that individuals

Table 6.4. D. S.'s BDI and POMS T Scores During the Challenge Phase

Challenge substance	Time	POMS factors						BDI
		Tension-anxiety	Depression-dejection	Anger-hostility	Vigor	Fatigue	Confusion-bewilderment	
Saccharin	Baseline	31	35	39	73	39	37	7
	1 hr	32	34	40	67	40	43	4
	24 hr	29	32	38	77	39	36	8
Caffeine	Baseline	37	35	38	43**	67**	61**	15*
	1 hr	39	34	42	40	73	58	15
	24 hr	38	32	37	69	37	36	4
Sucrose	Baseline	38	32	37	69**	37**	36**	4*
	1 hr	37	35	40	66	44	39	3
	24 hr	46	37	42	35	67	58	14
Equal	Baseline	29	32	37	77	34	34	4
	1 hr	29	32	37	75	34	34	4
	24 hr	28	32	37	81	34	33	3
Lactose	Baseline	28	32	37	81	34	33	3
	1 hr	28	34	37	69	38	39	3
	24 hr	27	34	37	83	34	30	5

Note. From Christensen, Krietsch, White, & Stagner (1985). Copyright 1985 by the American Psychological Association.
BDI = Beck Depression Inventory; POMS = Profile of Mood State.
*p < .06. **p < .05.

experiencing depressive symptoms may consume carbohydrates for their immediate mood-enhancing effect and disregard the more temporally distant effect of exacerbation and maintenance of negative affect. This postulated cyclical effect must, however, be verified in subsequent research.

Tryptophan

Over the past several decades, tremendous strides have been made in achieving an understanding of the causes of depression. One of the areas that has been investigated systematically is the biological or neurochemical aspects of affective disorder. Investigation of the neurochemical aspects of depression can be traced to the fortuitous discovery, in the early 1950s, of several drugs that were effective in the treatment of depression. Studies investigating the mechanism by which these drugs exerted their antidepression action revealed that they all had effects on brain neurotransmitters. The primary effect of these drugs was to increase the level of serotonin or the catecholamines in the synaptic cleft either by decreasing the breakdown of amines in the presynaptic terminal and synapse (the monoamine oxidase inhibitors or MAOIs) or by blocking the uptake of amines into the nerve terminal (McNeal & Cimbolic, 1986). These effects were thought to be associated with the therapeutic action of the antidepressant drugs, because these drugs should prolong the effects of serotonin or the catecholamines in the synapse.

The neurochemical effect of these antidepressant drugs as well as the results of a variety of other studies (see McNeal & Cimbolic, 1986 for a review) led to a deficiency hypothesis of depression. According to this hypothesis, depression was due to a deficiency of one or more crucial neurotransmitters and, therefore, the way to treat depression was to administer drugs that increased the level of these neurotransmitters in the neuronal synapse. More recently, the deficiency hypothesis has given way to a receptor sensitivity hypothesis and to a dysregulation hypothesis (Delgado, Price, Heninger, & Charney, 1992), because recent evidence has not supported the deficiency hypothesis. The receptor sensitivity hypothesis states that depression is more a function of abnormal receptor sensitivity than to deficiencies of neurotransmitters (Charney, Menekes, & Heninger, 1981). The dysregulation hypothesis has proposed that the mechanisms controlling the neurotransmitter functions are dysregulated and that the antidepressant drugs restore these systems to normal regulation (Siever & Davis, 1985).

We do not, at the present time, have a clear understanding of the biological or neurochemical underpinnings of depression. What does seem to be clear is that serotonergic and catecholaminergic neurotransmitters are involved. Of these two systems, the serotonergic system has received the most attention, because studies consistently reveal that serotonin is involved in the mechanism of antidepressant action. This is also the system that may be, at least in part, under dietary control. This is because, as was described in chapter 3, serotonin is synthesized from the amino acid tryptophan. Tryptophan loading not only increases the ratio of plasma tryptophan to the other large neutral amino acids, but it also seems to increase the synthesis of central serotonin.

Although the serotonergic system has been implicated in depression in a variety of studies ranging from those investigating platelet serotonin uptake to receptor binding studies (see Delgado et al., 1992, for a review), there are two types of studies that have implications for the role of diet and nutrition. The first group of studies are those in which researchers have investigated the relationship between plasma levels of tryptophan and depression. These researchers have attempted to determine whether the absolute level of either free or bound plasma tryptophan or the ratio of tryptophan to the other large neutral amino acids is related to depression. The underlying notion is that because serotonin is synthesized from tryptophan and the brain tryptophan level is dependent on both diet and uptake of tryptophan into the brain, decreasing the availability of tryptophan by restricting dietary intake of this amino acid should, therefore, decrease the amount of serotonin that can be synthesized. Biggio et al. (1974) demonstrated that depriving rats of dietary tryptophan for 24 hours resulted in 90% reduction of brain tryptophan and a 58% reduction of serotonin.

Researchers comparing the absolute level of plasma tryptophan in depressed and nondepressed individuals have provided somewhat conflicting results. Several earlier studies (Møller, Kirk, & Honoré, 1979; Riley & Shaw, 1976) did not reveal a difference between depressed and control groups. More recent studies (e.g., Coppen & Wood, 1978; Cowen, Parry-Billings, & Newsholme, 1989; Lucca, Lucini, Piatti, Ronchi, & Smeraldi, 1992) have demonstrated that the plasma tryptophan levels of the depressed are less than those of the nondepressed. This phenomenon may, however, exist primarily in individuals with major depression (Maes et al., 1990).

Although most studies have demonstrated that plasma tryptophan levels are decreased in depressed subjects, the crucial element is the tryptophan/LNAA ratio, because this ratio is the primary determinant of the amount of plasma tryptophan that crosses the blood–brain barrier and becomes available for synthesis to serotonin (Wurtman, Hefti, & Melamed, 1981). Researchers comparing the tryptophan/LNAA ratios in depressed and nondepressed individuals have rather consistently demonstrated that the depressed have a lower ratio than do the nondepressed (e.g., Cowen et al., 1989; Maes, DeRuyter, Hobin, & Suy, 1986; Russ, Ackerman, Banay-Schwartz, Shindledecker, & Smith, 1990). It is important to note that these studies have focused on individuals with major depression or individuals with major depression and melancholia, which suggests that only very severely depressed individuals have a reduced tryptophan/LNAA ratio. In support of this idea, Maes et al. (1990) found that individuals with minor depression had plasma tryptophan/LNAA ratios that were significantly greater than those of individuals with major depression and melancholia. Plasma tryptophan levels may, therefore, have implications only for individuals with major depression.

Table 6.5. Relapse of Depression During Rapid Tryptophan Depletion as a Function of Antidepressant Type

Antidepressant	Dose Mean mg/day (SD)	Number/ Relapse	% Relapse
Desipramine	200 (67)	2/11	18[a]
Fluoxetine	26 (10)	5/10	50
Fluvoxamine	233 (121)	5/6	83
Monoamine oxidase inhibitor[b]		6/6	100
Fluvoxamine/lithium	300/900	2/3	66
Desipramine/lithium	250 (87)/900	1/3	33
Fluoxetine/thioridazine	40/50	0/1	0
Bupropion	300	0/2	0
Nortriptyline	75	1/2	50
Imipramine	150	1/1	100
Amphetamine	20	1/1	100
Total		24/46	

Note. From Delgado et al. (1991).

Examples of the second type of study suggesting that tryptophan may contribute to depression include those reviewed in chapter 5, which showed that depleting tryptophan from the diet reduces brain serotonin function (Curzon, 1981; Fernstrom, 1977; Moja, Cipollo, Castoldi, & Tofanetti, 1989; Young, Ervin, Pihl, & Finn, 1989) in laboratory animals and probably in humans, because humans consuming a low-tryptophan or tryptophan-free amino acid diet experience a reduction in plasma tryptophan (Delgado et al., 1989; Rose, Haines, & Warner, 1954; Young, Hussein, Murray, & Scrimshaw, 1971). As I discussed in chapter 5, depleting tryptophan from the diet has the greatest effect on individuals who are vulnerable to depression. Depressed people who were not receiving antidepressant medication did not experience a mood-altering effect following consumption of a tryptophan-depleted amino acid drink (Miller et al., 1992). However, people whose depression was in remission experienced a return of their depression following consumption of the tryptophan-depleted amino acid drink (Delgado et al., 1990). Interestingly, 85% of the melancholic patients experienced a depressive relapse, whereas only 37% of the nonmelancholic patients experienced a relapse, suggesting that tryptophan depletion has a greater effect on more severely depressed individuals.

Delgado et al. (1991) have also demonstrated that the type of antidepressant medication that is effectively controlling depressive symptoms may be related to the experience of a depressive relapse during tryptophan depletion. Patients that were treated with desipramine or bupropion were much less likely to relapse than were patients treated with MAOIs or selective serotonin re-uptake inhibitors (see Table 6.5). These findings suggest that the availability of central serotonin is necessary for some drugs to achieve their therapeutic effectiveness.

Vitamins

The early studies investigating the efficacy of vitamin therapy in the treatment of disorders such as schizophrenia were unsuccessful and discouraged further investigation into the connection between vitamins and psychiatric disorders. In spite of these early negative results, reports have continued to appear in the literature suggesting that a substantial portion of the psychiatric population has low levels of a variety of vitamins. Although most of the literature has focused on folic acid, a small literature exists demonstrating that many psychiatric patients may be deficient in thiamin (B_1), pyridoxine (B_6), and cyanocobalamine (B_{12}) as well.

Thiamin, Pyridoxine, and Cyanocobalamin

Carney, Williams, and Sheffield (1979) assayed the thiamin (B_1) status of 154 psychiatric inpatients who had a history of poor diet and found low levels in 37%. Of the various psychiatric patients tested, those with a diagnosis of alcoholism (54%), schizophrenia (41%), and endogenous depression (40%) were most likely to have low B_1 levels. In a subsequent study, Carney, Ravindran, Rinsler, and Williams (1982) revealed that 30% of the 172 inpatients tested were low in B_1. Patients with a diagnosis of schizophrenia and alcoholism were most likely to have low B_1 levels, providing some support for Carney's earlier study.

Although these two studies suggest that a significant percentage of patients with alcoholism and schizophrenia may have a subclinical B_1 deficiency, it must be remembered that the participants were psychiatric inpatients and that, in the first study, the patients were specifically selected because they had a history of a poor diet. Additionally, in both studies a nonpsychiatric control group was not included, so it is not known what percentage of people in the general population would have low B_1 levels. It is, therefore, difficult to draw any conclusions other than that at the present time some psychiatric patients, particularly those with a diagnosis of alcoholism and schizophrenia, have low B_1 levels.

There are also several studies suggesting that a portion of psychiatric patients may have a pyridoxine (B_6) deficiency. Carney et al. (1979) found that 75% of the endogenously depressed individuals investigated had low B_6 levels. In a subsequent study, Carney et al. (1982) showed that individuals with a B_6 and riboflavin deficiency were more likely to have an affective illness. Stewart, Harrison, Quitkin, and Baker (1984) found that 21% of the psychiatric outpatients they investigated had low B_6 levels. These studies suggest that a portion of individuals with an affective disorder may have low B_6 levels. Like the B_1 studies, however, these studies did not include a nonpsychiatric control group; therefore, it is impossible to ascertain whether the percentage of psychiatric patients with low B_6 levels is greater than that of a nonpsychiatric group.

Table 6.6 summarizes the results of five studies that assayed cyanocobalamin (B_{12}) in a psychiatric population. As the table shows, a sub-

Table 6.6. Summary of Studies on the Incidence of Vitamin B_{12} Deficiency in Psychiatric Patients

Reference	Fluid	Definition of B_{12} deficiency	Type of patient	Psychiatric diagnosis	N	% with B_{12} deficiency
Carney (1970)	Serum	<150 pg/ml	Psychiatric inpatients	Organic psychosis	20	33
				Endogenous depression	12	21
				Neurotic depression	8	15
				Schizophrenia	9	15
				Other	4	4
Reynolds et al. (1970)	Serum	<200 pg/ml	Psychiatric inpatients	Depression	13	14
Carney & Sheffield (1978)	Serum	<150 pg/ml	Admitted to psychiatric hospital	Organic psychosis	17	52
				Endogenous depression	13	22
				Neurotic depression	16	31
				Schizophrenia	12	22
				Alcoholism	8	25
				Other	5	12
Levitt & Joffe (1989)	Serum	<100 pmol/l	Outpatients	Major depression	44	0
Kivela et al. (1989)	Serum	<170 pmol/l	Elderly outpatients	Depressed	39	5
				Nondepressed	39	13

stantial percentage of hospitalized psychiatric patients with organic psychosis, depression, and schizophrenia had low vitamin B_{12} levels. The incidence in depressed outpatients was substantially less and was no different than in a nondepressed population (Kivela, Pahkala, & Eronen, 1989). These findings suggest that B_{12} has more psychopathological significance for more severely disturbed patients. However, this conclusion must be tempered with the recognition that only a few studies have been conducted, and, as with the B_1 and B_6 studies, they did not include a comparable control group. Again, the only conclusion that can be drawn is that some severely disturbed psychiatric patients have low B_{12} levels.

Folic Acid

The vitamin that has received the most attention in recent years is folic acid. Interest in this vitamin seems to have been initiated following Herbert's (1962) report of the psychological effects produced by following a low folate diet. Consumption of 5 µg/day of folic acid (RDA = 150 to 200 µg/day depending on age and gender) for four months resulted in the development of sleeplessness, forgetfulness, and irritability. These symptoms disappeared within 48 hours of starting folate replacement therapy. Since that time a number of studies have been conducted, primarily in Great Britain, which have surveyed the folate status of psychiatric patients. These studies, summarized in Table 6.7, reveal that a substantial portion of hospitalized psychiatric patients have low folate levels, especially those diagnosed with depression, schizophrenia, and dementia. Three studies (Abou-Saleh & Coppon, 1989; Callaghan, Mitchell, & Cottier, 1969; Shaw et al., 1984) showed no more than 3% of individuals in control groups to be folate deficient, and Garry, Goodwin, and Hunt (1984) found that only 8% of 270 healthy individuals had low plasma folate levels. These findings suggest that the increased frequency of low folate levels in psychiatric patients seems to be related to their psychiatric status.

Although psychiatric patients, particularly those with depression, schizophrenia, and dementia, seem to be more susceptible to low folate levels, it is impossible to provide a relatively precise estimate of the extent to which such a folate deficiency exists. As Young and Ghadirian (1989) pointed out, the definitions of folate deficiency vary from study to study as do the methods by which folate levels are determined. In spite of this inability to identify the percentage of folate-deficient psychiatric patients, it is clear that folate-deficiency is characteristic of a significant percentage of psychiatric patients with a variety of diagnostic classifications.

If folate deficiency is relatively common in psychiatric patients, the obvious question is why? Decreased dietary intake or selection of foods with little folic acid could certainly contribute to a folate deficiency. It is known that disorders such as depression can result in not only a reduced appetite but also an alteration in food selection (Christensen & Somers, in press; Fernstrom et al., 1987). Although this hypothesis is logical, there is little support for it. Reynolds, Preece, Bailey, and Coppen (1970) found

Table 6.7. Studies on the Incidence of Folate Deficiency in Psychiatric Patients

Reference	Fluid	Definition of folate deficiency: Upper limit	Type of patient	Psychiatric diagnosis	n	% with folate deficiency	Comments
Hurdle & Williams (1966)	Serum	5 ng/ml	Geriatrics admitted to hospital	Mild physical disability, mentally normal	36	22	
				Severe physical disability, mentally normal	13	38	
				Mild physical disability	18	67	
Carney (1967)	Serum	2 ng/ml	Admitted to psychiatric hospital	Endogenous depression	75	35	
				Neurotic depression	71	29	
				Organic psychosis	90	24	
				Schizophrenia	78	20	
				Other (neurosis, drug addiction, abnormal personality, alcoholism, mania)	102	13	
Hunter et al. (1967)	Serum	3 ng/ml	Admitted to psychiatric hospital	Various	75	49	
Ibbotson et al. (1967)	Serum	2 ng/ml	Psychiatric inpatients	Various	48	15	
			Normal controls		61	0	
Shulman (1967)	Serum	6 ng/ml	Geriatrics admitted to hospital	Senile dementia	34	79	
				Arteriosclerotic dementia	7	100	
				Pre-senile dementia	5	60	
				Acute confusional state	4	100	
				Depression	5	80	
				Paraphrenia	4	75	

Reference	Sample	Cutoff	Population	Diagnosis	N	No. deficient	Comments
Callaghan et al. (1969)	Serum	2 ng/ml	Psychiatric inpatients	Schizophrenia, depression, or manic depression	40	15	
Hallstrom (1969)	Serum Whole blood	2.5 ng/ml 40 ng/ml	Normal controls Admitted to psychiatric hospital	Various	30 84 85	0 51 22	
Jensen & Olesen (1969)	Serum	2 ng/ml	Female psychiatric inpatients	Various	29	24	The patients with folate deficiency consisted of 4 with dementia, 1 with schizophrenia, 1 with manic-depressive psychosis, 1 with personality disorder.
Kallstrom & Nylof (1969)	Serum	3 ng/ml	Psychiatric inpatients, some with hematological deviations	Endogenous depression or intellectual deterioration	115	21	
Kariks & Perry (1970)	Serum	3.5 ng/ml	Admitted to psychiatric hospital	Various	411	33	
Reynolds et al. (1970)	Serum	2.5 ng/ml	Psychiatric inpatients	Depressed	91	24	The patients with low folate were more depressed on admission and discharge than those with normal folate. Serum folate was similar for patients with poor and good diets.
Reynolds et al. (1971)	Serum Red cells	2.5 ng/ml 100 ng/ml	Psychiatric inpatients	Schizophrenia, organic psychosis, or affective disorders	30 30	33 23	

table continues

Table 6.7. (Continued)

Reference	Fluid	Definition of folate deficiency: Upper limit	Type of patient	Psychiatric diagnosis	n	% with folate deficiency	Comments
Sneath et al. (1973)	Serum Red cells	2 ng/ml 200 ng/ml	Geriatrics admitted to hospital	Most mentally normal, a few with dementia	115 115	22 18	The 14 patients with dementia had a lower mean red cell folate than the rest.
Carney & Shef-field (1978)	Serum	2 ng/ml	Admitted to psychi-atric hospital	Organic Neurotic depression Endogenous depression Chronic alcoholism Schizophrenia Others	33 52 58 32 55 42	30 29 26 16 15 12	
Thornton & Thornton (1978)	Serum	6 ng/ml	Admitted to psychi-atric hospital Normal controls	Various	269 40	30 0	Inadequate diet oc-curred frequently among the patients but at the same fre-quency among those with or without fo-late deficiency.
Ghadirian et al. (1980)	Serum	2 ng/ml	Psychiatric inpatients Medical inpatients	Depressd Other (mainly schizophrenic) Various	16 13 19	50	Mean folate was less for depressed pa-tients than for psy-chiatric or medical patients.
Lowe et al. (1981)	Serum	3 ng/ml	Child psychiatric inpatients	Autistic Other neuropsychiatrics (aphasia, attention deficit disorder, chronic multiple ties, atypical development)	43 59	7 7	

Study	Folate measure	Cutoff	Population	Diagnostic group	n	Folate deficient	Comments
Shaw et al. (1984)	Not specified		Inpatients	Senile dementia	29	23	The incidence of folate deficiency is significantly different in patients with dementia and age-matched controls.
				Controls	35	3	
Bober (1984)	Not specified		Patients undergoing psychogeriatric assessment	Organic	114	18	
				Functional	62	23	
				Mixed	35	23	
				Miscellaneous	23	22	
Abou-Saleh, cited in Abou-Saleh & Coppen (1986)	Not specified			Controls	—	11	Anorexic patients diagnosed as clinically depressed had lower plasma folate concentrations than those who were not clinically depressed.
				Anorexic	49	37	
Gray & Leong (1986)	Serum	2.5 ng/ml	Admitted to adult psychiatric ward	Schizophrenic	23	0	
				Depression	12	8	
				Mania	10	0	
				Substance-induced organic mental disorder	7	0	
				Other psychotic disorders	8	0	
Abou-Saleh et al. (1986)	Serum	2.5 ng/ml	Geriatrics	Dementia	45	36	Folate deficient patients were significantly older than those with normal folate.
Levitt & Joffe (1989)	Serum	5.2 ng/ml	Outpatients	Depressed	44	2	

table continues

Table 6.7. (*Continued*)

Reference	Fluid	Definition of folate deficiency: Upper limit	Type of patient	Psychiatric diagnosis	n	% with folate deficiency	Comments
Abou-Saleh & Coppen (1989)	Plasma red cells	2.5 ng/ml	Inpatients & outpatients	Endogenous depression	71	16	
				Nonendogenous depression	24	13	
				Control depression	60	2	
Carney et al. (1990)	Plasma red cells	200 ng/ml	Inpatients & outpatients	Depressed	152	38	
				Euthymic	42	7	
				Mania	32	7	
				Schizophrenia	29	5	
				Alcoholic	30	12	
Godfrey et al. (1990)	Plasma red cells	200 ng/ml	Outpatients	Depression	76	31	
				Schizophrenia	47	36	

Note. Adapted from *Progress in Neuro-psychopharmacology and Biological Psychiatry, 13,* S. N. Young & A. M. Ghadirian, "Folic Acid and Psychopharmacology," pp. 841–863. Copyright 1989, with kind permission from Elsevier Science Ltd., The Boulevard, Langford Lane, Kidlington OX5 1GB, U.K.

no difference in the folate levels of patients whose diet was assessed as being poor, moderate, or good. Thornton and Thornton (1978) found that an inadequate diet occurred with the same frequency among patients with and without low folate levels. However, these studies relied on nutritional histories, which have been demonstrated to be inadequate in estimating the nutrient intake of individuals (Willett, 1990). Using a 3-day diet record, Somers and I (Christensen & Somers, 1994) found that only 2 out of 29 depressed participants had a deficiency in folate intake, which also suggests that a folate deficiency is not the result of inadequate dietary intake.

It is obvious that the contribution of food selection and intake to low folate levels in psychiatric patients is not settled. The studies that have been conducted are too few and most of the ones that have been conducted do not provide an adequate measure of food intake. Young and Ghadirian (1989) pointed out that it would be surprising if diet did not play some role given the decrease and alteration in food intake known to occur in various psychiatric disorders.

Another possible contributor to the low folate levels characteristic of many psychiatric patients is the use of certain drugs that can influence plasma folate levels (Swanwick, Manley, & McKeon, 1992). Drugs such as anticonvulsants and alcohol can diminish the absorption of folate from the gastrointestinal tract. Epileptics on anticonvulsants, for example, have a higher-than-usual incidence of psychiatric symptoms, and this increased incidence is associated with a folate deficiency (see Young & Ghadirian, 1989, for a review). However, studies on the prophylactic use of lithium have failed to show an association between folate status and the concomitant use of other drugs (e.g., McKeon, Shelley, O'Regan, & O'Broin, 1991). Therefore, it appears as though only certain types of drugs, such as anticonvulsants, contribute to lower folate levels, which suggests that the drug explanation would exist only in patients taking drugs that deplete or diminish the absorption of folate, a condition that probably does not apply to most psychiatric patients. Drugs do not, therefore, provide a good explanation for the low folate levels found in most psychiatric patients.

If folic acid does contribute to psychiatric disorders, there obviously has to be some metabolic explanation, because folic acid is involved in a variety of metabolic processes. The only theoretical explanation to date has focused on the potential mechanism by which a folate deficiency may affect depression. Reynolds and Stramentinoli (1983) have proposed a hypothesis that suggests that a methylation deficit exists in depression. This suggestion arose from the inadvertent discovery that S-adenosyl methionine (SAM) has antidepressant properties (Fazio et al., 1974; Muscettola, Galzenati, & Balbi, 1982), and SAM and folate have an intimate relationship. A major function of folate is the synthesis of methyl groups, which are subsequently used by SAM as the methyl donor in many methylation reactions. SAM is used in many important methylation pathways in the brain involving many of the neurotransmitters demonstrated to be involved in depression. Both SAM and folate alter the turnover of brain 5-HT, although the mechanism by which this occurs is uncertain. Reynolds and Stramentinoli (1983) proposed that neurotransmitter function, receptor sensitivity, or endocrine function in depression may be mediated by a membrane function disturbance, and this disturbance may be mediated by a folate deficiency.

Conclusion

The role that nutrition plays in depression has sparked renewed interest in recent years from a small group of investigators. These investigators have revealed that depressed people tend to consume more carbohydrates than do nondepressed people, mostly in the form of sucrose. Several researchers have suggested that increased consumption of carbohydrates may represent a form of self-medication to alleviate the symptoms of depression. However, other studies have indicated that elimination of sucrose from the diet of some depressed individuals can lead to an amelioration of their depression. It is possible that the temporary lift from carbohydrate consumption leads to further consumption, but that the continued consumption of sucrose can maintain the depression.

Studies have also implicated the role of the serotonergic and catecholaminergic neurotransmitters in depression. This is interesting from a dietary perspective, because these neurotransmitters are synthesized from dietary amino acids. The amino acid that has received the most attention is the serotonin precursor tryptophan. Studies have indicated that individuals with major depression have reduced tryptophan levels and reduced tryptophan/LNAA ratios. Depletion of tryptophan from the diet is an effective way of depleting brain serotonin levels. Use of this technique with nondepressed participants revealed that consumption of a tryptophan-free diet resulted in development of mild depression; formerly depressed individuals, primarily melancholic patients, experienced a return of their depression.

Apparently, there are some individuals for whom tryptophan and its presumed effect on central serotonin synthesis is more significant than for other individuals. Little information exists on the characteristics of nondepressed individuals that may be sensitive to tryptophan alteration. Research indicates that individuals with melancholia have a lower tryptophan/LNAA ratio, and these individuals seem to be the ones who relapse into depression following tryptophan depletion. This suggests that the more severely depressed individuals are more sensitive to alteration of plasma tryptophan and would seem to be more sensitive to alterations in their dietary intake of this amino acid. Perhaps this group of depressed individuals would be most responsive to a dietary tryptophan supplement.

Recent studies have also demonstrated that a significant percentage of patients with a variety of psychiatric disorders, including depression, have a deficiency in several vitamins such as thiamin, pyridoxine, cyanocobalamin, and folic acid. Folic acid has received the most attention and provides the most evidence for a relation between vitamin deficiencies and depression.

7

The Role of Carbohydrates in Seasonal Affective Disorder, Obesity, and Premenstrual Syndrome

Nutrition clearly seems to play a role in the depression experienced by many individuals, and although the exact role of both vitamins and carbohydrates has not been clearly identified, there is a sufficient body of evidence to indicate that nutrition needs to be given continued attention in the investigation of unipolar depression. In addition to unipolar depression, there are a number of other psychiatric disorders that also seem to have a nutritional component. Individuals with seasonal affective disorder and premenstrual syndrome, and obese individuals experiencing some degree of depression all seem to have a tendency to crave carbohydrates. The interesting component is that the presence of depression seems to be a common denominator related to the carbohydrate cravings characteristic of individuals with these disorders. In this chapter I discuss each of these disorders and end with a discussion of carbohydrate cravings, a phenomenon that is much more complex than it appears.

Seasonal Affective Disorder

People who suffer from seasonal affective disorder (SAD) seem to be depressed and down in the dumps every winter. Then, as spring approaches, they begin to pull out of the dumps and develop a cheerful attitude. Seasonal depressions have existed throughout recorded time. Hippocrates (1931) recorded the existence of seasonal depressions. Eight centuries later, Posidonius observed that "melancholy occurs in Autumn, whereas mania in Summer" (cited in Roccatagliata, 1986, p. 143). During the past two centuries and even in the early part of the 20th century, descriptions of annual episodes of depression beginning in the fall and remitting in the spring have continued to appear (Wehr & Rosenthal, 1989). Interestingly, Greco-Roman physicians were treating seasonal depression and lethargy with sunlight—essentially the same treatment used today.

Seasonal depressions were not systematically described or investigated until the 1980s. The recent interest in regularly recurring seasonal depressions was sparked by the account of an engineer who had documented his own seasonal mood swings for 15 years. He even hypothesized that light might have an influence on his mood state (Oren & Rosenthal, 1992). This report came to the attention of Rosenthal and his colleagues at the National Institute of Mental Health, who decided to further investigate the validity of this report.

The initial investigation consisted of several pilot studies to document the validity of the seasonal variation in affective episodes. One of these studies focused on a 29-year-old woman who consistently developed a depressive episode every winter since she was an adolescent. Over the course of several years she moved several times. When she moved north, her depressive symptoms began earlier in the fall, were more severe, and persisted longer into the next spring. On two occasions she took a winter vacation to Jamaica and within two days experienced a complete disappearance of her symptoms. The woman was treated with light therapy early in the morning (around 5:00 a.m. to sunrise) to determine whether exposure to a full spectrum light such as that which would be obtained from the sun would be effective in treating her symptoms. Within less than a week her depression ameliorated (cited in Rosenthal et al., 1984), and the light therapy continued to be successful throughout the fall and winter seasons. This pilot study as well as others (e.g., Rosenthal, Lewy, Wehr, Kern, & Goodwin, 1983) prompted Rosenthal and his colleagues to launch a full-scale investigation into the syndrome that has become known as seasonal affective disorder.

This investigation and others led to the classification of SAD as a psychiatric disorder included in the *DSM-III-R* (American Psychiatric Association, 1987). SAD seems to be a cross-cultural disorder: It has been identified in the United States, Europe, Africa, Asia, and Australia (Oren & Rosenthal, 1992). Several studies (e.g., Potkin, Zetin, Stamenkovic, Kripke, & Bunney, 1986; Rosen et al., 1990) have suggested that the prevalence of SAD increases with latitude (see Figure 7.1).

SAD is most frequently viewed as a disorder appearing in the fall and remitting in the spring as the days get longer. Recent evidence (Boyce & Parker, 1988) suggests that there may also be a group of individuals who experience a spring/summer affective disorder. However, this spring/summer disorder is not as well documented and has received much less attention. Regardless of the season when the disorder appears, the symptoms are similar (Boyce & Parker, 1988). In both instances, the depressed participants report typical symptoms of depression including dysphoria, concentration difficulties, decline in energy, irritability, anxiety, decreased libido, and social withdrawal. Some investigators believe that patients with SAD differ from classically depressed individuals in that they experience increased fatigue, sleep duration, appetite, and weight gain (Oren & Rosenthal, 1992). Garvey, Wesner, and Godes (1988), however, found a difference only in sleep duration and carbohydrate cravings.

The symptom or behavioral alteration of carbohydrate cravings seems to be one of the unique characteristics of this disorder and the one consistently identified across studies (e.g., Rosenthal et al., 1984, Takahashi et al., 1991). Increased preference for carbohydrate-rich foods not only has been reported by patients with SAD (Rosenthal et al., 1984) but also has been demonstrated in patients' reports of their food consumption during summer and winter months. Krauchi and Wirz-Justice (1988) had

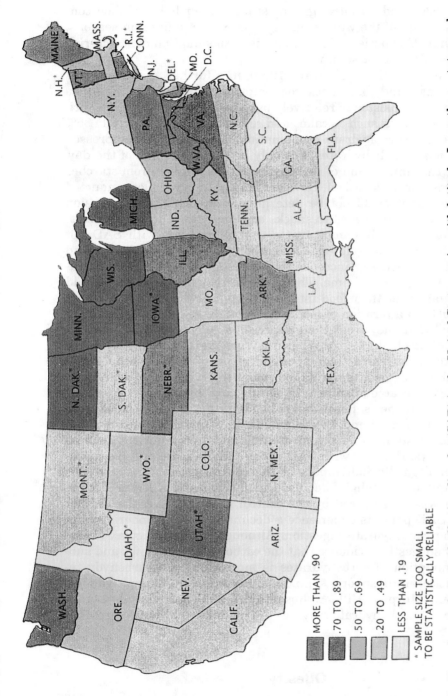

Figure 7.1. Prevalence of seasonal affective disorder (SAD) in the United States varies with latitude. In northern states such as Minnesota, SAD affects more than 100 people per 1,000, whereas in Florida it affects fewer than 6 people per 100,000. Asterisks indicate a sample that is too small to be reliable. The data were collected by Steven G. Potkin and his associates at the University of California at Irvine. From "Carbohydrates and Depression," by R. J. Wurtman & J. J. Wurtman. Copyright 1989 by Scientific American, Inc. All rights reserved.

patients with SAD and a control group estimate their habitual food consumption at the end of the winter, spring, summer, and autumn seasons. They found that SAD patients increased their consumption of starch-rich foods in all seasons except summer.

Krauchi, Wirz-Justice, and Graw (1990), in a further analysis of this data set, demonstrated that snack consumption, especially in the afternoon and evening, consisted of relatively pure carbohydrates obtained primarily from sweet foods such as cakes and represented approximately 85% of the total snack carbohydrate consumption. Light therapy suppressed the consumption of carbohydrates, but only in the second half of the day. Interestingly, the suppression of carbohydrate consumption from starches and sweets was almost identical. However, an analysis was not conducted by time of day, so it could not be determined whether the suppression occurred primarily with regard to snacks or equally to snacks and meals.

The evidence reliably demonstrates that individuals with SAD not only report an increased preference for carbohydrates during the fall and winter months but actually increase their consumption of this macronutrient during this period of time. The question that arises is, why would these individuals alter their food intake? There must be some motivation underlying such an alteration of food consumption. Anecdotally, these patients reported that they treat their depressive symptoms with carbohydrates (Leibenluft et al., 1993). When they consumed carbohydrate-rich foods, they experienced an activation or energizing effect (Rosenthal et al., 1984). Thus they may be attempting to combat their feelings of depression and the anergy that accompanies it by eating carbohydrates.

To test this hypothesis, Rosenthal et al. (1989) assessed the mood state of 16 patients with SAD and 16 individuals in a matched control group after they had consumed a carbohydrate-rich and a protein-rich lunch on two different days. Patients with SAD experienced a more positive mood-altering effect than did individuals in the control group. However, this effect was limited to a slight decrease in fatigue and a lesser decline in vigor than was experienced by the control group. The results did not suggest that SAD patients experience a decline in their dysphoric symptoms following carbohydrate ingestion. Although Rosenthal et al. (1989) provided only suggestive evidence that the carbohydrate cravings and subsequent consumption of carbohydrates is motivated by a carbohydrate-induced reduction in dysphoric symptoms, investigators (Joseph-Vanderpool, Jacobsen, Murphy, Hill, & Rosenthal, 1993) still speculate that behaviors such as carbohydrate cravings are modulated by brain serotonin systems.

Obesity

Obesity is considered to be a major health problem in the United States and in other affluent Western societies. Studies have repeatedly demonstrated that obesity has serious health consequences. Obesity increases the incidence of hypertension, diabetes, and cholesterol levels. Obese men have an elevated risk of colon, rectal, and prostate cancer, and obese women have an increased risk of cancer of the gallbladder, endometrium, cervix, ovaries, and breast (Simopoulos, 1987). Not only does obesity have serious health consequences, but also it can decrease life expectancy. Life insurance statistics clearly indicate that mortality increases for both men and women who carry excessive weight. Interestingly there is a direct relationship between weight and mortality for young individuals, whereas this relationship decreases when weight is gained later in life, suggesting that it is continuous obesity over many years that has the adverse effect on health and longevity (Bray, 1987).

There are also some serious psychological consequences of obesity. Obese people are universally disdained for their condition in most Western societies. They face discrimination in virtually all facets of their life. For example, obese individuals, identified by pictures sent with applications and personal interviews, are accepted by prestigious colleges at lower rates than are their normal-weight counterparts, even when they have equivalent credentials as determined by IQ scores, grades, attendance records, and extracurricular activities (Canning & Mayer, 1966). Employers rate overweight individuals as less desirable employees than normal-weight individuals even when they are believed to have the same abilities (Larkin & Pines, 1979).

Overweight individuals also seem to have a general disdain of their own bodies. Adolescent girls seem to be especially dissatisfied with their body weights and general appearance (Wadden & Stunkard, 1987) and experience a continued pressure to maintain a lean physical appearance as they move into adulthood. Societal sanctions against being overweight and the overwhelming emphasis placed on thinness has led to a preoccupation with dieting in many individuals. Lehrman (1987) revealed that, of 500 schoolgirls studied in the San Francisco area, almost 50% of the 9-year-olds and 80% of the 10- and 11-year olds stated that they were dieting. The continuing popularity of diet centers, health clubs, and exercise spas is one sign of our society's preoccupation with weight.

Obesity is defined as the excessive storage of energy in the form of fat (Simopoulos, 1987). Probably as the result of such definitions and the excessive weight of obese individuals, it has generally been taken as self-evident that overeating is the cause of obesity. Although research has demonstrated that this is an overly simplistic view, most treatments have consisted of efforts to reduce caloric intake (Bennett, 1987). These range from jaw wiring to behavior modification programs. While treatment programs are in effect, weight reduction does take place; however, people typically regain the weight following completion of the program and tend to experience repeated cycles of weight loss followed by weight gain.

Currently, the prevailing view seems to be that maintaining a focus on overconsumption of calories is counterproductive and will not contribute to our understanding of the causes and most effective treatment of obesity (Bennett, 1987). It is generally believed that obesity has multiple causes, including both genetic predisposition and a variety of environmental factors, only one of which is diet. Most of these variables have received considerable attention in articles and books (e.g., Pi-Sunyer, 1988) and will not be reiterated here. One of the variables that has received little attention is the potential effect that carbohydrate cravings can have on both the type and quantity of food ingested.

Among the population of obese individuals, as well as individuals of average weight, a large subgroup exists that describes powerful and frequent cravings for foods that are rich in carbohydrates (Wurtman, 1988). Wurtman, Wurtman et al. (1981) initially verified the existence of these carbohydrate cravers by having a group of healthy obese individuals who claimed to snack frequently on high carbohydrate foods live in a dormitory on the campus of the Massachusetts Institute of Technology and eat all their food there. In the dormitory they were given access to a vending machine that contained a variety of protein-rich and carbohydrate-rich snacks. This vending machine was controlled by a computer, and participants had to enter a personal three-digit access code to take the snack desired. The computer then recorded the snack taken, providing a record of the type and number of snacks obtained by each participant. Using this procedure, Wurtman, Wurtman et al. (1981) documented that individuals who were self-professed carbohydrate cravers consumed an average of 4.1 carbohydrate snacks versus only 0.8 protein snacks a day for the other participants.

When analyzing the caloric intake of these obese carbohydrate cravers, Wurtman, Wurtman, Reynolds, Tsay, and Chew (1987) found that they consumed an average of 1906 calories a day during mealtime. This was not considered to be excessive and corresponded to what might be expected from a sample of people in which 80% were women. However, the carbohydrate cravers also consumed an average of an additional 860 calories from snacks. Added to the mealtime calorie load, the total average calorie intake of 2766 calories was more than the recommended amount for a group composed of 80% women. These findings suggest that frequent carbohydrate snacking represents a variable that contributes to excessive caloric intake and probably contributes to obesity.

There are two interrelated hypotheses that have been postulated for the carbohydrate cravings experienced by many obese individuals. The first is that some obese individuals crave carbohydrates in an attempt to increase the synthesis and release of central serotonin. The second hypothesis is that metabolism of carbohydrates is impaired in obese individuals.

The basis for the serotonin hypothesis, as was discussed in chapter 3, is the research demonstrating that a carbohydrate load can increase brain serotonin levels. The increase in brain serotonin levels following this carbohydrate load was assumed to affect mechanisms that controlled appetite, especially for carbohydrates (Wurtman, Wurtman, et al., 1981). The increase in serotonin synthesis presumedly operates as a signal to diminish the likelihood that further carbohydrates will be consumed. When a protein-rich meal is consumed, the synthesis and release of serotonin is suppressed (Fernstrom & Wurtman, 1972), increasing the likelihood of eating more carbohydrates at the next meal (Wurtman & Wurtman, 1986).

Because many obese individuals crave carbohydrates and consume most of their snacks in the form of carbohydrates, it was assumed that this carbohydrate craving may be due to their attempt to increase their level of brain serotonin.

There are several strategies that have been used to test this hypothesis. Most of the studies have made use of drugs that increase serotonergic neurotransmission to determine whether administration of these drugs would suppress the cravings and intake of carbohydrates. In the first study, Wurtman, Wurtman, et al. (1981) investigated the effect d-fenfluramine, a drug that enhances serotonin-mediated neurotransmission (Garattini, Buczko, Jori, & Samanin, 1975), and tryptophan, the precursor of serotonin, would have on the ingestion of carbohydrate snacks. This experiment revealed that d-fenfluramine caused a significant reduction in the mean number of carbohydrate snacks consumed (4.2 during baseline and 2.4 following d-fenfluramine treatment) each day, whereas carbohydrate snacking did not change significantly following tryptophan or placebo conditions.

Given that d-fenfluramine decreased the absolute number of carbohydrate snacks consumed each day, Wurtman et al. (1985) wanted to determine whether the carbohydrate snacker not only selected snacks that are predominately composed of carbohydrates but also whether they chose disproportionately large amounts of carbohydrates at meals. They also wanted to determine whether d-fenfluramine affected mealtime nutrient intake. To obtain an answer to these questions, they measured food intake and snacking in 20 obese carbohydrate cravers before and after treatment with d-fenfluramine. They found that obese carbohydrate cravers consumed similar amounts of carbohydrates and protein at mealtime but that snacks were composed mostly of carbohydrates. D-fenfluramine produced a 22% reduction in mealtime carbohydrate intake, whereas snacking was reduced by 41%. Mealtime protein intake was not affected.

Wurtman et al. (1987) then extended this research to determine whether the effect of d-fenfluramine would be the same on carbohydrate noncravers, people who claimed to snack on both protein and carbohydrate foods. To test this hypothesis, it was necessary to identify both cravers and noncravers. These investigators found that it was very easy to identify carbohydrate cravers; however, after 18 months of newspaper, radio, television, and mass transit advertisements, only 25 noncravers were identified. Of these 25, three actually snacked almost exclusively on carbohydrate foods, which meant that only 22 carbohydrate noncravers were identified. Both groups of participants completed a 3-month trial of d-fenfluramine or placebo. Results revealed that d-fenfluramine significantly reduced carbohydrate snacking among carbohydrate cravers during all three drug treatment months, whereas a significant reduction in carbohydrate snacks did not occur for the noncravers until the third month. During mealtime, d-fenfluramine significantly reduced both carbohydrate and protein intake of carbohydrate cravers, whereas it had no effect on carbohydrate noncravers.

The studies conducted by the Wurtmans and their colleagues have clearly demonstrated that many obese individuals report that they crave carbohydrates, and those that report such cravings consistently select as snacks those foods that are rich in carbohydrates. The finding that carbohydrate snacking could be modified with drugs that enhance serotonergic neurotransmission seems to support the speculation that carbohydrate snacking results from an attempt to increase the synthesis and release of serotonin. However, the lack of a similar effect of d-fenfluramine at mealtime in one of the two studies tempers the suggestion that carbohydrates are regulated by brain serotonin levels.

Caballero (1987) and others have tested an interrelated hypothesis to explain why obese individuals crave and consume carbohydrates by extending the serotonin hypothesis to include the idea that the metabolic response to carbohydrate intake may be impaired in obese individuals. A number of studies (e.g., Ashley, Fleury, Golay, Maeder, & Leathwood, 1985) have demonstrated that obese people exhibit a blunted plasma amino acid response to insulin. In other words, the uptake of amino acids into peripheral cells following insulin secretion is not as great in obese individuals as it is in normal-weight individuals. If plasma amino acids do not fall as much in obese individuals after carbohydrate consumption, it follows that the tryptophan/LNAA ratio should decline at a lesser rate than for normal-weight individuals. Caballero, Finer, and Wurtman (1988) confirmed this fact by demonstrating that the tryptophan/LNAA ratio in a group of obese participants did not increase over the baseline level following a 30-, 50-, and 75-g carbohydrate load, in spite of the fact that the obese participants showed a significantly higher insulin response to the carbohydrate load than did those in the control group. This finding suggests that consumption of a carbohydrate load would have no effect on central serotonin for obese individuals. Based on the assumption that central serotonin does actually modulate carbohydrate intake, the insulin resistance exhibited by obese people would preclude the possibility that carbohydrate intake has any effect on central serotonin, because the feedback mechanism leading to a decrease in carbohydrate intake would not be triggered. In the absence of this feedback mechanism, obese people should constantly remain in a state of serotonin deficiency and continue to crave carbohydrates.

The explanation proposed by Caballero (1987) and others to account for the carbohydrate cravings of obese individuals is elegant but lacking in a number of respects. If the carbohydrate cravings are due to a deficit in central serotonin, enhanced carbohydrate consumption should occur during both mealtime and snacking. However, Wurtman et al. (1985) demonstrated that mealtime carbohydrate and protein intake were similar; the carbohydrate preference was demonstrated only for snack intake.

As I discussed in chapter 3, for a carbohydrate load to have any effect on central serotonin it must consist of almost pure carbohydrate, because as little as 5% protein can suppress the ability of a carbohydrate load to increase the tryptophan/LNAA ratio. Unless one consumes pure sucrose, it is almost impossible to eat a food that contains less than 5% protein. Even if enough carbohydrate were consumed, recent evidence indicates that serotonergic neurons are equipped with feedback mechanisms that limit the control that dietary variables can have on neurotransmitter activity. Therefore, it appears that dietary variables increase the availability of serotonin for release only when the neurons are stimulated (Garattini, 1989).

In several studies (e.g., Hrboticky, Leiter, & Anderson, 1985; Strain, Strain, & Zumoff, 1985; Wurtman, Wurtman, et al., 1981) researchers have administered various doses of tryptophan in an attempt to alter brain serotonin levels and, therefore, carbohydrate intake. These studies have been less than encouraging, demonstrating that either none or only a few subjects altered carbohydrate intake or that they reduced total energy intake. The Silverstone and Goodall (1986) study is one of the few demonstrating that carbohydrate intake is increasingly suppressed with increases in tryptophan dose.

Finally, Drewnowski, Kurth, Holden-Wiltse, and Saari (1992) have demonstrated that obese women demonstrate a preference for carbohydrate- and fat-rich foods and not just carbohydrate-rich foods, whereas obese men prefer protein- and fat-rich foods. As Drewnowski et al. (1992) have stated, the serotonin hypothesis does not suggest that carbohydrate cravings are restricted to obese females; Drewnowski et al. (1992) also suggested that "carbohydrate craver" may be a misnomer in that the foods most preferred are sweet, rich in fat, or both (Drewnowski, 1988).

If the carbohydrate cravings are not controlled by the impact of carbohydrate ingestion on central serotonin, what are they caused by? One suggestion is that because carbohydrate cravers prefer sweet-tasting foods, they demonstrate a preference for carbohydrates, but this explanation seems weak in light of studies such as the one conducted by Drewnowski, Kurth, and Rahaim (1991), who found that obese individuals have similar taste preferences for sweet and fat foods. Other researchers have suggested that carbohydrate cravers use snacks as a kind of self-medication to exert a positive effect on their moods. For example, in Wurtman and Wurtman's 1986 study, obese carbohydrate cravers described themselves as tense, restless, and unable to concentrate prior to consuming a carbohydrate snack and as calm, relaxed, and able to concentrate following the snack. This finding is consistent with Ganley's (1989) conclusion that obese individuals eat in certain emotional situations to exert a positive effect on their mood. To test this possibility, Lieberman, Wurtman, and Chew (1986) had obese carbohydrate cravers and noncravers complete a series of mood scales prior to and 2 hours after consuming a carbohydrate-rich lunch: the noncravers became more fatigued and sleepy and less alert, whereas the carbohydrate cravers reported being less depressed 2 hours after lunch.

Although these findings support the suggestion that obese carbohydrate cravers consume carbohydrates for their positive mood-altering effects, they should be interpreted with caution before any firm conclusions are reached.

Premenstrual Syndrome

The physical and psychological symptoms that occur in many women during the luteal phase of the menstrual cycle have been known and well documented since the time of Hippocrates. Unfortunately for women during medieval times, disturbances related to the menstrual cycle were shrouded by myth and superstition. It was believed that children conceived during menstruation would become drunkards, epileptic, psychopathological, or homicidal (Sutherland, 1892). Icard (cited in Rubinow, Hoban, & Grover, 1987) attributed disturbances such as kleptomania, nymphomania, hallucinations, and melancholia to disorders of menstruation.

Frank (1931) made the first clinical report of the premenstrual syndrome, commonly referred to as PMS, in which he described 15 women who developed premenstrual tension 7 to 10 days prior to the onset of menses and the disappearance of these symptoms following onset of menstruation. However, little significance or attention was attached to this report, and the syndrome remained in relative obscurity, even following Greene and Dalton's (1953) report in the British medical literature. However, in the late 1970s and early 1980s, the effects of PMS attracted widespread public and professional attention when two women attributed the murder they committed to PMS and had the charge reduced to manslaughter (Lauersen & Stukane, 1983).

Probably the most clinically useful definition refers to PMS as a "constellation of mood, behavior and/or physical symptoms which have a regular cyclical relationship to the luteal phase of the menstrual cycle, and remit by the end of menstrual flow with a symptom-free interval of at least one week each cycle" (Harrison, Rabkin, & Endicott, 1985, p. 789). The key characteristic of this definition is that there must be at least one symptom-free week following menses for a person to be diagnosed with PMS. Because the symptoms of PMS overlap with those of other disorders, it is necessary to differentiate PMS from other psychiatric disorders. Many patients with a broad range of psychiatric disorders, such as depression, anxiety disorder, schizophrenia, and borderline personality disorder, experience a premenstrual worsening of symptoms, and it is not uncommon for them to seek treatment for PMS rather than their more generalized psychiatric disorder (Harrison et al., 1985). For PMS to be considered clinically significant, a person has to meet the criterion of experiencing one symptom-free week following menses, the symptom changes must be at least of moderate severity, and some degree of social or occupational impairment must exist that is attributable to the symptoms (Harrison et al., 1985).

Numerous attempts have been made to approximate the prevalence of PMS. As would be expected, the estimates vary considerable from study to study. Neimeyer and Kosch (1988) stated that approximately 95% of premenopausal women report premenstrual symptoms. According to Reid (1985), however, only 5% to 10% of women report their symptoms to be severe or disabling. Only about 10% to 15% of women report an absence

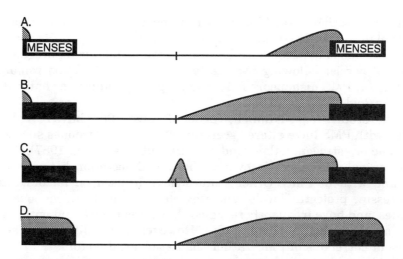

Figure 7.2.   Schematic diagram showing variability in the onset and duration of premenstrual symptoms. Most patients experience patterns A or B. From "Premenstrual Syndrome," by R. L. Reid, 1985, *Current Problems in Obstetrics, Gynecology, and Fertility, 8*, p. 13. Copyright 1985 by Mosby Year Book, Inc. Reprinted by permission.

of symptoms, whereas 50% report mild symptoms and 5% to 10% report severe symptoms (Reid, 1985).

The symptoms reported by women with PMS include a variety of physical and psychological complaints as well as a craving for carbohydrates. The physical symptoms may include weight gain, bloating, breast tenderness, headaches, and the psychological symptoms may include anger, irritability, fatigue, changes in libido, and depression. Reid (1985) has identified four different temporal patterns (see Figure 7.2) that describe the onset and duration of premenstrual symptoms. Patterns A and B are most characteristic; pattern D describes the most severely affected individuals, those who have only one symptom-free week out of the month.

Typically the first changes observed by women include breast swelling and tenderness, abdominal bloating, and constipation (Reid, 1985). These symptoms may be severe enough to warrant a change to looser fitting clothing as menses approaches. Concurrent psychological symptoms include fatigue, emotional lability, and depression. Psychological symptoms, which tend to accelerate as menses approaches, can lead to angry confrontations over minor issues, more severely affected individuals may completely withdraw from friends and family and prefer to isolate themselves. After the second or third day of menstruation the symptoms remit, although a few women report a dramatic lifting of symptoms several hours before onset of menstrual flow (Reid, 1985).

The acceptance of the syndrome of PMS has resulted in an attempt to identify its etiology. Most researchers have focused on identifying a hormonal or neuroendocrine cause for this disorder, because PMS is clearly tied to women's menstrual cycle. There is a reasonable database supporting the role of ovarian secretion in the etiology of PMS based on the following observations: "(a) PMS does not appear prior to activation of the hypothalamic-pituitary-ovarian axis at puberty; (b) PMS disappears during periods of hypogonadotropic amenorrhea and during pregnancy; (c) PMS will persist following hysterectomy if ovarian function remains intact; and (d) PMS disappears following surgically induced or natural menopause" (Reid, 1985, p. 21).

Some studies (e.g., Trunnell, Turner, & Keye, 1988) have revealed that women with PMS have altered secretion of ovarian hormones such as progesterone or estrogen. Other studies (e.g., Rubinow et al., 1987), however, do not reveal differences in ovarian hormonal secretion between women with and without PMS. Other studies have focused on factors, such as vasopressin, prolactin levels, glucose tolerance, and endogenous opiate peptides, and have frequently revealed that women with and without PMS differ on these factors (Reid, 1985). However, these differences seem to represent correlates of PMS rather than etiological factors.

Diet, in addition to neurochemical factors, has received a substantial amount of attention. Craving for sweet foods is commonly reported by women premenstrually. Smith and Sauder (1969), for example, reported that 62% of 289 nurses surveyed claimed to crave sweets. As Figure 7.3 shows, the women who reported such cravings did not demonstrate these cravings throughout the menstrual cycle; instead, these cravings gradually increased during the cycle, peaked just prior to menses, and declined rapidly thereafter (Bancroft, Cook, & Williamson, 1988). Other studies have shown parallel increases in preference for sweet foods (Bowen & Grunberg, 1990) and in appetite (Both-Orthman, Rubinow, Hoban, Malley, & Grover, 1988) during the luteal phase of the menstrual cycle.

Several studies (e.g., Dalvit, 1981; Manocha, Choudhuri, & Tandon, 1986) have demonstrated that women also significantly increase their energy intake during the luteal or premenstrual phase of the menstrual cycle, a logical outcome, given that appetite, consumption of carbohydrates, and cravings for sweet tasting foods increase during this phase. Dalvit-McPhillips (1983) verified this logic, demonstrating that the average carbohydrate intake of eight women was significantly greater during the 10 days preceding menses than it was during the 10 postmenstrual days (see Figure 7.4). Interestingly, because protein and fat consumption remained the same during this time, the increased energy intake during the premenstrual period seems to be due entirely to an increase in carbohydrate consumption. This finding was confirmed by Wurtman, Brzezinski, Wurtman, and Laferrere (1989), who found, however, that the increase in energy intake from increased carbohydrate consumption was characteristic only of individuals with premenstrual symptoms. Individuals without premenstrual symptoms had similar levels of energy and carbohydrate intake during both the follicular and luteal phases of the menstrual cycle.

Dalvit-McPhillips's (1983) finding that increased carbohydrate consumption was correlated with increased depression suggested that a relationship exists between these two variables. Wurtman et al. (1989) found that individuals who experienced a premenstrual increase in depression reported that feelings of depression, tension, anger, confusion, and fatigue

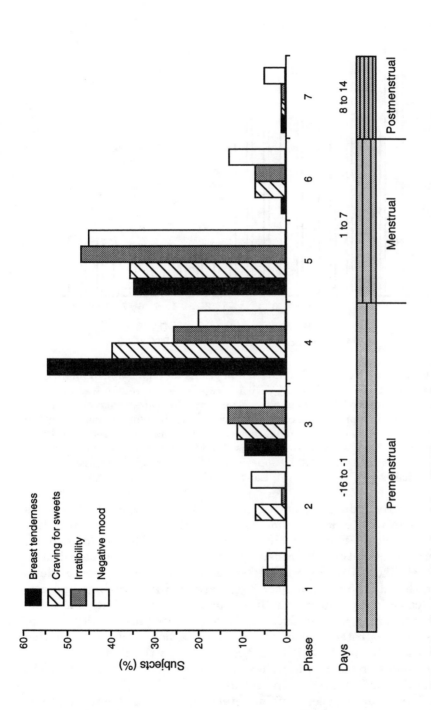

Figure 7.3. Distribution of peaks of four PMS symptoms—breast tenderness, craving for sweets, irritability, and negative mood—showing the percentage of participants experiencing symptoms in each phase (X^2 12, df = 36.95, $p < 0.001$). The method of dividing the cycle into phases is shown in the key at the bottom of the figure. From "Food Craving, Mood and the Menstrual Cycle," by J. Bancroft, A. Cook, & L. Williamson, 1988, *Psychological Medicine, 18,* p. 858. Copyright 1988 by Cambridge University Press. Reprinted with permission of Cambridge University Press.

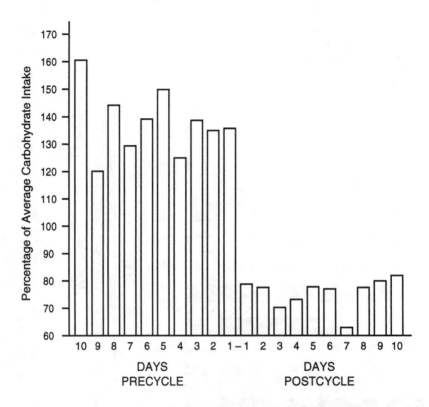

Figure 7.4. Averaged carbohydrate intake in grams for eight women for 10 days pre- and postmenstrual period. Daily carbohydrate for each woman was first converted to a percentage of that woman's average carbohydrate intake over the 60-day period. Each bar represents a composite average of all eight women on a given day of the cycle for both cycles—an average of 16 numbers. Reprinted from *Physiology & Behavior, 31*, S. P. Dalvit-McPhillips, "The Effect of the Human Menstrual Cycle on Nutrient Intake," p. 211. Copyright 1983, with kind permission from Elsevier Science Ltd., The Boulevard, Langford Lane, Kidlington OX5 1GB, U.K.

were significantly reduced following consumption of a carbohydrate-rich meal. If women with PMS consume carbohydrates to treat their negative mood state, it would follow that only women with PMS would increase their energy intake through consumption of additional carbohydrates. Brzezinski et al. (1990) have provided support for this suggestion by demonstrating that d-fenfluramine decreased carbohydrate cravings and carbohydrate consumption during the luteal phase in women with PMS. Because d-fenfluramine also produced a decrease in feelings of depression, this study demonstrated that depression and carbohydrate consumption and cravings are intimately tied together. Although the findings of these latter two studies are compelling, they must be replicated by others before complete faith can be placed in the results.

The relationship between caffeine intake and premenstrual symptoms has also been the subject of some study. In a series of three studies, Rossignol and her colleagues in the United States and China (Rossignol, 1985;

Rossignol & Bonnlander, 1990; Rossignol, Zhang, Chen, & Xiang, 1989) demonstrated that the prevalence and severity of premenstrual symptoms increased as the consumption of caffeine-containing beverages increased, regardless of whether the caffeine was obtained from tea, coffee, or soda. Although these studies do suggest a causal relationship, double-blind studies need to be designed to determine whether elimination of caffeine results in an amelioration of premenstrual symptoms and whether reintroduction of caffeine results in a return of symptoms.

The Problem of Defining Carbohydrate Cravings

Throughout this chapter I have discussed the fact that patients with SAD, PMS, and obesity who experience some degree of depression all have a strong propensity to crave carbohydrates. To many individuals the term *carbohydrate cravings* seems unambiguous and refers to an intense desire or longing for foods that are rich in carbohydrates. This definition, however, represents the nonscientific usage of the term. As Weingarten and Elston (1990) have pointed out, craving is a hypothetical construct and, therefore, it cannot be observed or measured directly. Unfortunately, little attention has been devoted to the development of an operational definition of cravings, and the measurement and definition of cravings are lacking.

In most cases carbohydrate cravers are identified through advertisements for individuals who "frequently crave carbohydrates" (Fernstrom, 1988). Self-report or consumption measures are typically used to verify whether people are carbohydrate cravers (Weingarten & Elston, 1990). The self-report measure requires people to rate the degree to which they crave or desire carbohydrates. The number on the scale is taken as an indication of the magnitude of the craving. Although such rating scales are appropriate to indicate whether one group has more intense cravings than another group, it is impossible to specify what merits the characterization of "craving" (Weingarten & Elston, 1990). Does a rating of 6 on a 10-point scale represent a craving, whereas a 5 does not?

Use of consumption measures to verify the existence of carbohydrate craving are also fraught with problems. As I discussed earlier in this chapter, Wurtman, Wurtman et al. (1981) verified the existence of obese carbohydrate cravers by recording the number of protein and carbohydrate-rich snacks that they consumed each day. Although this measure does represent an index of craving, it does not provide an indication of the magnitude of the craving; other factors, such as hunger, could also account for a portion of the food eaten.

The nutrient content of foods can also be a confounding factor. Carbohydrate cravers select foods that are rich in carbohydrates, but these foods also tend to contain considerable amounts of fat. Furthermore, the carbohydrate snacks used in most studies are significantly more appealing than the protein snacks (e.g., granola cookies vs. beef jerky). Because hedonic and sensory factors are also involved in the selection of snacks, verifying carbohydrate cravings on the basis of selection and consumption can also be confounded (Fernstrom, 1988b).

Fernstrom (1988b) has also pointed out that the type of carbohydrate craved by carbohydrate cravers has never been identified. Do they crave simple and complex carbohydrates equally? Does fat or protein content influence the cravings? As can be seen, defining *carbohydrate craver* is fraught with problems. What, on the surface, seems to be a simple construct is anything but simple. Yet, the construct is not superfluous and should not be eliminated from the scientific literature. As Weingarten and Elston (1990) have pointed out, "There can be no adequate explanation of human feeding without consideration of food cravings" (p. 241).

Conclusion

Several studies have verified that many individuals with SAD, PMS, and obesity who experience some degree of depression experience carbohydrate cravings that are manifested in increased carbohydrate consumption. Individuals with SAD consume more carbohydrates during the fall and winter months. Individuals with PMS increase their carbohydrate consumption premenstrually, but after menstruation both cravings and consumption decrease. The obese preferentially select carbohydrate-rich snacks over protein-rich snacks.

Most of the research stimulating investigation into the carbohydrate cravings of these individuals has focused on the role that carbohydrate ingestion may have in stimulating an increase in the synthesis and release of central serotonin. Studies that have investigated the effect that drugs such as fenfluramine have on carbohydrate ingestion, lended support for this hypothesis, but the research is lacking in a number of other respects. One consistent finding for all three of these disorders is that carbohydrate cravings seem to be stimulated following the experience of depressive symptoms. There is some evidence that carbohydrate ingestion is a form of self-medication, whereby individuals are motivated to seek out carbohydrates because they seem to alleviate depressive symptoms. This evidence, however, needs to be replicated and extended.

It must be acknowledged that, although carbohydrate cravings are experienced by many individuals, this phenomenon is a hypothetical construct that cannot be observed or measured directly. The term *carbohydrate cravings* is a useful one for investigating food intake, and it describes a real phenomenon. However, because it does not delineate specifically how cravings are to be measured or what constitutes a carbohydrate craving, more attention must be given to the measurement, cause, and definition of this phenomenon.

Part IV

The Use of Diet as Therapy

8

Efficacy of Dietary Interventions for the Treatment of Depression

It takes little effort to find books or magazine articles claiming that consumption or elimination of certain foods can have curative effects. Numerous publications (e.g., Duffy, 1975; Roberts, 1990a) promote the idea that certain foods, such as table sugar, can be detrimental to your physical and psychological health; others claim that certain diets can be used to treat various disorders (Scanlon & Strauss, 1991). Fortunately, research being conducted on the role of diet in disease and health is identifying the true effects of diet. It is not uncommon for one of the major news networks to report on the results of studies, such as those indicating that consumption of foods high in cholesterol may contribute to the development of heart attack disease or that consumption of high fiber foods can provide protection against colon cancer. Clearly, food does play a role in promoting health and ensuring freedom from disease.

Most of the research demonstrating the contribution of food to a person's health has focused primarily on physical health. The relationship that may exist between nutrition and psychological health has been studied as well; however, most of the relationships that have received the greatest publicity have been discounted. For example, as was stated in chapter 3, Feingold (1975a, 1975b) thought synthetic food additives were the cause of most cases of hyperactivity, but subsequent research (e.g., Harley, Matthews, & Eichman, 1978) did not support the claim. During the past decade a newer body of research has accumulated to suggest that some disorders, particularly depression, may have a nutritional component, and a few studies have shown that some kinds of depression may be treated effectively with diet. This research is the primary topic of this chapter.

L-Tryptophan

A series of studies conducted primarily during the 1960s and 1970s have investigated the effect that the amino acid L-tryptophan has on the treatment of depression. The rationale for these studies grew out of research demonstrating that some depressed and manic individuals have reduced levels of cerebrospinal fluid 5-HIAA or 5-hydroxyindoleacetic acid (e.g., van Praag, Korf, & Puite, 1970), the major metabolite of serotonin, and that suicide victims had lower brain levels of serotonin and 5-HIAA than did

Table 8.1. Double-Blind Studies of L-Tryptophan in Depression

Authors	Patients n	Patients Diagnosis	Dose of L-tryptophan (g/day)	Duration (days)	Other drugs	Design	Results
Bunney et al. (1971)	8	Manic-depressive and psychotic depression	8	16		vs. placebo	0/8
Coppen et al. (1972)	15	Primary depression	9	28	Ascorbic acid[a] Pyridoxine[b]	vs. imipramine (150 mg/day)	L-tryptophan as effective as imipramine
Murphy et al. (1974)	24	Primary affective disorder; 16 unipolar, 8 bipolar	9.6	20 ± 2	Ascorbic acid Pyridoxine	vs. placebo	1/16 improved in unipolar depression; 5/8 improved in bipolar depression
Mendels et al. (1975)	6	Unipolar and bipolar depression	3–16	42	Pyridoxine	vs. placebo	0/6
Dunner & Fieve (1975)	6	Primary affective disorder	8.4–9	10–18	Ascorbic acid Pyridoxine	vs. placebo	1/6 good antidepressant response
Jensen et al. (1975)	22	Endogenous depression	3–6	21		vs. imipramine (150 mg/day)	L-tryptophan as effective as imipramine
Lindberg et al. (1979)							

Rao & Broadhurst (1976)	9	Depressive illness	Ascorbic acid Pyridoxine	6	28	vs. imipramine (150 mg/day)	L-tryptophan as effective as imipramine
Herrington et al. (1976)	20	Primary diagnosis depression (MRC criteria)	Pyridoxine	6–8	28	vs. amitriptyline (150 mg/day)	L-tryptophan as effective as amitriptyline
Farkas et al. (1976)	16	Primary affective disorder: 10 unipolar; 6 bipolar	Ascorbic acid Pyridoxine	6–9	10–18	vs. placebo	UP 1/10 antidepressant response BP 3/6 antidepressant response
Chouinard et al. (1979)	17	Primary affective disorder; 10 unipolar; 7 bipolar	Nicotinamide[c] (1–1.5 g/day)	4–6	28	vs. imipramine (150 mg/day)	Tryptophan/nicotinamide (Tr/Ni) as effective as imipramine. No potentiation of imipramine by Tr/Ni. UP: 3/10 marked improvement; 5/10 moderate improvement. BP: 2/7 marked improvement; 0/7 moderate improvement.

Note. Reprinted by permission of Elsevier Science Inc. from "Management of Depression with Serotonin Precursors," by H. M. van Praag, *Biological Psychiatry, 16,* p. 298. Copyright 1981 by the Society of Biological Psychiatry.

[a]On the grounds that additional hydroxylase co-factor might be required for the hydroxylation of tryptophan to 5-HTP.
[b]On the grounds that additional decarboxylase co-factor might be required for decarboxylation of 5-HTP to 5-HT.
[c]To decrease the activity of tryptophan pyrrolase and herewith the breakdown of tryptophan in the liver.

individuals who did not commit suicide (e.g., Pare, Young, Price, & Stacey, 1969). Because it was assumed that many of the suicide victims were depressed, these studies suggested that depressed patients had a relative deficiency of brain serotonin.

During the 1960s it was known that, in animals, brain levels of tryptophan and serotonin increased when they were given a dose of L-tryptophan (Wurtman, Hefti, & Melamed, 1981). This research suggested that if the serotonin deficiency was causing the depression, then L-tryptophan should be effective in treating depression in humans. To date, there have been approximately two dozen studies investigating the relative efficacy of L-tryptophan in depression. Eleven of these were double-blind studies of the effect of L-tryptophan versus a placebo or one of several types of antidepressants.

The results of the 11 double-blind studies are summarized in Table 8.1. I focus on these because their data were not confounded by a placebo effect. As Table 8.1 shows, these studies yielded conflicting results. Those that compared L-tryptophan with placebo all indicated that L-tryptophan is no more effective than placebo in treating unipolar depression. Better results were found for bipolar depression: Murphy et al. (1974) and Farkas, Dunner, and Fieve (1976) found that 50% of these patients improved with tryptophan.

Five double-blind studies in which L-tryptophan was compared with either imipramine or amitriptyline demonstrated that L-tryptophan was just as effective as these antidepressants in ameliorating depression. These findings seem to contradict those comparing L-tryptophan with placebo because these studies indicated that L-tryptophan does not seem to be effective for treating depression. Van Praag and Lemus (1986) pointed out, however, that the number of participants used in most of the antidepressant studies was very small (typically less than 20) and that the antidepressants were administered in rather low doses (150 mg/day). When these two factors are taken into account, the apparent antidepressant effect of both L-tryptophan and the antidepressant may be construed as a placebo effect, which suggests that any effect obtained from L-tryptophan may be a placebo effect.

Most investigators (e.g., van Praag & Lemus, 1986), however, consider it premature to dismiss L-tryptophan on the basis that it may have a placebo effect. The most ambitious study conducted to date provided one very compelling argument for the antidepressant effect of L-tryptophan in mild to moderately depressed individuals. Thomson et al. (1982) administered L-tryptophan (3 g/day), amitriptyline (150 mg/day), the combination of these two compounds, or placebo in a double-blind format for 12 weeks to 115 mildly to moderately depressed individuals who met the *DSM-III* criteria for major depressive disorder. As Figure 8.1 shows, L-tryptophan and amitriptyline were equally effective in ameliorating depression and were superior to placebo, and the combination of these two was superior to either compound alone.

Tryptophan dosages may also explain the contradictory findings about the antidepressant effects of tryptophan. The doses used in the studies

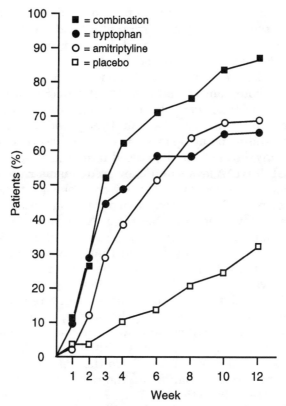

Figure 8.1. Comparison of the effects on amelioration of depression of L-tryptophan, amitriptyline, tryptophan and amitriptyline combined, and a placebo. The figure shows cumulative percentages of mildly to moderately depressed patients (N = 115) experiencing remission of depression (defined as 0—not depressed—on the global rating scale) during a 12-week treatment across the four conditions. From "The Treatment of Depression in General Practice," by J. Thompson, H. Rankin, G. W. Ashcroft, & C. M. Yates, 1982, *Psychological Medicine, 12,* p. 744. Copyright 1982 by Cambridge University Press. Reprinted with permission of Cambridge University Press.

listed in Table 8.1 varied considerably from 3 to 16 g/day. As I explained in chapter 3, tryptophan competes with tyrosine for entry into the brain. It may be that high doses of tryptophan used in some of these studies may have reduced the level of tyrosine entering the brain. Because tyrosine is the precursor for the catecholamines, a diminished level of tyrosine could result in a decline in catecholamine synthesis. And because the catecholamines are related to depression, a diminished catecholamine synthesis resulting from excessive levels of tryptophan administration could counteract any beneficial effect that may have accrued from the tryptophan. Chouinard, Young, Annable, and Sourkes (1979) provided support for this suggestion by indicating that a "therapeutic window" exists for L-tryptophan. These investigators found that the effectiveness of L-tryptophan decreased as the dose of L-tryptophan decreased as well as increased ($\geq$6 g/

day). The decreased effect was presumed to be due to a catecholamine deficit caused by the competition of tryptophan and tyrosine for entry into the brain. This study must be replicated, however, before the concept of a therapeutic window can be considered valid.

Finally, one other reason for not dismissing the potential antidepressant value of L-tryptophan is that treatment outcome studies have only recently begun to consider variables other than tryptophan that are also related to serotonin synthesis. As van Praag and Lemus (1986) have pointed out, serotonin metabolism seems to be disturbed in depression. For example, many, but not all, depressed individuals have lowered baseline levels of CSF-5-HIAA levels and a lowered plasma ratio of tryptophan/LNAA. Thus depressed people with a lowered plasma tryptophan/LNAA ratio would be more likely to respond to a dose of L-tryptophan than would those with normal tryptophan/LNAA ratio. A study by Møller, Kirk, and Honoré (1980) supported this speculation. The Møller, Kirk, and Honoré (1980)'s study is the only study I found that provides direct support for the contention that tryptophan may be effective primarily with a select group of depressives. However, related studies (e.g., Møller, 1990; Møller et al., 1990) of the relative efficacy of several different antidepressants (e.g., 5-HT uptake inhibitors and tricyclic antidepressants) for depressed participants who have normal versus low plasma tryptophan/LNAA ratios have consistently demonstrated people with the low plasma tryptophan/LNAA ratios responded most effectively to the antidepressants.

The efficacy of antidepressants and the role of low plasma tryptophan/LNAA ratios need to be investigated further in future research. At present, there are too few data. Young (1991b) reviewed the literature on the use of tryptophan in combination with other antidepressants and concluded that tryptophan potentiates MAO inhibitors but not the tricyclics. However, the studies he reviewed were all conducted more than 20 years ago and did not include metabolic factors such as plasma tryptophan/LNAA ratios. The only conclusion that can be drawn at present is that tryptophan seems to have some antidepressant properties, perhaps with a select group of individuals, and this amino acid may also be capable of potentiating the efficacy of antidepressant drugs.

Before leaving the discussion of therapeutic uses of tryptophan, it is worth reviewing briefly three other somewhat minor realms in which therapeutic tryptophan use has been investigated: for schizophrenia and mania and as a home remedy. Studies of the use of tryptophan in schizophrenia are not encouraging (see van Praag & Lemus, 1986, for a review), which is not surprising given that there is hardly any theoretical basis for assuming that tryptophan would be of benefit in schizophrenia. Studies of the therapeutic value of tryptophan in treating mania have been more encouraging: Murphy et al. (1974), Chouinard et al. (1985), and Prange, Wilson, Lynn, Alltop, and Stikeleather (1974), have all suggested that high doses of tryptophan, 6 to 12 gm/day may be effective in the treatment of manic states and may be even more effective in treating hypomanic states. There are two caveats to drawing this conclusion. First, three studies form too small a research base from which to draw a firm conclusion. Second, very high doses of tryptophan were used in these studies; therefore, it is possible that the therapeutic effect comes from the decrease in catecholamine synthesis due to the competition with tyrosine for entry into the brain and not from an increased synthesis of serotonin (van Praag & Lemus, 1986).

Because of its highly publicized antidepressant properties and its ready availability in health food and other stores, during the 1980s, individuals increasingly turned to tryptophan as a home remedy for disorders such as depression and insomnia. Roberts (1990b) has estimated that at least 10 million people in the United States have taken tryptophan. In the spring of 1989, physicians began reporting the occurrence of a previously rare disorder called eosinophilia-myalgia, which is characterized by muscle pain, edema, dermatological problems, and pulmonary difficulties. Many individuals were hospitalized with this disorder, and several have died.

Epidemiological studies revealed that almost all individuals with eosinophilia-myalgia were consuming relatively large amounts of tryptophan to combat conditions such as depression, insomnia, or PMS. Because tryptophan was strongly implicated, it was assumed to be the cause, and the product was taken off the market to ensure that subsequent cases of this disorder did not continue to appear (Nightingale, 1990). It seemed that the epidemiological studies were correct, because additional cases have not appeared since tryptophan was taken off the market.

Yet the idea that taking a tryptophan supplement could cause a disorder as potentially severe as eosinophilia-myalgia is surprising, and it seems unlikely that the tryptophan itself could have been the cause of the disorder. We all need a certain amount of tryptophan in our daily diet to maintain nitrogen balance (Altman & Dittmer, 1968); a normal diet supplies 1 to 1.5 g of tryptophan per day (Cole, Hartmann, & Brigham, 1980). Tryptophan supplements typically supplied 250 mg, 500 mg, or 1 g per capsule. Subsequent research has traced the syndrome of eosinophilia-myalgia to tryptophan manufactured during a single timeframe by a single Japanese manufacturer (Slutsker et al., 1990). The exact cause of the syndrome has yet to be identified, but it appears to be linked to a trace contaminant that was present in the tryptophan capsule. Presumably, this particular problem with tryptophan can be solved by identifying and eliminating this unwanted contaminant. However, tryptophan continues to remain unavailable to the general public without a prescription from a physician.

Tyrosine

The rationale for the use of tyrosine in the treatment of depression is essentially identical to that which stimulated the investigation of the efficacy of the use of tryptophan for treating depression. The catecholamine hypothesis of depression, formulated by Schildkraut (1965), stated that, in at least some patients, depression was the result of a deficiency in the availability or function of norepinephrine. This hypothesis was supported by the fact that many of the drugs that have been used to treat depression appear to enhance neurotransmission of the catecholamines.

In light of the catecholamine hypothesis and the experimental evidence indicating that tyrosine can increase the synthesis of the catecholamines in depressed patients, Gelenberg and his colleagues conducted a series of experiments designed to determine whether depression could be treated with a tyrosine supplement. In the first study (Gelenberg, Wojcik, Growdon, Sved, & Wurtman, 1980), positive results were found following treatment of one 30-year-old depressed woman with 6 g/day of tyrosine. Two weeks after starting the tyrosine treatment the patient's depression had ameliorated, and this amelioration was reversed following placebo treatment during the next 18 days. Following this initial positive experiment, Goldberg (1980) reported improvement in symptoms for two depressed patients who had previously responded to amphetamine.

Following these successes, Gelenberg (reported in Gelenberg, Wojcik, Gibson, & Wurtman, 1983) conducted a small double-blind study comparing tyrosine (100 mg/kg/day) with placebo in outpatients suffering from major depression for a 4-week period: 67% of those treated with tyrosine and 38% of the control group experienced an amelioration of depression. Gelenberg and his colleagues conducted a larger trial comparing tyrosine to both placebo and imipramine (Gelenberg et al., 1990). In this study 65 outpatients with a diagnosis of major depression were randomly assigned to tyrosine (100 mg/kg/day), imipramine (2.5 mg/kg/day), or placebo for at least four weeks. At the end of treatment, outpatients in all groups had improved, but the imipramine group showed a trend toward greater improvement. There was no difference in the placebo and tyrosine groups.

This study represents the most ambitious attempt to test the efficacy of tyrosine in the treatment of depression; however, it provides little support for the use of tyrosine to treat depression. Further investigation does not seem warranted, although, as Gelenberg et al. (1990) have suggested, it is still possible that a subgroup of people with depression may be responsive to tyrosine.

Folic Acid

Since the discovery of vitamins in the early 20th century and recognition that a vitamin deficiency could produce a variety of psychological symptoms, individuals have advocated that various psychological disorders could be treated with vitamin supplements. Watson and his colleagues (e.g., Watson & Currier, 1960), for example, conducted several studies during the 1950s and 1960s in which they claimed to have demonstrated that vitamin supplements could be used to treat psychiatric patients. One of the difficulties with this research is that these studies only classified participants as being "emotionally disturbed" or as having one of several psychiatric disorders. As was characteristic of research during that time, the basis for this classification was not specified. Additionally, Watson's research did not specify how to identify subjects that would profit from vitamin supplementation. In fact, he even stated that vitamin supplementation could exacerbate some individuals' psychiatric disorders (Watson, 1965).

As I mentioned in chapter 6, the topic of vitamin deficiency in psychiatric disorders has again resurfaced; research findings (e.g., Carney et al., 1979) have indicated that a portion of psychiatric patients are deficient in several vitamins including thiamin, pyridoxine, cyanocobalamin, and folic acid. Perhaps because individuals with depression, schizophrenia, and dementia seem to be particularly prone to a folate deficiency, most of the research has focused on folic acid as a possible treatment for depression. The emphasis on the use of folic acid to treat depression as opposed to schizophrenia or dementia may be due to the fact that depressed individuals are the larger population and that several studies (e.g., Ghadirian et al., 1980) have indicated that depressed individuals seem to have lower folate levels than those with schizophrenia.

Two studies have (Carney & Sheffield, 1970; Guaraldi, Fava, Mazzi, & La Greca, 1993) suggested that folic acid may be effective in treating depression in some individuals. However, because both were open-trial studies, confounding variables, such as a placebo effect, may have contributed to the overall treatment outcome. Although it is difficult to draw any firm conclusions from these studies, several controlled studies have also suggested that folic acid replacement therapy may be beneficial in treating some depressed individuals.

Coppen, Chaudhry, and Swade (1986) found that participants with unipolar but not bipolar depression who received a 200-mg folic acid supplement as well as lithium carbonate for a year were significantly less depressed than those receiving only lithium carbonate. Those subjects with the highest plasma folate levels at the end of the study were least depressed. Godfrey et al. (1990) found that, at the end of a 6-month treatment with 15 mg methylfolate or placebo, the folate group's clinical outcome score was significantly lower than that of the placebo group for both depressed and schizophrenic participants. However, there was no difference in other indices of depression. It must be pointed out that the participants in this study, as in the Coppen et al. (1986) study, were also taking psychotropic medication. Consequently, the study really represents a measure of whether methylfolate enhances the effectiveness of psychotropics. Passeri, Ventura, Abate, Cucinotta, and La Greca (1991) were the only researchers to compare folate to an antidepressant, finding that 5-methyltetrahydrofolate was as effective as trazodone in treating depression accompanying senile organic mental disorder in elderly patients.

Both open and double-blind trials of folic acid or 5-methyltetrahydrofolate have indicated that folic acid has potential beneficial effects. However, the double-blind studies have focused on the use of folic acid for enhancing antidepressants, and the only study to compare folic acid with placebo was subject to contamination by other factors such as a placebo effect. Consequently, it is impossible to state whether folic acid has any real antidepressant properties by itself. Probably the most accurate conclusion to draw at this time is that folic acid does seem to be able to enhance the effectiveness of antidepressants in people with low folate levels and that it may have antidepressant properties by itself. These conclusions must be viewed as tentative until supported by subsequent research.

Selenium

The first studies of the effects of selenium focused on the elderly, on the assumption that selenium, along with vitamin E, may offer some protection against cellular damage. To study the effects of selenium on mood, researchers have used supplements containing the antioxidants Vitamin E and selenium (Tolonen, Halme, & Sarna, 1985) or an antioxidant cocktail containing selenium, zinc, vitamin C, vitamin A, vitamin B_6, and vitamin E (Clausen, Nielsen, & Christensen, 1989). Tolonen et al.'s (1985) supplement resulted in a significant improvement in mood on dimensions such as depression and anxiety. Clausen et al. (1989) found only a trend toward an improvement in mood. Although these studies do suggest that antioxidants can improve the mood of the elderly, they do not specifically pinpoint selenium. This may be because, in animals, many diseases are caused by simultaneous deficiencies of selenium and vitamin E, and they can be prevented or cured by supplementation with either nutrient alone (National Research Council, 1983).

When Benton and Cook (1991) investigated the effect of selenium supplementation, administering 100 mcg to healthy individuals over a 5-week interval in a double-blind placebo-controlled design, they found that those receiving the supplement experienced an improvement in overall mood, specifically anxiety and confusion, when compared to the placebo group. The interesting component of this study is that the participants were physically and emotionally healthy. Whether a similar mood-altering effect may occur in a population with psychiatric disorders is not known. Alertsen, Aukrust, and Skaug (1986) showed that levels of selenium in blood and serum did not differ for psychiatric patients and control-group participants. However, this finding does not mean that a subclinical deficiency may not exist or that, as Benton and Cook (1991) have demonstrated, a selenium supplement may not have a positive effect on both a psychiatric and a nonpsychiatric population. This should be explored in future research.

Caffeine and Sucrose

During the past decade, my colleagues and I have been investigating the influence that caffeine and sucrose, or table sugar, can have on emotional distress. Our research was stimulated by a number of reports suggesting that both of these dietary substances can exert a detrimental effect on affect. Green (1969), Powers (1973), and Von Hilsheimer (1974), for example, reported case studies of children whose behavioral disturbances, irritability, hyperactivity, and short attention span improved following a dietary change consisting of a high protein/low-carbohydrate diet and the inclusion of various vitamin supplements. Mikkelsen (1978) and Greden (1974) reported case studies in which paranoid delusions, headaches, anxiety symptoms, depression, and insomnia were eliminated or dramatically reduced following elimination or reduction of caffeine. Winstead (1976) and Greden, Fontaine, Lubetsky, and Chamberlain (1978) found that caffeine consumption was related to anxiety and depression in a population of adults with psychiatric disorders.

These reports, although they represented correlational and case studies, suggested that carbohydrates, especially sucrose, and caffeine may have a detrimental effect on a portion of the population and that the primary effect was psychological in nature. Consequently, we focused on these two substances in our research.

We recognized from the outset that only certain individuals would potentially profit from a diet that consisted of elimination of caffeine and refined sucrose, so we attempted to devise a method of selecting sensitive individuals. Prior research we had conducted indicated that individuals expressing symptoms characteristic of hypoglycemia often reported beneficial effects following adherence to a diet that eliminated caffeine and sucrose. In our first study, we reported on the successful amelioration of the emotional distress of four individuals using a single-subject reversal design (Christensen, Krietsch, White, & Stagner, 1985). Figure 8.2, which depicts the MMPI scores of two of these individuals, reveals that, at baseline, they were both experiencing significant emotional distress. However, following a 2-week dietary intervention consisting of elimination of all caffeine and refined sucrose, their emotional distress declined considerably and then returned when baseline conditions were reinstituted.

In this study we also attempted to eliminate a placebo explanation by conducting double-blind challenge studies following the initial dietary intervention when the participant had received maximum amelioration of distress and prior to reinstituting baseline conditions. Each participant was asked, on consecutive days, to consume placebo, caffeine, or sweeteners including saccharin, aspartame, sucrose, and fructose. The substance administered on each day was randomly determined. Each day of the challenge, the participant provided ratings (e.g., of fatigue, depression, and irritability) every 5 minutes on a symptom rating scale for 55 minutes. The first three ratings were baseline ratings. Then the challenge substance was introduced, and the next eight ratings were designed to assess the reaction to the sweeteners or caffeine.

Figure 8.3 depicts the results for one subject. This figure shows that the ratings for symptom severity during the caffeine challenge began to increase at the 40-minute time interval and continued to increase during the remainder of the challenge. The next day this participant stated that he did not know what we gave him but "don't do it again," because he felt progressively worse during the rest of the day. This comment was consistent with the results of the challenge portion of the study indicating that

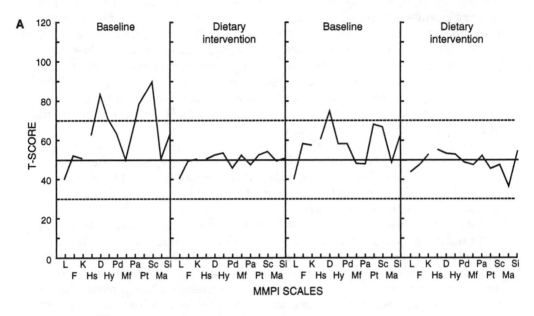

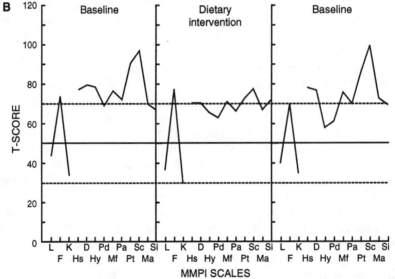

Figure 8.2. Effect on depression of eliminating caffeine and sucrose from the diet, as represented by MMPI scores of two individuals (*A*, C. C.; *B*, W. B.) during baseline and after a 2-week intervention. (Hs = Hypochondriasis; D = Depression; Hy = Hysteria; Pd = Psychopathic Deviate; Mf = Masculinity-Femininity; Pa = Paranoia; Pt = Psychasthenia; Sc = Schizophrenia; Ma = Hypomania; Si = Social Introversion) From Christensen, Krietsch, White, and Stagner (1985). Copyright 1985 by the American Psychological Association.

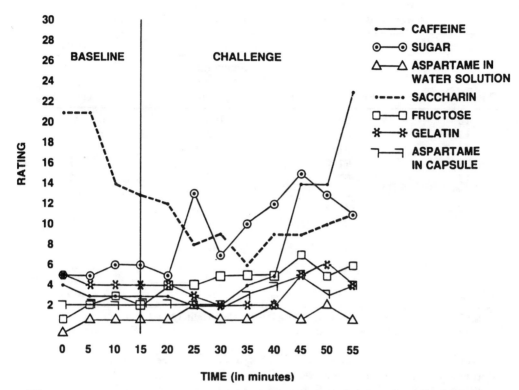

Figure 8.3. One participant's ratings of symptom severity during baseline and challenge phases of a dietary challenge with caffeine, sugar, sweeteners, and placebo. From Christensen, Krietsch, White, and Stagner (1985). Copyright 1985 by the American Psychological Association.

the participant was sensitive to caffeine and that this substance was contributing to his emotional distress. Interestingly, our research program has revealed that sucrose, rather than caffeine, is the more frequent contributor to emotional distress.

This participant's belated reaction to caffeine, as well as subsequent research we have conducted, have suggested to us that the duration of the challenge must be extended. Recent research has indicated that many individuals do not begin to experience a detrimental effect for several days. Currently, we use six-day challenges to identify whether a person is sensitive to either caffeine or sucrose.

Identifying Dietary Responders

Our initial study (Christensen, Krietsch, White, & Stagner, 1985) provided rather convincing evidence that caffeine and sucrose do contribute to the emotional distress of some individuals and that elimination of these substances from their diet could improve their emotional state. However, we knew that the sensitive individuals represented only a portion of the distressed population and that we needed to be able to identify the sensitive

Table 8.2. Sensitivity and Specificity of the CDDI for Various Cutoff Scores

Cutoff score	Sensitivity		Specificity
	Responders	Responders plus probable responders	Nonresponders
12	100	100	33
13	100	100	67
14	87.5	86	67
15	71.4	79	67
16	57	64	89
17	57	57	89
18	43	36	89
19	29	36	89
20	29	36	89
21	14	14	89
22	14	14	89
23	14	14	89
24	14	14	100

Note. From Christensen, Krietsch, & White (1989). Copyright 1989. Canadian Psychological Association. Reprinted with permission.

individuals. In our next study (Krietsch et al., 1988), we attempted to determine whether dietary responders could be identified by their presenting symptoms and psychological characteristics.

To accomplish this purpose, we identified a group of dietary responders, individuals who responded to the elimination of refined sucrose and caffeine, and a group of nonresponders, individuals who did not respond to the dietary intervention, using a single-subject and double-blind placebo controlled design. Dietary responders were individuals who not only profited from the dietary intervention but also demonstrated a return of their emotional distress following double-blind challenge of caffeine or refined sucrose but not placebo. Nonresponders, as might be expected, were those individuals who did not respond to the dietary intervention. Interestingly, the dietary responders and nonresponders did not differ on any of the psychological measures included in the study: They did not differ in terms of presenting symptoms, MMPI scores, MMPI two- and three-point codes, or on a variety of mood measures such as the BDI (Beck et al., 1961).

Our inability to differentiate dietary responders in terms of presenting symptoms or on a variety of psychological tests led us to develop a psychometric test, the Christensen Dietary Distress Inventory (CDDI; Christensen, 1990). This 34-item scale (see Appendix A) has a test–retest reliability coefficient of .87 and a predictive validity coefficient of 0.48 (Christensen et al., 1989). Table 8.2 presents the sensitivity and specificity of this scale.

The ideal cutoff score is obviously one that has a sensitivity and specificity of 100, because this would represent the perfect diagnostic instrument. However, because no instrument is perfect, one must identify the value, or cutoff score, that results in the fewest false classifications. This means that the best cutoff score would be one that had the highest sensitivity and specificity value. For the CDDI, a cutoff score of 13 seems to be most efficient, because it will identify all dietary responders (a sensitivity of 100) while producing a 33% false positive rate (a specificity of 67).

This scale has been successfully used for identifying dietary responders in subsequent research (Christensen & Burrows, 1990). However, I must point out that multiple inclusion criteria were used to select participants. They had to have been diagnosed with a current episode of major depression, have a BDI score of 16 or more and have an MMPI score of 70 or more. As a result of these multiple cutoff scores, the participants selected were quite depressed (M BDI > 27). Interestingly, it appears that it is the more seriously depressed individual that is more likely to respond to a refined sucrose and caffeine free diet. We do not know now whether the CDDI is capable of identifying dietary responders from a general population or from an introductory pool that represents the population that is used for many psychological studies.

Even after devising a method for identifying dietary responders, we still had not been able to identify the specific type of individual that would benefit most from dietary intervention. Because we had consistently found that dietary responders not only expressed symptoms of depression but also scored very high on measures of depression, such as the BDI, we decided to focus subsequent research (Christensen & Burrows, 1990) on individuals experiencing an episode of major depression. Using the criteria described earlier, we selected individuals who were experiencing an episode of major depression and who had cutoff scores of 13 or more on the CDDI, 16 or more on the BDI, and 70 or more on the MMPI. Twenty participants meeting these inclusion criteria were randomly assigned to an experimental (elimination of refined sucrose and caffeine) or control (elimination of red meat and artificial sweeteners) group.

As Table 8.3 shows after three weeks on the diet, the experimental group's level of depression declined significantly more than that of the control group and did so to a mild or nondepressed level. Improvements that existed at the end of the treatment period were maintained at a 3-month follow-up. This study seems to confirm that a dietary intervention that excludes refined sucrose and caffeine can be effective in the treatment of *some* depressed individuals. Again, however, these findings are in need of replication before they are considered to be robust.

Recommendations for Implementing Dietary Interventions

The procedure for investigating the efficacy of a dietary intervention consisting of elimination of refined sucrose and caffeine seems relatively simple. Some individuals are randomly assigned to a group that eliminates caffeine and refined sucrose from the diet, and an equivalent number are assigned to a group that eliminates a similar dietary element. Then the efficacy of the intervention is measured with selected outcome instruments. Conduct of such a study is, however, never as simple as it seems.

Table 8.3. Mean Pretest and Posttest Depression Scores of Participants Adhering to a Three-Week Dietary Intervention

	Pretest		Posttest	
Depression index	*M*	*SD*	*M*	*SD*
MMPI-D*				
Experimental	90.10	6.71	63.30	14.63
Control	85.80	11.94	81.20	15.87
BDI*				
Experimental	27.00	8.88	9.50	8.29
Control	27.40	8.69	23.10	9.12
SCL-90 Depression Scale*				
Experimental	53.40	4.33	34.90	5.04
Control	56.30	4.81	50.10	6.38

Note. MMPI-D = MMPI Depression Scale; BDI = Beck Depression inventory; SCL-90 = Symptom Checklist-90. The MMPI-D and SCL-90 Depression Scale scores are T-scores. *n* = 10 for experimental and control groups. The experimental group eliminated dietary caffeine and refined sucrose. The control group eliminated artificial sweeteners and red meat. From Christensen & Burrows (1990). Copyright 1990 by *Behavior Therapy*. Reprinted with permission.
*$p < .05$.

As I have already discussed, it is necessary, first, to identify and select individuals who are likely to respond to dietary intervention. Then, participants have to be instructed to avoid caffeine and sucrose. I recommend (see Christensen, 1991) telling participants that they can consume only foods that do not contain refined sucrose and caffeine, placing no restriction on how much is eaten as long as something is eaten at each meal and the restricted substances are not consumed.

Unfortunately, caffeine and refined sucrose are ubiquitous substances and not easily avoided; therefore, participants must read the labels of all packaged, bottled, and canned products and be able to accurately interpret their contents. Sugar products are especially problematic. Sweeteners come in a variety of forms other than sugar or sucrose. Products containing glucose or dextrose should be avoided. If a sweetener is required, an artificial sweetener such as Nutrasweet is recommended, although most sensitive subjects tolerate fructose and corn sweeteners if used in small quantities, probably because the metabolic pathway for fructose is different than that for sucrose, which results in a smaller rise in serum glucose or insulin (Crapo et al., 1982). Interestingly, foods that contain naturally occurring sucrose, such as apples, can be tolerated and, according to the research I have conducted, they do not restrict the effects of dietary interventions. Foremost, participants need to avoid added sugar or refined sucrose.

To aid participants in adhering to dietary restrictions, it is helpful to provide a sample diet, as well as a list of caffeine and refined-sucrose foods, such as the one that appears in Appendix B. Many individuals feel overwhelmed when faced with the task of deleting these substances, and a sample diet can assist in implementation.

Participants should adhere to a diet for at least two weeks. The maximum benefit seems to occur within this timeframe, although most individuals experience an improvement in affect within the first week. If a benefit has not occurred within the first two weeks, it is unlikely that the dietary intervention will be effective.

It is also important to alert participants to possible withdrawal effects, primarily from the elimination of caffeine: Headaches frequently begin to occur within 12 to 24 hours following caffeine elimination. Other less common symptoms include fatigue, anxiety, irritability, confusion, insomnia, and various muscle pains or stiffness.

Whereas some individuals experience no withdrawal effects from elimination of caffeine, others experience very severe effects. At present, there are no predictors of severity of withdrawal effects or who will experience them. One female participant (Christensen & Burrows, 1990) was consuming up to 20 cups of coffee a day, apparently to combat the anergy accompanying her depression, and she had no withdrawal effects. Other participants who consumed 3 to 5 cups of coffee a day had very painful withdrawal effects that did not begin to abate for at least a week; a slight headache was still present at the end of two weeks. Most individuals will experience tolerable withdrawal effects for 2 to 4 days. I consider it important to inform participants of the possibility of withdrawal effects and to let them know that they will typically last from 2 to 4 days.

Sucrose can also produce withdrawal effects in some individuals. A few individuals report feeling shaky and dizzy and develop an increased sense of "internal nervousness" during the first few days on the diet. In most instances, participants can handle these effects by eating something, such as an apple or peanuts, as soon as the symptoms occur. They should then try to anticipate the occurrence of the symptoms and eat something prior to their occurrence. These withdrawal effects should disappear within the first week on the diet, although for some they may last longer.

If the dietary change proves to be effective in reducing depression or depression-related symptoms, it is important to determine whether the offending substance is caffeine or sucrose, because few people are sensitive to both substances. To accomplish this task, each substance must be introduced individually into the diet and should be done so in the context of a double-blind placebo controlled design.

When administering a diet within the context of an outpatient treatment program, it may be useful to employ an open procedure, whereby participants would consume one of the target substances, such as caffeine-containing products, for up to two weeks, and the researcher would monitor symptoms during this time. If symptoms do not return, participants would be instructed to consume a large quantity of sucrose-containing foods such as donuts, sweet rolls, candy, or any sugary food not containing caffeine for up to two weeks. Again, symptoms should be monitored; if they return following sucrose but not caffeine consumption, the researcher could conclude that the participant is sucrose sensitive. It must be remembered, however, that open trials are subject to a placebo effect.

When conducting the challenge portion of a study, regardless of whether a double-blind or open-challenge procedure is used, one of the issues that must be confronted is the amount of caffeine or sugar to be consumed by the participant. I recommend trying to match the amount of caffeine to the amount that the subject consumed prior to the dietary intervention. This approach has been effective in my research for identifying caffeine-sensitive individuals. In estimating the amount of caffeine, a guideline that can be used is that a cup (150–237 ml) of caffeinated coffee contains about 100 mg of caffeine; an 8-oz (237 ml) glass of tea contains about 50 mg of caffeine; and a 12-oz (355 ml) cola drink contains about 50 mg. It is more difficult to estimate the amount of sucrose, because it is virtually impossible to determine the amount of sucrose added to products. As an alternative, I have had participants consume a half-gallon of Kool-Aid a day for up to six days. This seems to be sufficient to identify most sucrose responders.

I want to point out that once sensitive individuals and the offending substance have been identified, this substance must be continually avoided to eliminate its negative effect. Although there is little data on this topic, there is some indication that minor violations can be tolerated well. My experience and that of Egger et al. (1985) suggests that some individuals' sensitivity to certain foods declines below a threshold of producing symptoms following a period of abstinence. Minor transgressions may be tolerated well, but repeated consumption of the offending substance will probably result in a reemergence of symptoms.

Conclusion

During the last decade, diet–behavior research has begun to focus more attention on the effects of food on psychological health, particularly on depression. Because tryptophan and tyrosine are precursors of the neurotransmitters serotonin and norepinephrine, a deficiency of which has been linked to depression, a number of researchers have investigated their potential benefits for treating depression. Tryptophan studies have revealed that tryptophan is no more effective in treating depression than is placebo but is just as effective as antidepressants. However, because the dose of the antidepressant used in these studies was rather low, any effect may have been due to placebo.

The most recent and extensive study found tryptophan to be more effective than placebo with mild to moderately depressed individuals. Moreover, most studies have not taken into consideration metabolic variables, such as the plasma tryptophan/LNAA ratio. Recent research has revealed that depressed people with low tryptophan/LNAA ratios are more likely to respond to tryptophan and more likely to potentiate the effect of antidepressants. This finding suggests that tryptophan does have antidepressant properties but primarily in certain individuals. Tryptophan has not been found to be effective in treating schizophrenia, but large doses do seem to have some effect in treating hypomanic individuals, probably because large doses compete with tyrosine for entry into the brain and thereby reduce catecholamine synthesis.

Results from initial clinical trials suggested that tyrosine may be an effective treatment modality for depression. However, the most recent and largest study did not support this conclusion. Other researchers have found that folate and selenium may have antidepressant properties and that depressed people with low levels of these substances may benefit from dietary supplementation. However, these findings are tentative and must be replicated and extended to identify the antidepressant properties of these two substances.

Several studies have also focused on the antidepressant properties of elimination of caffeine and sucrose, consistently demonstrating that some emotionally distressed individuals are sensitive to these substances and that elimination of these substances can ameliorate their distress. These studies also suggest that depressed individuals are most likely to respond to this dietary intervention.

9 _____

Efficacy of Dietary Interventions for the Treatment of Disorders in Children and Adolescents

Children and adolescents are treated in a variety of mental health settings for disorders ranging from anxiety and depression to hyperactivity. Although it is agreed that the mental health needs of children are relatively great, there are little data on the extent to which specific children suffer from different types of dysfunctions (Kazdin, 1988). Several epidemiological studies in the United States and Great Britain have estimated that clinical dysfunction exists among approximately 12% of children. However, the estimated range varies considerably (6%–37%) among the different studies (Gould, Wunsch-Hitzig, & Dohrenwend, 1980). We do know that problems such as hyperactivity, autism, and aggressive behavior do exist and are in need of effective treatment, and strides have been made.

Nutritional approaches, in addition to the more traditional pharmacological and psychotherapeutic approaches, have been proposed as effective treatment of a number of disorders. Most nutritional approaches have focused on megavitamin therapy—the use of massive doses of vitamins and large amounts of minerals in the treatment of psychological disorders. The popularity of this approach increased dramatically when Linus Pauling, a two-time Nobel Prize winner, supported its use and proposed that large quantities of vitamins are critical for optimal mental functioning (Pauling, 1968). Pauling coined the term *orthomolecular psychiatry* to describe this type of treatment. This term has since been adopted to describe megavitamin therapy. Practitioners using this approach have even formed a medical society, the Academy of Orthomolecular Psychiatry (Ross, 1986), to promote orthomolecular treatment, including through its own scholarly journal. Although the megavitamin approach has probably dominated, orthomolecular psychiatrists as well as more traditional medical and mental health professionals have also focused on using specific foods such as simple carbohydrates. In this chapter I focus on the types of disorders that have received attention from nutritionally minded investigators and summarize the current state of knowledge regarding the role of nutrition in these disorders.

Attention-Deficit Hyperactivity Disorder

One area of child psychopathology that has received considerable attention in the past several decades is attention-deficit hyperactivity disorder

(ADHD). This disorder has, in the past, gone by myriad names including minimal brain damage, minimal brain dysfunction, hyperkinetic reaction of childhood, hyperkinetic-impulsive disorder, hyperactivity, and attention deficit disorder (with and without hyperactivity). The label in vogue at any one time seems to roughly parallel the prevailing belief regarding the primary deficit inherent in this disorder (Hoza & Pelham, 1993).

The primary symptoms of ADHD are inattention, impulsive behavior, and hyperactivity. Problems of inattention include difficulty in completing tasks or in persisting at a given play activity, difficulty in concentrating on tasks requiring sustained attention such as doing homework or assigned deskwork, being easily distracted, and not attending to instructions. Impulsive behavior includes acting without thinking, which causes a disruption such as blurting out in class or barging into a game others are playing; having difficulty taking turns; and having difficulty in controlling one's own behavior. The hyperactivity dimension is perhaps the one that most attracts the attention of parents, because it involves excessive movement such as running, climbing, fidgeting, and not staying seated at school.

For a child to be given the diagnosis of ADHD, he or she must manifest the symptoms by age 7, and the symptoms must have persisted for at least six months. Interestingly, ADHD symptoms may be completely absent when children are engaged in an activity that they are very interested in or when they are interacting one-to-one with another person. For this reason, it is very difficult to make a diagnosis from just observing the child in a doctor's office. An accurate diagnosis can be made only by observing the child's behavior in his or her natural environment across many settings.

ADHD is the most frequently diagnosed childhood behavior disorder. It has been estimated that 3% to 5% of all children have ADHD (Pelham, Gnagy, Greenslade, & Milich, 1992), with boys outnumbering girls by a ratio of 6 to 1 based on clinic samples (Barkley, 1990). The most common treatment of ADHD is medication consisting primarily of either dextroamphetamine, methylphenidate, or magnesium pemoline (Zametkin & Rapoport, 1987). However, it has been suggested that concurrent treatment with medication and behavior therapy is preferable to the singular use of either treatment (Pelham, 1989), because neither treatment alone tends to completely correct the disorder and the positive effects of either treatment are apparent only while the treatment is being administered (Hoza & Pelham, 1993).

Although medication and behavior therapy are the recommended treatments of choice, neither treatment is effective for all children. About one third of all children fail to respond to either type of treatment. This statistic has further stimulated the belief that a combined approach would be more effective (Hoza & Pelham, 1993). The failure to effectively treat one third of all children and the anxiety many parents have regarding maintaining their children on medication (Gath, 1986) has stimulated both the scientific community and parents to search for and try alternative treatments. Over the past several decades, a variety of nutritional treatments have been advocated, and some of these have received considerable attention from the general public. Perhaps the most notable of these is the Feingold diet.

The Feingold Diet

Feingold, a physician working in the Department of Allergy at the Kaiser-Permanente Medical Center in San Francisco, California, proposed that some children have a sensitivity to synthetic food additives, particularly butylated hydroxyanisol (BHA), a food color, and butylated hydroxytoluene (BHT), an antioxidant (1975b). Feingold proposed that ingestion of these substances by sensitive children results in ADHD and that elimination of these items from the diet results in a dramatic improvement and even a cure of ADHD (referred to as hyperactivity during the 1970s when this theory was in vogue). According to Feingold (1975b), approximately 50% of all ADHD children adhering to the diet should experience a positive response.

Given the concern that parents had about maintaining their children on medication, the possibility of controlling ADHD dietarily was extremely appealing. Feingold was invited to hold a press conference at the annual meeting of the American Medical Association in 1973 and 1974, which provided worldwide publicity for his observations and assertions (Feingold, 1981). The public interest generated by the press conferences prompted publishers to approach him to write a popular book on the dietary management of ADHD. This book stimulated the formation of numerous parent associations in several countries, which were dedicated to compiling lists of permissible foods as well as providing support groups. Many pediatricians and family physicians were convinced of the potential efficacy of this diet and recommended the diet to parents of ADHD children (Bennett & Sherman, 1983).

The considerable public interest in and acceptance of the Feingold diet sparked the interest of the scientific community. The Nutrition Foundation and the U.S. Department of Health, Education, and Welfare independently formed working groups to review Feingold's data, concluding ultimately that the data were based on clinical findings and not rigorous experimental research (Williams & Cram, 1978). Following this evaluation, a number of investigators (e.g., Conners, Goyette, Southwick, Lees, & Andrulonis, 1976; Harley, Matthews, & Eichman, 1978) attempted to assess the validity of Feingold's claims and the efficacy of his dietary intervention in treating ADHD. Reviewers of this research (e.g., Kavale & Forness, 1983; Mattes, 1983) as well as other independent researchers (e.g., Harley, Ray, et al., 1978) have consistently arrived at the same conclusion: The Feingold diet was not effective for managing ADHD except, perhaps, for a very small percentage of children. Although the advocates of this treatment modality did not accept these conclusions (e.g., Rimland, 1983), these conclusions did finally seem to make an impact. Little attention is currently given to the Feingold diet, and most people seem to agree that it is of little, if any, benefit for most children with ADHD.

Restriction of Sugar

As interest in the Feingold diet declined, a corresponding interest in the potential detrimental effect of sugar on children's behavior began to emerge (Varley, 1984). Parents reported that the behavior of their children changed rapidly and dramatically following the ingestion of sugar, and this belief pervaded for children with or without ADHD (Milich, Wolraich, & Lindgren, 1986). A belief in the detrimental effect of sugar also pervaded the medical profession; 45% of physicians surveyed reported that they periodically recommended that parents of children with ADHD restrict their sugar intake (Bennett & Sherman, 1983). And, as I stated in chapter 4, 90% of teachers surveyed in one study reported that they believed that sugar adversely affected children's classroom behavior and academic performance (McLoughlin & Nall, 1988).

Some anecdotal reports and case studies (e.g., Crook, 1975; Rapp, 1978) also supported a detrimental effect of sugar. Rapp has even produced a videotape visually demonstrating the behavioral alteration that can occur following ingestion of food to which a child is supposedly sensitive. The arguments against sugar have been buttressed by statistics estimating that the consumption of sucrose per person rose from 35 lbs. a year at the turn of the century to 100 lbs. in 1972 (Lecos, 1985). Although sucrose consumption has declined since other sweeteners have appeared on the market, per capita consumption was still high at approximately 65 lbs. in 1986.

Unfortunately, belief in the adverse effect of sugar on children's behavior did not grow out of controlled experimental studies; controlled studies did not begin to appear until after widespread acceptance of this belief. And, unfortunately, one of the earliest studies conducted provided support, although it was correlational and did not demonstrate causality. Prinz et al. (1980) examined the relationship between dietary intake and behavior in hyperactive and nonhyperactive children and found sugar consumption to be correlated with destructive-aggressive and restless behavior in hyperactive children but not in nonhyperactive children. This finding also suggested that sugar consumption may be a factor in ADHD. Attempts to replicate this study were either unsuccessful (Barling & Bullen, 1984) or provided only mild support (Wolraich, Milich, Stumbo, & Schultz, 1985). An alternative hypothesis may be that more active and disruptive children may seek out sugar-laden foods. Fortunately, this hypothesis has been explored in controlled experimental studies.

In a number of dietary challenge studies (e.g., Rosen et al. (1988), children with ADHD were given sucrose, another sweetener, or a placebo in a double-blind fashion. Reviewers of these studies (e.g., Kinsbourne, 1994; Kruesi, 1986; Milich et al., 1986) have reached the same conclusion: There is no convincing evidence that sugar ingestion has a detrimental effect on the behavior of hyperactive children. This is a general conclusion and does not mean that a few hyperactive children may not respond adversely to sugar, as was demonstrated by Egger et al. (1985). Several researchers (e.g., Behar, Rapoport, Adams, Berg, & Cornblath, 1984) even found that sugar ingestion had the positive effect of inducing a slight calming effect on hyperactive children.

Vitamin Therapy

The notion that megadoses of vitamins can be used to effectively treat children with ADHD seems to be based on the belief that these children suffer from a biochemical imbalance that can be corrected (Kershner & Hawke, 1979). This assumption has received support from clinical trials in which children with ADHD were effectively treated with vitamin supplements (Brenner, 1982; Cott, 1972). In an attempt to provide further support for the clinical trials, several researchers (e.g., Arnold, Christopher, Huestis, & Smeltzer, 1978; Haslam, 1992) have conducted double-blind placebo controlled experiments using only children who seemed to benefit from vitamin supplementation during clinical trials. These researchers have consistently reached the same conclusion: Vitamin supplementation is not an effective treatment for ADHD. Apparently, the positive effects noted from the earlier clinical trials were due to a placebo effect or some other variable and not to the vitamin supplement the children were receiving.

Elimination of Food-Induced Allergies

With all the rhetoric and attention given to the potential contribution of food to the development of ADHD, it would be surprising if reference were not also made to the role of food allergies in this childhood disorder. Although the potential etiological contribution of allergy in ADHD is very controversial (Atkins, 1986), the notion still has its advocates. A relationship between allergic reactions and disordered behavior was hypothesized as early as 70 years ago. Shannon (1922) described eight children who were suffering from complaints such as nervousness, irritability, unruliness, insomnia, decreased appetite, and poor school performance, which he believed to be due primarily to reactions to certain foods. He reported that elimination of these foods from the diet resulted in a marked improvement in seven of these children. Since this early description, additional reports (e.g., Randolph, 1974; Speer, 1958) have continued to suggest that the behavior of at least a portion of children with ADHD may be due to an allergic reaction to foods.

Other researchers have found that the incidence of food allergies is greater in hyperactive children than nonhyperactive children. Tryphonas and Trites (1979) found that 47% of 90 hyperactive children were allergic to at least one food when tested by the radioallergosorbent test (RAST). Rapp (1978) found that 66% of children who had been prescribed Ritalin for their hyperactivity had a history of classic respiratory or cutaneous allergy. These rates are far above those found in the general population. Epidemiology studies have found an incidence of 6.6% (Arbeiter, 1967) and 7.5% (Buckley & Metcalfe, 1982) of food allergy in children and an incidence of 23.7% (Appel, Szanton, & Rapaport, 1961) and 24% (Arbeiter, 1967) of any form of allergy.

Trites, Ferguson, and Tryphonas (1980) compared the behavior of 19 hyperactive children with allergies with the behavior of 15 children without allergies using a double-blind crossover treatment and control diet. The treatment diet eliminated the foods to which the children with allergies had shown positive RAST results. Results, based on a blind clinical judgment of both parent and teacher ratings, revealed that 58% of the allergic children improved on the treatment diet, whereas none of the non-allergic children received a rating of being improved. Similar results were found by Rapp (1978).

Egger et al. (1985) assessed the effect of an oligoantigenic diet on 76 children diagnosed as being either hyperactive or overactive, based on suggestions in the literature that children with ADHD may be reactive to certain foods or have a food allergy. This diet restricted the child's food consumption to two meats such as lamb and chicken, two carbohydrate sources (e.g., potatoes and rice), two fruits, vegetables, calcium, and vitamins. Eighty-two percent of the children following this restricted diet responded positively by demonstrating an improvement in their symptoms, although only 27% recovered completely. Following recovery or improvement in symptomatology, Egger et al. (1985) reintroduced the foods eliminated on the oligoantigenic diet weekly and one at time to begin to identify the offending foods. Table 9.1 lists the foods that caused a reemergence of symptoms in the children. The interesting component of this table is the variety of foods to which the children were sensitive. Additionally, some children were sensitive to more than one food, and different children were sensitive to a different combination of foods. This finding suggests that food sensitivities have no generalizability among children but that each child may have an idiosyncratic response to foods. To verify that the identified foods were really having an effect, Egger et al. (1985) conducted a double-blind placebo controlled crossover trial with 28 of the children who had improved on the oligoantigenic diet. All evaluations indicated that the children's behavior was significantly better on the placebo than during the food challenge, supporting the finding that elimination of the offending foods resulted in a behavioral improvement.

The Egger et al. (1985) study stands in direct contrast to most of the other dietary studies of the relationship between ADHD and food. The difference is that Egger et al. eliminated many foods in addition to preservatives and food colors. Interestingly, several researchers (Boris & Mandel, 1994; Carter et al., 1993) have replicated the Egger et al. study, indicating that when multiple foods are eliminated, positive effects are found.

Boris and Mandel (1994) followed a procedure similar to that of Egger et al. (1994) but added the component of ensuring that all children participating met *DSM-III-R* criteria for ADHD. In this study, the children completed an open-elimination diet, eliminating dairy products, wheat, corn, yeast, soy, citrus, egg, chocolate, and peanuts. Seventy-three percent of the children showed improvement on this diet. In challenges with the

Table 9.1. Reactions of Children Diagnosed as Hyperactive or Overactive to Foods Administered in an Olioantigenic Diet

Foods universally tested	Number tested N = 76	Number reacted (%)	Foods rarely‡ tested and positive	Number tested	Number reacted
Colorant &			Plums	9	2
preservatives	34	27 (79)	Rabbit	6	3
Soya*	15	11 (73)	Sago	5	2
Cow's milk	55	35 (64)	Duck	4	3
Chocolate	34	20 (59)	Foods tested only in		
Grapes	18	9 (50)	patients who re-		
Wheat	53	28 (49)	acted to antigeni-		
Oranges	49	22 (45)	cally related foods		
Cow's cheese	15	6 (40)	To cow's milk:		
Hen's eggs	50	20 (39)	Goat's milk	22	15
Peanuts	19	6 (32)	Ewe's milk	12	4
Maize	38	11 (29)	To wheat:		
Fish	48	11 (23)	Rye	29	15
Oats	43	10 (23)	Foods to which there		
Melons	29	6 (21)	was no reaction		
Tomatoes	35	7 (20)	Cabbages	54	
Ham/bacon	20	4 (20)	Lettuces	53	
Pineapple	31	6 (19)	Cauliflowers	50	
Sugar†	55	9 (16)	Celery	49	
Beef	49	8 (16)	Goat's cheese	4	
Beans	34	5 (15)	Duck eggs	2	
Peas	33	5 (15)			
Malt	20	3 (15)			
Apples	53	7 (13)			
Pork	38	5 (13)			
Pears	41	5 (12)			
Chicken	56	6 (11)			
Potatoes	54	6 (11)			
Tea	19	2 (10)			
Coffee	10	1 (10)			
Other nuts	11	1 (10)			
Cucumbers	32	3 (9)			
Bananas	52	4 (8)			
Carrots	55	4 (7)			
Peaches	41	3 (7)			
Lamb	55	3 (5)			
Turkey	22	1 (5)			
Rice	51	2 (4)			
Yeast	28	1 (4)			
Apricots	34	1 (3)			
Onions	49	1 (2)			

Note. From "Controlled Trial of Oligoantigenic Treatment in the Hyperkinetic Syndrome," by J. Egger, C. M. Carter, P. J. Graham, D. Gumley, & J. F. Soothill, 1985, *Lancet, 1,* p. 540–545. Copyright 1985 by *The Lancet Ltd.* Reprinted with permission.

*Given only to those who reacted to cow's milk.

†5 reacted to both beet and cane sugar. 3 to cane sugar only, and one to beet sugar only. The parents of several other patients thought that large quantities of sugar provoked symptoms, without definite confirmation.

‡Tested in <10 patients.

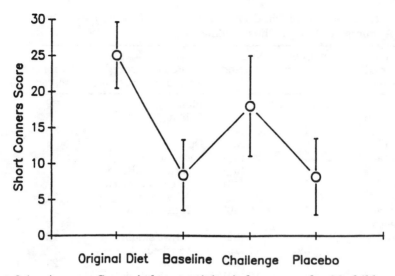

Figure 9.1. Average Conner's hyperactivity index scores for 26 children diagnosed with ADHD, after a 2-week open-elimination diet. From "Foods and Additives Are Common Causes of the Attention Deficit Hyperactive Disorder in Children," by M. Boris & F. S. Mandel, 1994, *Annals of Allergy, 72,* p. 446. Copyright 1994 by the American College of Allergy and Immunology. Reprinted with permission.

eliminated foods during the subsequent month, these children reacted to several of the foods that had been previously eliminated. This finding is consistent with those of both Egger et al. (1985) and Carter et al. (1993).

More important, these children also reacted to these substances when they were presented in the context of a double-blind placebo controlled challenge. As Figure 9.1 shows, the children's average scores on the hyperactivity index of the Conners Parent Rating Scale-48 (Goyette, Conners, & Ulrich, 1978) declined during the baseline period when the elimination diet was followed. During the double-blind challenge portion of the study, hyperactive behavior remained low following placebo administration and increased when challenged with the suspected offending food.

The Egger et al. (1985), Carter et al., (1993), and Boris and Mandel (1994) studies consistently demonstrate that more than 70% of the children tested in these studies reacted to foods and additive-containing foods. This finding suggests that a large portion of children with ADHD can be assisted by close monitoring of food reactions. It is also important to emphasize that a portion of children with ADHD do not seem to be sensitive to any food substance, which indicates the heterogeneity of this disorder. These studies are also instructive in consistently revealing that most reactive children are sensitive to multiple foods and that studies investigating only one food or substance are doomed to failure. Additionally, the combination of foods to which a child may be sensitive seems to be idiosyncratic to that child. This speaks to the necessity of starting out with a broad elimination diet rather than attempting to focus on one substance such as sugar.

Although these studies support the belief that allergies can contribute to ADHD in some children, they do not provide any rationale for the connection between food sensitivities and ADHD. Marshall (1989) has argued that an allergic sensitivity results in an imbalance between the adrenergic and cholinergic activity in the autonomic and central nervous system. This imbalance can contribute to a poorly regulated arousal system that can be manifested in attentional problems and other behaviors exhibited by children with ADHD. Whether this is an accurate explanation of the connection between ADHD and food sensitivities remains to be seen.

Autism

Autism is a devastating disorder that affects about three to five children out of every 10,000 births. Boys are affected about four times as frequently as girls. Children born with this disorder typically have a profound and pervasive deficit in social attachment and behavior. They do not bond with parents or develop emotional attachments with others. About 50% of autistic children have an impairment in language, and those that do speak typically have a speech pattern that is very different from that of other children. They prefer routine and become distressed with changes in their environment or routine. Many autistic children engage in self-stimulatory behavior such as rolling their heads or rocking their bodies. Sometimes they inflict damage to themselves by banging their heads or biting their hands or wrists. Coupled with this compilation of unusual behavior is unusual affect. Some autistic children seem very placid, whereas others throw a raging tantrum at the slightest provocation (Schreibman, Loos, & Stahmer, 1993).

Early theories suggested that autism was psychogenic in origin, with parents, especially the mother, being the causative agent. Autism is now believed to be organic, but the etiology is unknown. Nonetheless, there are treatments for autism. Behavior therapy has been most effective, and pharmacotherapy is used to decrease some of the behavioral symptoms that accompany the disorder.

The only dietary substance that may have some positive benefit is vitamin B_6. In a study of the effects of an experimental vitamin regimen (vitamin C, vitamin B_6, niacinamide, and pantothenic acid) for 200 autistic children, Rimland (1974) noted that vitamin B_6 appeared to be the key factor in producing the positive changes observed. To more completely investigate this possibility, 16 autistic children who improved on the experimental vitamin regimen participated in an experimental trial of the effect of inclusion and exclusion of vitamin B_6 (Rimland, Callaway, & Dreyfus, 1978). Both parents and teachers rated each child's behavior during each stage of the experiment. Results revealed that removal of the vitamin led to a deterioration in behavior, and subsequent ingestion led to a behavioral improvement.

In a similar study, Lelord et al. (1988) found that 47% of autistic children improved with vitamin B_6 and magnesium. In a survey of 318 parents who were administering some form of drug or vitamin therapy, Rimland (1988) found that 43% of the parents stated that their child profited from vitamin B_6 and magnesium treatment, as compared to only 29% of parents citing the drug deanol as the next most helpful agent.

The available data suggest that vitamin B_6 and magnesium may be useful in the treatment of autism; however, these findings must be accepted with caution because of the possible existence of confounding factors. Survey reports from parents are subject to numerous potential biases such as a placebo effect. The Lelord et al. (1988) study provided few data on the characteristics of the individuals for whom treatment was successful, so it is difficult to differentially identify the children who may profit from this treatment. The Rimland (1978) study is problematic in that the parents and their children were located in a widely spaced geographical area (Florida to California). Because it was necessary to give parents and teachers instructions by mail and telephone, it was not possible to ensure that either the instructions or the requirements of the study were understood. Additionally, the children were consuming a variety of other agents including vitamins, minerals, and other drugs that could have contributed to any beneficial effect.

Down's Syndrome

Down's syndrome is a chromosomal abnormality occurring in about 1 in every 700 live births. As the mother ages the probability of giving birth to a Down's syndrome child increases: The risk of a 35- to 39-year-old woman having a Down's syndrome child is 6.5 times greater than that of a 20- to 24-year-old and 20.5 times greater for a 40- to 44-year-old woman (Batshaw & Perret, 1992). Most children with Down's syndrome have an extra copy of chromosome 21 or trisomy 21. Apparently there is a critical region of chromosome 21 that, if present, produces Down's syndrome, and if absent, even though the rest of chromosome 21 is present, does not. This means that the genes producing the characteristics for Down's syndrome reside in this lower region of chromosome 21 (Batshaw & Perret, 1992).

Individuals with Down's syndrome have a distinctive set of physical and mental features. IQs range from being extremely low, to an average of 40 to 50 to a high of about 80. Down's syndrome children have small heads that are flattened at the back; the eyes, which are slanted upwards, and mouth are small; hands and feet are short; and necks are broad and stocky. These children frequently have a variety of medical problems ranging from middle ear infections to obesity, seizures, and depression (Batshaw & Perret, 1992).

Although there is no known cure for Down's syndrome, a variety of treatments have been attempted, including fetal cell therapy and administration of glutamic acid, pituitary extract, 5-hydroxytryptophan, vitamin and mineral supplements, and dimethyl sulfoxide (Pruess, Fewell, & Bennett, 1989). The idea that providing large doses of vitamins and minerals may be useful in treating Down's syndrome has a long history and periodically reemerges in the scientific literature. Turkel, in 1940, probably initiated one of the first studies investigating the treatment of Down's syndrome with a combination of ingredients that included many vitamins and minerals (Turkel, 1975). He claimed that this combination of supplements resulted in an improvement in intellectual functioning as well as in physical attributes.

Turkel's claims were based on his own observations, which increases the likelihood of bias; however, other researchers have found deficiencies in nutrients such as zinc, copper, and vitamin B_6 in children with Down's syndrome and other children as well (Justice et al., 1988; Pruess et al., 1989), thus providing at least some additional support for the suggestion that a nutritional deficiency exists in Down's syndrome.

In the early 1980s Harrell, Capp, Davis, Peerless, and Ravitz (1981) conducted a study that renewed interest in the possible benefit of megavitamin therapy for Down's syndrome. These investigators based their study on the *genetotrophic hypothesis*, which states that a disease can be caused by a genetically determined insufficiency of one or more specific nutrients. If these nutrients are supplied, the disease can be prevented or at least ameliorated.

On the basis of a report of the successful treatment, with megadoses of vitamins and minerals, of a severely retarded child, Harrell et al.'s (1981) goal was to confirm this hypothesis in the context of an experimental study. At the end of the first four months of the study, the IQ scores of the children who received the vitamin–mineral supplement increased an average of 5 points, whereas the children who took the placebo showed no change. At the end of eight months, those who took the supplement during this entire time interval increased their IQ scores by an average of 13.5 points, and those who changed from placebo to the supplement increased their IQ scores by 10.2 points. The Down's syndrome children showed the greatest increase of from 10 to 25 IQ points and also demonstrated improvement in eyesight and physical appearance.

This study yielded encouraging results and suggested that vitamin–mineral supplements may be of benefit for mentally retarded children and particularly for those with Down's syndrome. Harrell et al. (1981) stated that the benefit was particularly evident in the younger children. Unfortunately, there were several difficulties with the Harrell et al. (1981) study that have weakened these conclusions. The children were matched only on IQ and not on sex, age, and parental education, which have been related to variations in intelligence test performance. Additionally, of the 22 children beginning the study, only 16 completed it, and most of the dropouts were in the group that initially received the supplement. Finally, during the last phase of the study when all children received the supplement, the researchers were not blind to the condition the children were in. All of these factors could have biased the study in the direction of showing a greater change in IQ than really existed.

Because of the potential importance of this study, several other investigators have attempted replication but, unfortunately, have been unsuccessful. In four of the studies (see Pruess et al., 1989, for a review), no benefit of the vitamin–mineral supplement used by Harrell et al. (1981) was found for institutionalized mentally retarded young adults. It is difficult to draw conclusions from these studies because the participants differed considerably from those studied by Harrell et al. (1981). Fortunately several other researchers (see Pruess et al., 1989, for a review) did, like Harrell et al. (1981), study only children with Down's syndrome who were also living at home, the children that had received the most benefit from the supplement. Still, none of these studies could demonstrate a benefit for the vitamin–mineral supplement, not even when only young children were used (Weathers, 1983). Taken together, the studies of the efficacy of megavitamin therapy in the treatment of mental retardation, and specifically Down's syndrome, is very disappointing. There are virtually no good data suggesting that any intellectual benefit can be obtained from administering large doses of vitamins and minerals.

Juvenile Delinquency

During the 1980s, one theory that received considerable attention from correctional personnel as well as from some criminologists was that diet was somehow related to antisocial behavior. This theory seems to have originated in studies conducted in the earlier part of the 20th century, wherein individuals with hypoglycemia performed a variety of antisocial acts (e.g., Wilder, 1947). This theory even made its way into the courtroom. The most famous example is the "Twinkie defense" that was used in the murder trial of Dan White, a former San Francisco supervisor. White climbed into city hall through a window to avoid a metal detector and proceeded to the office of Mayor George Moscone, where he shot the mayor nine times. White then proceeded to kill Supervisor Harvey Milk. White's actions seemed to have been prompted by the fact that he had resigned his seat on the city's board of supervisors, changed his mind and requested his seat back, then learned that Moscone was going to give the seat to a political rival. Apparently he shot Milk, too, because he had frequently opposed him on the board ("Depression as a Defense," 1979).

There seemed to be no question that White had committed premeditated murder. But the defense attorney argued that White had a tendency to consume large amounts of junk food—Twinkies, Cokes, and doughnuts—and that this prodigious consumption of sugar exacerbated his depression. This exaggerated depressive state diminished his mental capacity, leaving him unable to act in a premeditated, deliberate manner. Similarly, a Virginia man was acquitted of burglary after his defense attorney successfully argued that he had committed the crime because of a vitamin deficiency. John Hinckley, who attempted to assassinate President Ronald Reagan in 1981, as well as his parents and attorney, apparently received letters suggesting that hypoglycemia be incorporated into Hinckley's defense (cited in Gray, 1986).

Anecdotes and testimonials such as those just described seem to have formed the primary basis for the belief that a link exists between crime and diet. Others (e.g., Hippchen, 1981) have argued that factors such as cerebral allergies and environmental contaminants can also contribute to delinquent behavior. On the basis of beliefs such as these, Schoenthaler (1983a, 1983b, 1983c, 1983d, 1983e) conducted a series of experiments designed to investigate the role that diet, particularly sucrose, has on antisocial behavior of juveniles. The focus of attention was on sucrose because Schoenthaler (1983b) believed that hypoglycemia was caused by consumption of large quantities of sucrose, and hypoglycemia was presumed to contribute to antisocial behavior.

In these studies, Schoenthaler (1982, 1983a, b, c, d, e) investigated the influence of a dietary change on the number of disciplinary actions imposed on juveniles placed in a detention facility. Each of these studies used a time-series design. The number of disciplinary actions or incidents were recorded prior to and following implementation of a dietary change. The dietary change consisted of decreasing sugar availability by replacing sugar with honey; soft drinks and Kool-Aid with fruit juice; and high-sugar cereals, desserts, and snacks with foods thought to be lower in sucrose. The exception was a study in which Schoenthaler (1983c) compared the disciplinary records of juveniles during a 6-month period in which milk and water were served with meals with a 6-month period in which orange juice was served with meals. In each of these studies Schoenthaler reported that the number of disciplinary incidents was significantly less following dietary intervention than they were prior to intervention.

Without critically analyzing the experimental design used by Schoenthaler, these results seem to offer considerable hope for treating the antisocial behavior of juvenile delinquents with a dietary change. In fact, the uncritical acceptance of these data have led correctional facilities in several states to change inmates' diets. Some of these facilities have even provided megavitamin supplements and have tested for hypoglycemia, food allergies, and "subclinical" nutritional deficiencies (Gray, 1986).

Fortunately, Schoenthaler's studies have now been critically analyzed by competent researchers, and awareness of their limitations seems to be reversing the initial enthusiasm over the potential benefit of a dietary change. Gray (1986), Harper and Gans (1986), and others have correctly pointed out that Schoenthaler's studies are littered with confounding variables that make it impossible to determine whether the dietary change had any effect on antisocial behavior. For example, in virtually all of his studies, the population prior to and following dietary intervention was not the same. In one of the first studies he conducted, the percentage of nonwhite inmates decreased from 31% to 18% and the percentage of female inmates increased from 0% to 29%. These are changes that should lead to a decrease in number of reported incidents (Gray, 1986), which is exactly what Schoenthaler found. Consequently, the change in the population seems to represent a better explanation for the decline in antisocial behavior and not the dietary change.

Schoenthaler also did not conduct double-blind experiments, in spite of his claim to have done so. It is impossible to disguise, for example, the fact that sugar is no longer available at meal time but honey is, or that orange juice is now available. Schoenthaler also relied on the institutional personnel to provide a measure of the disciplinary actions. No data were supplied regarding the reliability or consistency of recording such actions. Finally, there was no control group to detect changes that would naturally occur over time from having been placed in a detention facility. One would expect that antisocial behavior would decline as time in the detention facility increased.

Fortunately, more recent studies have shed more light on the relation between diet and antisocial behavior and on the existence of metabolic imbalances in juvenile delinquents. Longhurst and Mazer (1988) conducted an experiment that addressed many of the shortcomings inherent in Schoenthaler's studies. They randomly assigned 14 cottages, each housing 12 delinquents, to an experimental and a control group. The experimental group received a diet consisting of foods that had a low glycemic value, foods that elicit low blood glucose values (Jenkins et al., 1981). The control group received foods that contained carbohydrates high in glycemic value or foods that would produce a high glucose response. The experimental and control diets were administered for 35 consecutive days. Both groups completed a variety of assessment measures consisting of an index of "troublesome incidents," adaptive behavior, and mood prior to and following the 35-day dietary treatment period. Longhurst and Mazer found that behavior or mood was not affected by the high glycemic diet, which suggests that alterations in the blood sugar level that are induced by diet have no detrimental effect on delinquents' behavior.

A similar conclusion was reached by Gans et al. (1990). These investigators compared the nutritional status and blood and insulin values of a group of Black delinquents, White delinquents, and White nondelinquents, finding both nutritional status and their metabolic reactions to an oral sucrose tolerance test (OSTT) to be similar. The delinquent groups also did not react negatively to the OSTT. Instead, their mood ameliorated with time, and they reported feeling more awake two hours into the OSTT, which would be inconsistent with the assumption that sucrose consumption creates an adverse affect.

When the performance of these three groups was compared following consumption of a breakfast consisting of sucrose or aspartame-sweetened cereal, it was found that White delinquents performed better following the sucrose breakfast (Bachorowski et al., 1990). However, when the delinquents, both Black and White, were separated into hyperactive and nonhyperactive groups, the hyperactive delinquents performed better following the sucrose breakfast and the nonhyperactive delinquents performed better following the aspartame breakfast. The White nondelinquents were not differentially affected by the type of breakfast.

This study further suggests that sucrose ingestion does not adversely affect the performance of juvenile delinquents. In fact, the delinquents who were described by their teachers as being most disruptive performed better following the sucrose breakfast. However, the fact that the nonhyperactive delinquents generally performed worse following the sucrose breakfast alerts us once again to the fact that individual difference variables, such as the extent to which hyperactive symptoms are present, may interact with diet. Such variables must be taken into consideration when conducting diet–behavior studies to gain a complete understanding of the relationship that exists between these two variables. Currently, the most accurate statement that can be made is that sucrose does not compromise delinquent performance.

Conclusion

In an attempt to identify an effective treatment for many of the disorders affecting children and adolescents, some investigators have proposed that altering their dietary intake may represent an effective treatment modality. These nutritional treatments have spanned the range from advocating increases in vitamins and minerals to eliminating foods such as table sugar.

The disorder that has received the most attention is ADHD. In the 1970s Feingold proposed that approximately 50% of all children with ADHD could be treated by having them adhere to a diet that eliminated items such as food colors, food additives, and antioxidants. Unfortunately, Feingold's initial studies of the efficacy of his diet were flawed, and controlled investigation of the diet revealed that children with ADHD derive little, if any, benefit from it.

Attention then turned to the possible contribution of table sugar to ADHD. In one of the first scientific studies, a relationship between sugar and ADHD was found. Subsequent findings, however, indicated that sugar not only does not adversely affect ADHD but also may have a calming effect on these children. This finding did not preclude the involvement of food in ADHD: Recent studies have indicated that children with ADHD may be reacting adversely to one or more foods and that elimination of the offending food can result in an improvement in behavior. However, the offending food is frequently different for different children, and most sensitive children respond adversely to a combination of foods that is unique to them.

Studies have postulated that the addition of certain vitamins and minerals contribute to the improvement in disorders such as autism and Down's syndrome. But because the data supporting this contribution are confounded and insufficient, firm conclusions cannot be drawn. At present it seems clear that these nutrients are not effective in treating Down's syndrome or for enhancing IQ in other mentally retarded individuals.

A number of poorly conducted studies have suggested that the antisocial behavior that is characteristic of juvenile delinquents can be reduced by reducing or eliminating the ingestion of sugar. Well-controlled studies have not supported these claims, but they do indicate that the effect of sugar may interact with the presence of hyperactive symptoms. Juvenile delinquents with hyperactive symptoms seem to profit from sugar ingestion, whereas nonhyperactive delinquents do not and may experience a detrimental effect.

10

Recommendations for Applying Diet Therapy

Throughout this book I have discussed a number of dietary manipulations that seem to have some benefit in treating several behavioral disorders, most of which involve depression. The research is consistent with the beliefs of many individuals who strongly advocate that "we are what we eat" and that nutrition strongly affects behavior. A nutritional intervention, however, does not possess magical powers that can be used to cure all or even a large portion of behavioral disorders. Unfortunately, myths and inaccuracies pervade this field. To apply nutrition appropriately to behavioral problems, it is imperative to correct and replace inaccurate information.

It would, for example, be inappropriate to assume that anyone could change their mood or improve their performance dramatically merely by eating more or less of a certain food such as carbohydrates. If any mood or behavioral change did take place, it would probably be a subtle and weak effect. For some other depressed individuals the effect could be dramatic. Consider the following case of an individual who participated in one of my research studies.

Nancy represents a dramatic example of the benefits that can accrue from a sugar-free diet. Nancy's problems began shortly after the birth of her first child. She first experienced flu-like symptoms about once a month, which, over the course of a year, developed into weak, shaky spells. After Nancy gave birth to her second child she began experiencing an increasing array of symptoms including chills, sleepy spells, weakness, shakiness, headache, blurred vision, inability to concentrate, and memory lapses. Nancy consulted several physicians, who speculated that she might be hypoglycemic, have a hormone imbalance, or even have a brain tumor. She was scheduled for numerous tests, including a CAT scan, but all the tests came back negative, and none of the recommendations given by the numerous physicians she consulted provided anything but temporary relief. Over time Nancy's symptoms got worse and she became fearful, apprehensive, agitated, and depressed.

Several years later, Nancy gave birth to her third child. By this time her condition had deteriorated to the point that she could no longer handle her job as well as be a mother and wife, so she quit. However, her symptoms continued to get progressively worse. She lost her appetite, her sexual desire declined, and she felt extremely fatigued, exhausted, and weak. Thoughts of suicide entered her mind and gradually became a permanent part of her life. When Nancy responded to my advertisement for participants for the depression study I was conducting, her condition had so deteriorated that she was crying repeatedly without any reason, was very irritable, felt guilty about screaming at her children, and seldom had the energy to even fix a meal for her family.

When I first met Nancy she displayed a distinct lack of affect but expressed serious concern over her condition. After explaining the dietary study (Christensen & Burrows, 1990) to her, we administered the Structured Clinical Interview for the *DSM-III-R* (SCID) to obtain a psychiatric diagnosis. Based on the SCID, Nancy met the criteria for major depression. She then completed the Beck Depression Inventory (BDI), and the Symptom Checklist-90 (SCL-90). She scored above 30 on the BDI, indicating that she was severely depressed, and her CDDI score of 26 indicated that she might profit from a dietary intervention (a score of 13 indicates that a person may be a dietary responder).

Nancy was then given instructions to totally eliminate refined sucrose and caffeine from her diet for the next three weeks, to keep a dietary record for three designated days during the week, and to return once a week to allow us to answer any questions and to monitor her progress. When Nancy returned each week, she turned in the dietary record, which was inspected, and any deviations from the diet were discussed as well as ways to eliminate these deviations. (Most of the research participants, including Nancy, adhered closely to the prescribed diet.) At this time any questions Nancy had were also discussed.

At the completion of the study, Nancy told us that she had left the psychology clinic the first time feeling very discouraged, because she had no faith that a mere diet would change her life. But after only two days on the diet, Nancy reported that she had chuckled and that she was laughing by the end of the week. At the end of the three-week dietary intervention, Nancy again completed the assessment instruments. At this time, not only did she not meet *DSM-III-R* criteria for depression, but also her BDI score had dropped to 11, indicating only mild depression.

One of the prime criterion for any treatment is the persistence of the observed change. In this study, we conducted a 3-month follow up of dietary responders such as Nancy. All but one of the individuals who responded to the diet maintained the amelioration in depression demonstrated at the end of the 3-week dietary intervention, and most of them continued to demonstrate a further amelioration in depression. Nancy's BDI score, for example, continued to fall; at 3-month follow-up it was below 10, indicating an absence of depression.

Cases such as Nancy's illustrate the benefit that a dietary alteration can have for some individuals. I want to emphasize, however, that the benefit derived is only for *some* individuals. Not everyone can and will experience a benefit from altering diet, and most individuals should not expect to experience much of a change in mood or behavior from changing the way they eat. Because there is a pervasive belief among a large segment of the population that dietary alterations are beneficial, I want to provide some suggestions and guidelines that might be useful when considering a dietary intervention.

Unipolar Depression

Depression seems to be the one disorder that is most responsive to diet. It is also the disorder that has been the subject of a lot of speculation and comments in popular magazines. I have had individuals participating in my studies who are consuming numerous vitamins and minerals on the assumption that this will correct their depression. Others have asked about tryptophan, stating that they have heard that this amino acid will correct depression.

What is the status of nutritional intervention in depression, and what should a client be told? The answer to this question seems to be tied to the type and nature of the depression a person is experiencing. Diet is clearly involved in unipolar depression and in depression associated with PMS, SAD, and obesity.

Most of the attention and work relating diet to depression has focused on unipolar depression. There are consistent reports that individuals with unipolar depression consume greater amounts of carbohydrates, especially refined simple carbohydrates, and that at least some of them respond favorably to dietary interventions. At present, I think a very conservative approach should be taken when considering using a dietary intervention with such an individual. A client with unipolar depression should be informed that dietary interventions have been successful in helping some individuals. Tryptophan seems to be helpful with individuals experiencing mild to moderate levels of depression. The problem with trying tryptophan is that it is no longer available to the general public. Consequently, it is impossible to try this approach, unless a prescription can be obtained from a physician.

Vitamin supplements have been advocated as having antidepressant effects. Most of the research has focused on folic acid and has consistently demonstrated that a portion of depressed individuals are deficient in this vitamin. However, it has not been convincingly demonstrated that folic acid supplementation can ameliorate depression. This does not mean that depressed clients should not try folic acid. If they are so inclined, I would recommend that they try 200 μg/day. At this level there seems to be little risk, and the client may receive some benefit from the supplementation. Currently, the most promising dietary intervention seems to be the elimination of caffeine and refined carbohydrates to ameliorate depression for *some* sensitive individuals, that is, those who are identified as being likely to respond to treatment. However, to ensure the success of this approach, the procedure outlined in chapter 8 should be followed.

Dietary approaches that are used with people suffering from unipolar depression must be considered to be adjunctive. You should not consider it to be a panacea. Some individuals may need only a dietary intervention, but most individuals experiencing depression will also need psychotherapy. Typically, a person who is responsive to a dietary intervention may experience a benefit but still have many other situational issues that must be resolved. Therefore, I recommend a combined psychotherapy and dietary intervention approach.

Consider, for example, the case of Linda, a participant in the Krietsch et al. (1988) study. When I first saw Linda, she stated that her son, daughter-in-law, and ex-husband were all living with her. She was providing food and shelter for them, but they did little or nothing to help her clean the house, cook, or even do the dishes after she prepared a meal. To make matters worse, she paid most of the bills. Yet they would criticize her for being selfish and not thinking of them. They constantly asked more and more of her, and she would never tell them no. Linda was unable to confront them and demand that they help or leave. She felt worthless; nothing she did was good enough. To Linda, this was the cause of her depression.

Without inquiring further, it would have been easy to attribute her depression to this unhealthy family situation. Further questioning, however, revealed that Linda—who currently was in her 60s, had experienced depression since she was a young woman. Linda had, throughout her adult life, periodically received counseling for her depression. At the time I saw her she was in counseling with another psychologist and taking antidepressant medication prescribed by a psychiatrist. The important issue was that Linda's depression was not just tied to her current family situation but that she had experienced depression prior to this time. This, as well as her symptoms, suggested that diet might be beneficial to her.

To obtain an index of degree of emotional distress Linda was experiencing and to determine whether she might be a dietary responder, we administered the BDI, MMPI, Profile of Mood States (POMS) and CDDI. The SCID was not included because Linda participated in one of the first studies I conducted. At that time I was trying to demonstrate the value of dietary intervention and did not realize that it had primary benefit for individuals suffering from depression. Linda's CDDI score was 18, which indicated that she might respond to dietary intervention. Her BDI score was 46, indicating that she was severely depressed. Depression was confirmed by her MMPI depression scale score of 84 and a POMS depression score of 62. In fact, Linda scored above 70 on eight of the MMPI scales, suggesting that she was quite emotionally distressed.

Linda was instructed to remain on a refined sucrose-free and caffeine-free diet for 2 weeks, to maintain a diet record for three days during each week, and to return at a designated time each week to allow us to monitor her diet and to answer any questions she may have. When Linda returned at the end of the first and second weeks, she reported that her depression was lifting and that she was decreasing her antidepressant medication. During the course of the study, she continued decreasing her medication until she quit taking it altogether. As her mood improved, she became more assertive with her free-loading family and insisted that they contribute their fair share.

At the end of the two-week intervention, Linda again completed the BDI, POMS, and MMPI. Although the MMPI depression scale score showed little change, the BDI dropped from the original score of 46 to 22, and the POMS depression score dropped from 62 to 38. Both scores supported her self-report of an amelioration in depression. In addition to providing another illustration of the benefit of dietary intervention, Linda's case also clearly illustrates a situation in which psychotherapy is also needed. Linda's BDI score of 22 indicates that she was still moderately depressed and in need of additional treatment. No dietary intervention could eliminate the unhealthy family interactions, and she needed continued counseling to help her deal with her kids and ex-husband.

Premenstrual Syndrome, Seasonal Affective Disorder, and Obesity

The research on PMS, SAD, and obesity in people who experience some depression provides a limited but very similar picture. These individuals experience carbohydrate cravings simultaneous with the appearance of depression. A small body of data indicates that the consumption of carbohydrates results in a lifting of their depressed mood and suggests that consumption of carbohydrates may have a therapeutic benefit. Based on these data, it would be tempting to recommend that these individuals increase their carbohydrate consumption, but such a recommendation would be premature given that refined carbohydrate consumption seems to lead to depression in some unipolarly depressed individuals. If these individuals want to try a dietary approach, I recommend having them experiment by trying different carbohydrates and observing the alteration in mood. They should try both simple and complex carbohydrates, and then they should try eliminating simple carbohydrates to determine if this strategy works better than consuming either simple or complex carbohydrates. Clients should be informed that little is known about therapeutic benefits to be derived; we do know that these individuals not only crave carbohydrates but also consume more of them than their nondepressed counterparts.

Individuals with PMS should also try eliminating caffeine during the luteal phase of the menstrual cycle, because research has revealed that caffeine consumption is related to the appearance of symptoms. Again, clients who are encouraged to try such approaches should be cautioned that there is little evidence indicating that these dietary approaches work and that what evidence exists is only suggestive.

Attention-Deficit Hyperactivity Disorder

Over the past 25 years, considerable attention has been given to the role that diet plays in attention-deficit hyperactivity disorder (ADHD). The literature has focused extensively on the use of the Feingold diet and the role of sugar in ADHD. Although research conducted in the last decade has shown the Feingold diet to be less effective than was originally claimed, several studies have confirmed that diet does play a role in ADHD and that a dietary alteration can be very helpful in some instances. This literature also reveals that a child's response to diet is very idiosyncratic, which means that the offending foods have to be identified for each child and that a general statement regarding a specific food cannot be made.

The literature indicates that one or several dietary substances may be contributing to ADHD. I recommend that parents be informed that identification of an offending dietary substance will be a lengthy process that will require extensive commitment on the part of the family. Parents may find it encouraging to know that at least one study revealed that 73% of the children studied showed improvement following a dietary approach. It is important to convey to parents that a dietary approach may help their child but to also make clear that not all children with ADHD respond to such an approach.

If the parents are committed to a dietary approach, they must follow the procedure described in chapter 9 and be ready to accept the fact that their child may not be responsive to diet. It should also be emphasized that, even if behavior does improve with a dietary change, the dietary change may not totally eliminate the behavioral disorder. Many parents seem to think that diet is a panacea and can provide a complete cure. There are even cases in which the objective data indicate that a child did not respond positively to elimination of a substance such as sugar, but parents were so convinced that the child was reactive that they would not believe the objective data and continued to advocate that their child was sugar reactive.

Conclusion

There seem to be only two types of behavioral disorders that are responsive to dietary intervention—depression and ADHD. In the case of depression, only some sensitive individuals will respond, and, even for these individuals it is imperative that the dietary approach is considered to be an adjunctive therapy. For most individuals, psychotherapy or pharmacotherapy will also be needed to obtain maximum improvement.

For other types of behavioral disorders, little evidence exists to suggest that a dietary approach will be beneficial. It seems certain that the dietary approaches attempted to date for treatment of mental retardation and schizophrenia are of no value. For other disorders, such as autism, there is insufficient data to provide even a tentative conclusion regarding the potential benefit or lack thereof of a dietary approach.

Appendix A ⸺⸺⸺⸺⸺

Christensen Dietary Distress Inventory [CDDI]

Administration Booklet

Larry Christensen, PhD

DIRECTIONS

This inventory consists of 34 questions and statements each with five alternative answers. Read each question or statement carefully and decide if the question or statement applies to you. If it does **NOT** apply to you **skip to the next question or statement.** If the question or statement does apply to you read the alternative answers and select the one answer that most accurately applies. If two or more alternative answers seem to apply **PICK ONE ANSWER THAT IS MOST ACCURATE** and fill in the appropriate circle on the answer sheet. **Be sure to read all alternative answers before choosing the ONE that is most accurate.**

---

1. **How do you feel after getting a good night's sleep (7 to 9 hours per night) for several nights in a row?**
   a. Refreshed.
   b. Refreshed and energetic.
   c. Drowsy or still tired right after you wake up, but within 10 or 20 minutes you feel refreshed and energetic.
   d. Drowsy and tired for some time because you have had too much sleep.
   e. Drowsy and tired as though you have not had enough sleep, like you are still fatigued and need more sleep and if you must get up, you have to drag yourself out of bed.

CONTINUE ON THE NEXT PAGE

---

2. How do you feel after taking a short nap in the afternoon?
   a. Refreshed.
   b. Refreshed and energetic.
   c. Drowsy or still tired right after you wake up, but within 10 or 20 minutes you feel refreshed and energetic.
   d. Drowsy and tired for some time because you have had too much sleep.
   e. Drowsy and tired as though you have not had enough sleep, like you are still fatigued and need more sleep and you continue to feel that way after being up for some time.

3. When you experience depression at what time of the day does it seem to occur?
   a. In the morning.
   b. During midmorning and/or afternoon.
   c. At noon.
   d. In the evening.
   e. There does not seem to be a specific time at which it occurs.

4. What is the most frequent cause of your depression when you experience it?
   a. Your job, school, or money.
   b. Something someone (e.g. friend, spouse, parent, or roommate) has said or done to you, or you have said or done to them.
   c. Recreational drugs.
   d. Illness or the medication taken for an illness.
   e. There does not seem to be any reason for the depression you experience. Sometimes you all of a sudden feel depressed for no apparent reason.

5. When you get angry what usually causes it?
   a. Something someone else has said or done.
   b. Something you have said or done.
   c. Some little unimportant thing such as stopping at a stop sign or putting something in the wrong place, or some other little thing that really should not make you angry.
   d. Something relating to money.
   e. Something relating to your job or school.

CONTINUE ON THE NEXT PAGE

---

6. How frequently do you have a headache that is not caused by drugs, illness, or alcohol?
   a. Every day.
   b. Every other day.
   c. Several times a week.
   d. About once a week.
   e. Less than once a week.

7. What would be the most frequent cause of your starting to sweat when you are sitting in a comfortable room?
   a. Tension.
   b. Being in a situation that makes you nervous.
   c. Illness.
   d. You can't identify a cause. Most of the time you start sweating when there is nothing that should make you sweat.
   e. Medication.

8. When you experience inner tension or trembling what usually causes it?
   a. Tension.
   b. Being in a situation that makes you nervous.
   c. Illness or the medication taken for the illness.
   d. Nothing that you can identify. Sometimes you seem to feel an inner tension or trembling for no apparent reason.
   e. Recreational drugs.

9. When your muscles ache, the usual cause is:
   a. Exercise.
   b. Tension.
   c. Injury.
   d. Illness.
   e. Some reason that you cannot identify.

10. When you lose your appetite, it is usually because:
   a. You have just eaten.
   b. of medication taken.
   c. of some reason that you cannot identify.
   d. of excitement or being upset about something.
   e. of tension.

CONTINUE ON THE NEXT PAGE

11. When you experience mental confusion it is usually due to:
   a. Alcohol.
   b. Medication or recreational drugs.
   c. Illness.
   d. Having many things to be done in a short period of time.
   e. Many things seem to be going on in your head at the same time and you can't separate them out or make them clear.

12. When your eyesight blurs it is usually due to:
   a. Eye strain.
   b. Illness.
   c. Medication.
   d. Some unidentified reason. It just blurs at different times of the day.
   e. Not using your glasses, or a problem with contact lenses.

13. You seem to be uncoordinated and are always running into things:
   a. When you are tired.
   b. When you are in a hurry.
   c. When you are angry.
   d. For no specific reason, you just seem to be uncoordinated.
   e. When you are not feeling good.

14. When your joints ache it is usually due to:
   a. Exercise.
   b. Illness or injury.
   c. Lack of sleep or when awakening from sleep.
   d. The weather.
   e. Something that you can't identify.

15. When you worry, it is usually about:
   a. Money.
   b. Your job.
   c. Societal concerns such as nuclear war, prejudice, etc.
   d. Other people such as friends, parents, spouse, roommate.
   e. Little unimportant things that you should not worry about.

16. When you have to make a decision:
   a. You take your time to think it over and make a sound decision.
   b. You make it very rapidly.

CONTINUE ON THE NEXT PAGE

---

    c. You have a hard time doing so and you change your mind a lot.
    d. You try to get other people to make the decision for you.
    e. You avoid doing so for as long as you can.

17. How frequently do you feel as though you must have something sweet to eat?
    a. Several times a day.
    b. Once a day.
    c. Every other day.
    d. A couple of times a week.
    e. Once a week or less.

18. When do you become moody?
    a. Just about all the time. It seems to come and go and nothing specific seems to cause it.
    b. When you are tired.
    c. When you are sick.
    d. When you have many things to do and are under a lot of pressure.
    e. When something bad has happened to you and everything seems to be going wrong.

19. How frequently do you feel like you are going "crazy," as though you need some psychological help?
    a. Every day.
    b. Every other day.
    c. A couple of times a week.
    d. Once a week.
    e. Less than once a week.

20. What would cause you to have an itching and crawling sensation on your skin?
    a. An illness or disease.
    b. Something you can't identify.
    c. Being chilled.
    d. An allergic reaction.
    e. An insect bite.

21. How frequently do you feel as though you are smothering?
    a. Every day.
    b. Every other day.

CONTINUE ON THE NEXT PAGE

    c. A couple of times a week.
    d. Once a week.
    e. Less than once a week.

22. When you get angry what seems to be the most frequent cause?
    a. Your job or school.
    b. Just about anything. You seem to have a short fuse.
    c. Money.
    d. Other people.
    e. Being tired.

23. When you are around noise produced by a TV, stereo, or radio:
    a. It bothers you because you just seem to be very sensitive to noise.
    b. You enjoy it most of the time.
    c. You can tune it out so that it does not bother you.
    d. It helps you because you seem to need some noise in the background.
    e. You are not bothered nor do you enjoy such noise.

24. How frequently do you need a cup of coffee, tea, or a soft drink to get going?
    a. Every day.
    b. Every other day.
    c. A couple of times a week.
    d. Once a week.
    e. Less than once a week.

25. When you suddenly feel very weak, as if the energy was just drained out of you, the usual cause is:
    a. Exercise or finishing an emotionally and/or physically draining task.
    b. Illness or injury.
    c. Not eating correctly.
    d. There does not seem to be any reason, it just happens even though you have not been exercising.
    e. Not enough sleep.

26. How frequently do you feel very thirsty?
    a. Several times a day.
    b. Once a day.

CONTINUE ON THE NEXT PAGE

---

   c. Every other day.
   d. A couple of times a week.
   e. Once a week or less.

27. **What would you say your attitude was about yourself, others, and the things going on around you?**
   a. You just don't care.
   b. Most of the time you don't care.
   c. Some of the time you don't care.
   d. Most of the time you do care.
   e. You are concerned all the time.

28. **When you are with a group of people, how do you usually feel?**
   a. You join in with the group all of the time.
   b. You join in with the group most of the time.
   c. You are somewhat shy so you don't contribute much.
   d. You feel as though you are just with the group but don't join in.
   e. You feel as though you are detached from them, like they are on TV and you are standing back looking at them and not part of the group.

29. **How often do you find that it is very difficult to handle stress or pressure and that it makes you feel worse?**
   a. Every day.
   b. Every other day.
   c. A couple of times a week.
   d. Once a week.
   e. Less than once a week.

30. **When you are unable to fall asleep when you go to bed at night, it is usually because:**
   a. Something is bothering you or you are excited about something.
   b. You are thinking about all of the things that you must do.
   c. A physical illness.
   d. No specific reason. Once you lie down you are all of a sudden wide awake even though you are tired.
   e. You are overtired.

CONTINUE ON THE NEXT PAGE

---

31. When you wake up in the middle of the night and are not able to go back to sleep, it is usually because:
    a. Something is bothering you or you have had a bad dream.
    b. You are thinking of all the things you must do.
    c. You have a physical illness.
    d. No specific reason. Sometimes you awaken and can't return to sleep.
    e. Something excites you or you hear something.

32. How often do you have nightmares?
    a. Every night.
    b. Every other night.
    c. A couple of times a week.
    d. Once a week.
    e. Less than once a week.

33. What usually makes you cry?
    a. Just about anything makes you cry, even when there is no reason for crying.
    b. A death of a friend or a relative.
    c. Being real tired.
    d. Medication.
    e. Hearing something sad, being hurt by others, or things going wrong.

34. How would you assess your energy level?
    a. Extremely energetic.
    b. Energetic.
    c. About what I would expect.
    d. Much less than I think it should be.

SCORING KEY

The CDDI is scored by assigning a value of −1, 0, 1, or 2 to the response alternatives provided for each question. The scale is scored by summing the weight given to the response alternatives across all questions, and the total sum represents the CDDI scale score. The response alternatives given a weight of −1, 1, or 2 for each question are listed below. All other response alternatives are given a weight of 0.

Question	Response alternative	Weight	Question	Response alternative	Weight
1.	d.	1	18.	a.	2
	e.	1		b.	2
2.	c.	2	19.	a.	1
	e.	2	20.	b.	1
3.	e.	1	21.	a.	1
4.	e.	2	22.	b.	1
5.	a.	1	23.	b.	1
6.	a.	2	24.	a.	1
	b.	2	25.	c.	1
7.	e.	−1		d.	1
8.	d.	2	26.	a.	1
9	b.	1	27.	b.	2
10.	c.	2		d.	2
	e.	2	28.	d.	1
11.	e.	1		e.	1
12.	a.	−1	29.	a.	1
13.	a.	1	30.	a.	1
14.	a.	1	31.	d.	1
15.	e.	1	32.	b.	2
16.	a.	1		c.	2
	e.	1	33.	a.	1
17.	a.	1	34.	d.	1
	b.	1			

Appendix B _____

Dietary Instructions and Sample Diet

For each of the three meals that you eat, select from the items listed below. There is no restriction on how much you eat as long as you eat something at each meal. If you begin to feel light-headed, shaky, or nervous between meals, eat something selected from the items listed under *Snacks* or any other acceptable food.

The success of the dietary program requires that you adhere completely to the following instructions. Please do not eat anything that is not on this list.

Breakfast

Cereals: oatmeal, shredded wheat, grape nuts, Kellogg's Nutri-Grain cereals (wheat, corn, barley, rye), Wheatena
    Eggs
    Toast
    Milk
    Any juice made from frozen concentrate (not a juice drink or something like Tang)
    Butter or margarine
    Honey on toast
    Sweetener: Equal or another artificial sweetener

Lunch and Dinner

Meat: chicken, fish, turkey, or any red meat (do not eat barbecued meats)
    Any fresh or frozen vegetable (not canned)
    Any fresh fruit
    Salad using any type of lettuce and other fresh fruits and vegetables
    Salad dressings: Use only Marie's brand (Blue Cheese, Avocado Goddess, or Italian Garlic) or vinegar and oil
    Potatoes, rice, and other complete carbohydrates
    Beverages: milk, water, or any juice (e.g., apple, orange, or grapefruit) made from concentrate and unsweetened

_____

From Christensen (1991). Copyright 1991 by the American Psychological Association.

Sandwiches: tuna, cheese, hamburger
Equal or another artificial sweetener
Kraft Light mayonnaise
No prepackaged or prepared meals

Eating Out

During the course of the study it is preferred that you do not eat out. However, if you do, select Mexican food because this closely corresponds to the demands of the dietary program.

Snacks

Pretzel sticks, cheese, saltine crackers, Triscuit wafers, popcorn (plain or with salt or butter if desired), any type of fruit, unsweetened nuts or seeds of any type, plain yogurt, ice cream or yogurt sweetened with Nutrasweet (aspartame).

Headache Medication

Acetaminophen or plain aspirin

Drinks

Diet 7-Up and Diet Slice are the two acceptable soft drinks; any other caffeine-free soft drink that is artificially sweetened is acceptable. The only other acceptable beverages are water and unsweetened fruit juice. If you eat out and select a juice such as orange juice, make sure it is unsweetened.

Sample Diet

Breakfast

Two eggs scrambled in margarine
Sliced wheat toast with margarine
Orange juice, milk, or water

Noon meal

Tuna, water packed
Mayonnaise

Celery
Margarine
Fresh orange
Milk, water, Diet Slice, or Diet 7-Up

Evening meal

Fresh spinach salad
Marie's salad dressing
Broiled pork loin
Cooked peas
Asparagus spears
Margarine (served on vegetables)
Bread with margarine or butter
Water, juice, Diet Slice, or Diet 7-Up

Cautions

If you should purchase a packaged, bottled, or canned product for consumption, read the label and avoid products that contain added sucrose,
glucose, dextrose, or caffeine.

References

Abbott, F. V., Etienne, P., Franklin, K. B. J., Morgan, M. J., Sewitch, M. J., & Young, S. N. (1992). Acute tryptophan depletion blocks morphine analgesia in the cold-pressor test in humans. *Psychopharmacology, 108,* 60–66.

Abou-Saleh, M. T., & Coppen, A. (1986). The biology of folate in depression: Implications for nutritional hypothesis of the psychosis. *Journal of Psychiatric Research, 20,* 91–101.

Abou-Saleh, M. T., & Coppen, A. (1989). The efficacy of low-dose lithium: Clinical, psychological and biological correlates. *Journal of Psychiatric Research, 23,* 157–162.

Abram, H. S. (1972). The psychology of chronic illness. *Journal of Chronic Diseases, 25,* 659–664.

Abramson, L. Y., Seligman, M. E., & Teasdale, J. D. (1978). Learned helplessness in humans: Critique and reformation. *Journal of Abnormal Psychology, 7,* 49–74.

Alertsen, A. R., Aukrust, A., & Skaug, O. E. (1986). Selenium concentrations in blood and serum from patients with mental diseases. *Acta Psychiatry Scandinavia, 74,* 217–219.

Altman, P. L., & Dittmer, D. S. (1968). *Metabolism.* Bethesda, MD: Federation of the American Society of Social and Experimental Biology.

American Psychiatric Association. (1980). *Diagnostic and statistical manual of mental disorders* (3rd ed.). Washington, DC: Author.

American Psychiatric Association. (1987). *Diagnostic and statistical manual of mental disorders* (3rd ed., rev.). Washington, DC: Author.

Amsterdam, J. D., Maislin, G., Winokur, A., King, M., & Gold, P. (1987). Pituitary and adrenocortical responses to the ovine corticotropin releasing hormone in depressed patients and healthy volunteers. *Archives of General Psychiatry, 44,* 775–781.

Anderson, G. H., & Hrboticky, N. (1986). Approaches to assessing the dietary component of the diet–behavior connection. *Nutrition Reviews, 44*(Suppl.), 42–50.

Anderson, R. A. (1986). Chromium metabolism and its role in disease process in man. *Clinical Physiology and Biochemistry, 4,* 31–41.

Anderson, R. A., & Guttman, G. N. (1988). Trace minerals and exercise. In E. S. Horton & R. L. Terjung (Eds.), *Exercise, nutrition and energy metabolism* (pp. 180–195). New York: Macmillan.

Anderson, R. A., Polansky, M. M., Bryden, N. A., Bhathena, S. J., & Canary, J. J. (1987). Effects of supplemental chromium on patients with symptoms of reactive hypoglycemia. *Metabolism, 36,* 351–355.

Appel, S. J., Szanton, V. L., & Rapaport, H. G. (1961). Survey of allergy in a pediatric population. *Pennsylvania Medical Journal, 64,* 621–625.

Arbeiter, H. I. (1967). How prevalent is allergy among United States school children? A survey of findings in the Munster (Indiana) school system. *Clinical Pediatrics, 6,* 140–142.

Arnold, L. E., Christopher, J., Huestis, R. D., & Smeltzer, D. J. (1978). Megavitamins for mineral brain dysfunction: A placebo-controlled study. *Journal of the American Medical Association, 240,* 2642–2643.

Arrington, L. R. (1959). Foods of the Bible. *Journal of the American Dietetic Association, 35,* 816–820.

Ashcroft, G. W., Crawford, T. B. B., Cundall, R. L., Davidson, D. L., Dobson, J., Dow, R. C., Eccleston, D., Loose, R. W., & Pullar, I. A. (1973). 5-Hydroxytryptamine metabolism in affective illness: The effect of tryptophan administration. *Psychological Medicine, 3,* 326–332.

Ashley, D. V., Barclay, D. V., Chauffard, F. A., Moennoz, D., & Leathwood, P. D. (1982). Plasma amino acid responses in humans to evening meals of differing nutritional composition. *The American Journal of Clinical Nutrition, 36,* 143–153.

Ashley, D. V. M., Fleury, M. O., Golay, A., Maeder, E., & Leathwood, P. D. (1985). Evidence for diminished brain 5-hydroxytryptamine biosynthesis in obese diabetic and non-diabetic humans. *American Journal of Clinical Nutrition, 42,* 1240–1245.

Ashley, D. V. M., Liardon, R., & Leathwood, P. D. (1985). Breakfast meal composition influences plasma tryptophan to large neutral amino acid ratios of healthy lean young men. *Journal of Neural Transmission, 63,* 271–283.

Atkins, F. M. (1986). Food allergy and behavior: Definitions, mechanisms and a review of the evidence. *Nutrition Reviews, 44*(Suppl.), 104–112.

Bachorowski, J., Newman, J. P., Nichols, S. L., Gans, D. A., Harper, A. E., & Taylor, S. L. (1990). Sucrose and delinquency: Behavioral assessment. *Pediatrics, 86,* 244–253.

Bancroft, J., Cook, A., & Williamson, L. (1988). Food craving, mood and the menstrual cycle. *Psychological Medicine, 18,* 855–896.

Banderet, L. E., & Lieberman, H. R. (1989). Treatment with tyrosine, a neurotransmitter precursor, reduces environmental stress in humans. *Brain Research Bulletin, 22,* 759–762.

Bandura, A. (1977). Self-efficacy: Toward a unifying theory of behavioral change. *Psychological Review, 84,* 191–215.

Bandura, A. (1982). Self-efficacy mechanism in human agency. *American Psychologist, 37,* 122–147.

Barkley, R. A. (1990). *Attention deficit hyperactivity disorder: A handbook for diagnosis and treatment.* New York: Guilford Press.

Barling, J., & Bullen, G. (1984). Dietary factors and hyperactivity: A failure to replicate. *The Journal of Genetic Psychology, 146,* 117–123.

Barnes, L. (1979). Olympic committee endorses vitamin. *Physical Sports Medicine, 7,* 17–18.

Barnett, P. A., & Gotlib, I. H. (1988a). Dysfunctional attitudes and psychosocial stress: The differential prediction of subsequent depression and general psychological distress. *Motivation and Emotion, 12,* 251–270.

Barnett, P. A., & Gotlib, I. H. (1988b). Psychosocial functioning and depression: Distinguishing among antecedents, concomitants, and consequences. *Psychological Bulletin, 104,* 97–126.

Barrett, S., & Herbert, V. (1981). *Vitamins and health foods.* Philadelphia: George F. Stickley.

Batshaw, M. L., & Perret, Y. M. (1992). *Children with disabilities: A medical primer.* Baltimore: Paul H. Brookes.

Beaton, G. H., Milner, V., McGuire, V., Feather, T. E., & Little, J. A. (1983). Source of variance in 24-hour dietary recall data: Implications for nutrition study design and interpretation of carbohydrate sources, vitamins and minerals. *American Journal of Clinical Nutrition, 37,* 986–995.

Beck, A. T. (1967). *Depression: Causes and treatment.* Philadelphia: University of Pennsylvania Press.

Beck, A. T., Rush, A. J., Shaw, B. F., & Emery, G. (1979). *Cognitive therapy of depression.* New York: Harper & Row.

Beck, A. T., Ward, C. H., Mendelson, M., Mock, J., & Erbaugh, J. (1961). An inventory for measuring depression. *Archives of General Psychiatry, 4,* 561–571.

Behar, D., Rapoport, J. L., Adams, A. J., Berg, C. J., & Cornblath, M. (1984). Sugar challenge testing with children considered behaviorally "sugar reactive." *Nutrition and Behavior, 1,* 277–288.

Bell, E. C. (1958). Nutritional deficiencies and emotional disturbances. *The Journal of Psychology, 45,* 47–74.

Bennett, F. C., & Sherman, R. (1983). Management of childhood "hyperactivity" by primary care physicians. *Developmental and Behavioral Pediatrics, 4,* 88–93.

Bennett, W. (1987). Dietary treatments of obesity. *Annals of the New York Academy of Sciences, 499,* 250–263.

Benton, D., & Cook, R. (1991). The impact of selenium supplementation on mood. *Biological Psychiatry, 29,* 1092–1098.

Biggio, G., Fadda, D., Fanni, P., Tagliamonte, A., & Gessa, G. L. (1974). Rapid depletion of serum tryptophan, brain tryptophan, serotonin and 5-hydroxyindoleacetic acid by a tryptophan-free diet. *Life Science, 14,* 1321–1329.

Bjerner, B., & Swensson, A. (1953). Shift work and the rhythmus. *Acta Medica Scandinavia*, *145*(Suppl. 278), 102–107.

Blake, M. J. F. (1971). Temperament and time of day. In W. P. Colquhoun (Ed.), *Biological rhythms and human performance* (pp. 109–148). London: Academic Press.

Blaney, P. H. (1986). Affect and memory: A review. *Psychological Bulletin, 99*, 229–246.

Blouin, A. G., Blouin, J. H., Braaten, J. T., Sarwar, G., Bushnik, T., & Walker, J. (1991). Physiological and psychological responses to a glucose challenge in bulimia. *International Journal of Eating Disorders, 10*, 285–296.

Bober, M. J. (1984). Senile dementia and nutrition. *British Medical Journal, 288*, 1234.

Boris, M., & Mandel, F. S. (1994). Foods and additives are common causes of the attention deficit hyperactive disorder in children. *Annals of Allergy, 72*, 462–468.

Both-Orthman, B., Rubinow, D. R., Hoban, M. C., Malley, J., & Grover, G. N. (1988). Menstrual cycle phase-related changes in appetite in patients with premenstrual syndrome and in control subjects. *American Journal of Psychiatry, 145*, 628–631.

Bowen, D. J., & Grunberg, N. E. (1990). Variations in food preference and consumption across the menstrual cycle. *Physiology & Behavior, 47*, 287–291.

Brenner, A. (1982). The effects of megadoses of selected B complex vitamins on children with hyperkinesis: Controlled studies with long-term follow-up. *Journal of Learning Disabilities, 15*, 258–264.

Brown, G. W., & Harris, T. O. (1978). *Social origins of depression: A study of psychiatric disorder in women*. New York: Free Press.

Boyce, P., & Parker, G. (1988). Seasonal affective disorder in the southern hemisphere. *American Journal of Psychiatry, 145*, 96–99.

Bray, G. A. (1987). Overweight is risking fate. Definition, classification, prevalence, and risks. *Annals of the New York Academy of Sciences, 499*, 14–28.

Breland, T. (1974). *Rating the diets*. Chicago: Rand McNally.

Brody, S., & Wolitzky, D. L. (1983). Lack of mood changes following sucrose loading. *Psychosomatics, 24*, 155–162.

Brown, G. G., & Nixon, R. (1979). Exposure to polybrominated biphenyls: Some effects on personality and cognitive functioning. *Journal of the American Medical Association, 242*, 523–527.

Brown, G. G., Preisman, R. C., Anderson, M. D., Nixon, R. K., Isbister, J. L., & Price, H. A. (1981). Memory performance of chemical workers exposed to polybrominated biphenyls. *Science, 212*, 1413–1415.

Bruch, H. (1970). The allure of food cults and nutrition quackery. *Journal of the American Dietetic Association, 57*, 316–320.

Brzezinski, A. A., Wurtman, J. J., Wurtman, R. J., Gleason, R., Greenfield, J., & Nader, T. (1990). d-fenfluramine suppresses the increased calorie and carbohydrate intakes and improves the mood of women with premenstrual depression. *Obstetrics & Gynecology, 76*, 296–301.

Buchwald, D., Sullivan, J. L., & Komaroff, A. L. (1987). Frequency of chronic active Epstein-Barr virus infection in a general medical practice. *Journal of the American Medical Association, 17*, 2303–2307.

Buckley, R. H., & Metcalfe, D. (1982). Food allergy. *Journal of the American Medical Association, 248*, 2627–2631.

Bunney, W. E., Brodie, H. K. H., Murphy, D. L., & Goodwin, F. D. (1971). Studies of alphamethyl-para-tyrosine, L-dopa, and L-tryptophan in depression and mania. *American Journal of Psychiatry, 127*, 872–881.

Burks, R., & Keeley, S. (1989). Exercise and diet therapy: Psychotherapists' beliefs and practices. *Professional Psychology: Research and Practice, 20*, 62–64.

Caballero, B. (1987). Brain serotonin and carbohydrate craving in obesity. *International Journal of Obesity, 11*(Suppl. 3), 179–183.

Caballero, B., Finer, N., & Wurtman, R. J. (1988). Plasma amino acids and insulin levels in obesity: Response to carbohydrate intake and tryptophan supplements. *Metabolism, 37*, 672–676.

Callaghan, N., Mitchell, R., & Cottier, P. (1969). The relationship of serum folic acid and vitamin B_{12} levels to psychosis in epilepsy. *Irish Journal of Medical Science, 2*, 497–505.

Canning, H., & Mayer, J. (1966). Obesity—Its possible effects on college admissions. *New England Journal of Medicine, 275,* 1172–1174.

Carney, M. W. P. (1967). Serum folate values in 423 psychiatric patients. *British Medical Journal, iv,* 512–516.

Carney, M. W. P. (1970). Serum vitamin B12 values in psychiatric in-patients. *Diseases of the Nervous System, 31,* 566–569.

Carney, M. W. P., Charv, T. K., Laundy, M., Bottiolieri, T., Chanarin, I., Reynolds, E. H., & Toone, B. (1990). Red cell folate concentrations in psychiatric patients. *Journal of Affective Disorders, 19,* 207–213.

Carney, M. W. P., Ravindran, A., Rinsler, M. G., & Williams, D. G. (1982). Thiamine, riboflavin, and pyridoxine deficiency in psychiatric inpatients. *British Journal of Psychiatry, 141,* 271–272.

Carney, M. W. P., & Sheffield, B. F. (1970). Associations of subnormal serum folate and vitamin B_{12} values and effects of replacement therapy. *The Journal of Nervous and Mental Disease, 150,* 404–412.

Carney, M. W. P., & Sheffield, B. F. (1978). Serum folic acid and B12 in 272 psychiatric inpatients. *Psychological Medicine, 8,* 139–144.

Carney, M. W. P., Williams, D. G., & Sheffield, B. F. (1979). Thiamine and pyridoxine lack in newly-admitted psychiatric patients. *British Journal of Psychiatry, 135,* 249–254.

Carter, C. M., Urbanowicz, M., Hemsley, R., Mantilla, L., Strobel, S., Graham, P. J., & Taylor, E. (1993). Effects of a few food diet in attention deficit disorder. *Archives of Disease in Childhood, 69,* 564–568.

Carpenter, K. J. (1986). *The history of scurvy and vitamin C.* Cambridge, England: Cambridge University Press.

Carver, C. S., & Scheier, M. F. (1981). *Attention and self-regulation.* New York: Springer-Verlag.

Cassileth, B. R., Lusk, E. J., Strouse, T. B., Miller, D. S., Brown, L. L., Cross, P. A., & Tenaglia, A. N. (1984). Psychological status in chronic illness: A comparative analysis of six diagnostic groups. *The New England Journal of Medicine, 311,* 506–511.

Centers for Disease Control. (1984). Evaluation of consumer complaints related to aspartame use. *Morbidity and mortality weekly report, 33,* 605–607.

Charney, D. S., Menekes, D. B., & Heninger, G. R. (1981). Receptor sensitivity and the mechanism of action of antidepressant treatment. *Archives of General Psychiatry, 38,* 1160–1180.

Cheraskin, E., & Ringsdorf, W. M. (1976). *Psychodiatetics: Food as the key to emotional health.* New York: Bantam Books.

Chouinard, G., Young, S. N., & Annable, L. (1985). A controlled clinical trial of L-tryptophan in acute mania. *Biological Psychiatry, 20,* 546–557.

Chouinard, G., Young, S. N., Annable, L., & Sourkes, T. L. (1979). Tryptophan-nicotinamide, imipramine and their combination in depression. *Acta Psychiatry Scandinavia, 59,* 395–414.

Christensen, L. (1990). *Christensen Dietary Distress Inventory Manual.* (Available from the author.)

Christensen, L. (1991). Issues in the design of studies investigating the behavioral concomitants of foods. *Journal of Consulting and Clinical Psychology, 59,* 874–882.

Christensen, L. (1993). Effects of eating behavior on mood: A review of the literature. *International Journal of Eating Disorders, 14,* 173–183.

Christensen, L., & Archer, S. (1990). Similarity assessment and attribute scaling of sucrose and aspartame in grape drink. *Journal of the American College of Nutrition, 9,* 44–47.

Christensen, L., & Burrows, R. (1990). Dietary treatment of depression. *Behavior Therapy, 21,* 183–193.

Christensen, L., & Redig, C. (1993). Effect of meal composition on mood. *Behavioral Neuroscience, 107,* 346–353.

Christensen, L., & Somers, S. (1994). Adequacy of the dietary intake of depressed individuals. *Journal of the American College of Nutrition, 13,* 597–600.

Christensen, L., & Somers, S. (in press). Comparison of nutrient intake among depressed and nondepressed individuals. *International Journal of Eating Disorders.*

Christensen, L., Krietsch, K., & White, B. (1989). Development, cross-validation, and assessment of the reliability of the Christensen Dietary Distress Inventory. *Canadian Journal of Behavioral Science, 21,* 1–15.

Christensen, L., Krietsch, K., White, B., & Stagner, B. (1985). Impact of a dietary change on emotional distress. *Journal of Abnormal Psychology, 94,* 565–579.

Christensen, L., White, B., & Krietsch, K. (1985). Failure to identify an expectancy effect in nutrition research. *Nutrition and Behavior, 2,* 149–159.

Christie, M. J., & McBrearty, E. M. (1979). Psychophysiological investigations of post lunch state in male and female subjects. *Ergonomics, 22,* 307–323.

Clark, L. A., & Watson, D. (1988). Mood and the mundane: Relations between daily life events and self-reported mood. *Journal of Personality and Social Psychology, 54,* 296–308.

Clark, L. A., & Watson, D. (1991). Tripartite model of anxiety and depression: Psychometric evidence and taxonomic implications. *Journal of Abnormal Psychology, 100,* 316–336.

Clarke, A. G., & Prescott, F. (1943). Studies in vitamin B deficiency with special reference to mental and oral manifestations. *British Medical Journal, 2,* 503–505.

Clausen, J., Nielsen, S. A., & Kristensen, M. (1989). Biochemical and clinical effects of an antioxidative supplementation of geriatric patients. *Biological Trace Element Research, 20,* 135–151.

Cole, J. O., Hartmann, E., & Brigham, P. (1980). L-tryptophan: Clinical studies. In J. O. Cole (Ed.), *Psychopharmacology update* (pp. 119–148). Lexington: Collamore Press.

Condiotte, M. M., & Lichtenstein, E. (1981). Self-efficacy and relapse in smoking cessation programs. *Journal of Consulting and Clinical Psychology, 49,* 648–658.

Conners, C. K., Goyette, C. H., Southwick, D. A., Lees, J. M., & Andrulonis, P. A. (1976). Food additives and hyperkinesis: A controlled double-blind experiment. *Pediatrics, 58,* 154–166.

Cooper, L. F., Barber, E. M., Mitchell, H. S., & Rynbergen, H. J. (1950). *Nutrition in health and disease.* Philadelphia: Lippincott.

Coppen, A., Chaudhry, S., & Swade, C. (1986). Folic acid enhances lithium prophylaxis. *Journal of Affective Disorders, 10,* 9–13.

Coppen, A., Whydrow, P. C., Noguera, R., Maggs, R., & Prange, A. J. (1972). The comparative antidepressant value of L-tryptophan and imipramine with and without attempted potentiation by liothyronine. *Archives of General Psychiatry, 26,* 234–241.

Coppen, A., & Wood, K. (1978). Tryptophan and depressive illness. *Psychology and Medicine, 8,* 49–57.

Cosman, M. P. (1983). A feast for Aesculapius: Historical diets for asthma and sexual pleasure. *Annual Review of Nutrition, 3,* 1–33.

Cott, A. (1972). Megavitamins: The orthomolecular approach to behavioral disorders and learning disabilities. *Academic Therapy, 7,* 245.

Cowen, P. J., Parry-Billings, M., & Newsholme, E. A. (1989). Decreased plasma tryptophan levels in major depression. *Journal of Affective Disorders, 16,* 27–31.

Craig, A. (1986). Acute effects of meals on perceptual and cognitive efficiency. *Nutrition Reviews, 44*(Suppl.), 163–171.

Craig, A., Baer, K., & Diekmann, A. (1981). The effects of lunch on sensory-perceptual functioning in man. *International Archives of Occupational and Environmental Health, 49,* 105–114.

Craig, A., & Richardson, E. (1989). Effects of experimental and habitual lunch-size on performance, arousal, hunger and mood. *International Archives of Occupational and Environmental Health, 61,* 313–319.

Craighead, W. E. (1980). Away from a unitary model of depression. *Behavior Therapy, 11,* 122–128.

Crapo, P. A., Scarlett, J. A., Kolterman, O. G., Sanders, L. R., Hofeldt, F. D., & Olefsky, J. M. (1982). The effects of oral fructose, sucrose, and glucose in subjects with reactive hypoglycemia. *Diabetes Care, 5,* 512–517.

Crook, W. G. (1975). Food allergy—The great masquerader. *Pediatric Clinics of North America, 22,* 227–238.

Curzon, G. (1981). Relationships between plasma, CSF and brain tryptophan. *Journal of Neural Transmission, 15*(Suppl.), 93–105.

Curzon, G., & Sarna, G. S. (1984). Tryptophan transport into the brain: Newer findings and older ones reconsidered. In H. G. Schlossberger, W. Kochen, B. Linzen, & H. Steinhart (Eds.), *Progress in tryptophan and serotonin research* (pp. 145–160). New York: Walter de Gruyter.

Cutrona, C. E. (1983). Causal attributions and perinatal depression. *Journal of Abnormal Psychology, 92,* 161–172.

Dalvit, S. P. (1981). The effect of the menstrual cycle on patterns of food intake. *American Journal of Clinical Nutrition, 34,* 1811–1815.

Dalvit-McPhillips, S. P. (1983). The effect of the human menstrual cycle on nutrient intake. *Physiology & Behavior, 31,* 209–212.

Darby, W. J., Ghalioungui, P., & Grivetti, L. (1977). *Food: The gift of Osiris.* New York: Academic Press.

deCastro, J. M. (1987). Circadian rhythms of the spontaneous meal pattern, macronutrient intake, and mood of humans. *Physiology & Behavior, 40,* 437–446.

Delgado, P. L., Charney, D. S., Price, L. H., Aghajanian, G. K., Landis, H., & Heninger, G. R. (1990). Serotonin function and the mechanism of antidepressant action. *Archives of General Psychiatry, 47,* 411–418.

Delgado, P. L., Charney, D. S., Price, L. H., Landis, H., & Heninger, G. R. (1989). Neuroendocrine and behavioral effects of dietary tryptophan restriction in healthy subjects. *Life Sciences, 45,* 2323–2332.

Delgado, P. L., Price, L. H., Heninger, G. R., & Charney, D. S. (1992). Neurochemistry. In E. S. Paykel (Ed.), *Handbook of affective disorders* (pp. 219–254). New York: Guilford Press.

Delgado, P. L., Price, L. H., Miller, H. L., Salomon, R. M., Licinio, J., Krystal, J. H., Heninger, G. R., & Charney, D. S. (1991). Rapid serotonin depletion as a provocative challenge test for patients with major depression: Relevance to antidepressant action and the neurobiology of depression. *Psychopharmacology Bulletin, 27,* 321–329.

Depression as a defense [Editorial]. (1979, May 28). *Time,* p. 57.

Dews, P. B. (1982). Caffeine. *Annual Review of Nutrition, 2,* 323–341.

Doll, R., & Peto, R. (1981). The causes of cancer. *Journal of the National Cancer Institute, 66,* 1197–1208.

Drake, M. E. (1986). Panic attacks and excessive aspartame ingestion. *Lancet, 2,* 631.

Dreisbach, R. H., & Pfeiffer, C. (1943). Caffeine-withdrawal headache. *Journal of Laboratory and Clinical Medicine, 28,* 1212–1219.

Drewnowski, A. (1988). Changes in mood after carbohydrate consumption. *American Journal of Clinical Nutrition, 46,* 703.

Drewnowski, A., Kurth, C., Holden-Wiltse, J., & Saari, J. (1992). Food preferences in human obesity: Carbohydrate versus fats. *Appetite, 18,* 207–221.

Drewnowski, A., Kurth, C. L., & Rahaim, J. E. (1991). Taste preferences in human obesity: Environmental and familial factors. *American Journal of Clinical Nutrition, 54,* 635–641.

Duffy, W. (1975). *Sugar Blues.* New York: Warner Books.

Dunner, D. L., & Fieve, R. R. (1975). Affective disorder: Studies with amine precursors. *American Journal of Psychiatry, 26,* 364–366.

Duval, S., & Wicklund, R. (1972). *A theory of objective self-awareness.* New York: Academic Press.

Eckenrode, J. (1984). Impact of chronic and acute stressors on daily reports of mood. *Journal of Personality and Social Psychology, 46,* 907–918.

Egger, J., Carter, C. M., Graham, P. J., Gumley, D., & Soothill, J. F. (1985). Controlled trial of oligoantigenic treatment in the hyperkinetic syndrome. *Lancet, 1,* 540–545.

Farkas, T., Dunner, D. L., & Fieve, R. R. (1976). L-tryptophan in depression. *Biological Psychiatry, 11,* 295–302.

Fazio, C., Andreoli, V., Agnoli, A., Casacchia, M., Cerbo, R., & Pinzello, A. (1974). Therapy of schizophrenia and depressive disorders with S-adenosyl-L-methionine. *IRCS Medical Science-Nervous System, 2,* 1015.

Feingold, B. (1975a). Hyperkinesis and learning disabilities linked to artificial food flavors and colors. *American Journal of Nursing, 75,* 797–803.

Feingold, B. (1975b). *Why is your child hyperactive?* New York: Random House.

Feingold, B. F. (1981). Dietary management of behavior and learning disabilities. In S. A. Miller (Ed.), *Nutrition and behavior* (pp. 235–246). Philadelphia: The Franklin Institute Press.

Fenigstein, A., & Levine, M. P. (1984). Self-attention, concept activation and the causal self. *Journal of Experimental Social Psychology, 20,* 231–245.

Fernstrom, F. D. (1977). Effects of the diet on brain neurotransmitters. *Metabolism, 26,* 207–223.

Fernstrom, F. D. (1986). Acute and chronic effects of protein and carbohydrate ingestion on brain tryptophan levels and serotonin synthesis. *Nutrition Reviews, 44*(Suppl.), 25–36.

Fernstrom, J. D. (1988a). Carbohydrate ingestion and brain serotonin synthesis: Relevance to a putative control loop for regulating carbohydrate ingestion and effects of aspartame consumption. *Appetite, 11*(Suppl.), 35–41.

Fernstrom, J. D. (1988b). Tryptophan, serotonin and carbohydrate appetite: Will the real carbohydrate craver please stand up! *Journal of Nutrition, 118,* 1417–1419.

Fernstrom, F. D., & Faller, D. V. (1978). Neutral amino acids in the brain: Changes in response to food ingestion. *Journal of Neurochemistry, 30,* 1531–1538.

Fernstrom, M. H., Krowinski, R. L., & Kupfer, D. J. (1987). Appetite and food preference in depression: Effects of imipramine treatment. *Biological Psychiatry, 22,* 529–539.

Fernstrom, J. D., & Wurtman, R. J. (1971a). Brain serotonin content: Increase following ingestion of carbohydrate diet. *Science, 174,* 1023–1025.

Fernstrom, J. D., & Wurtman, R. J. (1971b). Brain serotonin content: Physiological dependence on plasma tryptophan levels. *Science, 173,* 149–172.

Fernstrom, J. D., & Wurtman, R. J. (1972a). Brain serotonin content: Physiological regulation by plasma neutral amino acids. *Science, 178,* 414–441.

Fernstrom, J. D., & Wurtman, R. J. (1972b). Elevation of plasma tryptophan by insulin in rat. *Metabolism, 21,* 337–341.

Fernstrom, J. D., & Wurtman, R. J. (1974). Nutrition and the brain. *Scientific American, 230,* 84–91.

Frank, R. T. (1931). The hormonal causes of premenstrual tension. *Archives of Neurology and Psychiatry, 26,* 1053–1057.

Fritz, M. F. (1933). The field of psychodietetics. *Psychological Clinics, 22,* 181–189.

Frost, R. O., Graf, M., & Becker, J. (1979). Self-devaluation and depressed mood. *Journal of Consulting and Clinical Psychology, 47,* 958–962.

Ganley, R. M. (1989). Emotion and eating in obesity: A review of the literature. *International Journal of Eating Disorders, 8,* 343–361.

Gans, D. A., Harper, A. E., Bachorowski, J., Newman, J. P., Shrago, E. S., & Taylor, S. L. (1990). Sucrose and delinquency: Oral sucrose tolerance test and nutritional assessment. *Pediatrics, 86,* 254–262.

Garattini, S. (1989). Further comments. *Integrative Psychiatry, 6,* 235–238.

Garattini, S., Buczko, W., Jori, A., & Samanin, R. (1975). The mechanism of action of fenfluramine. *Postgraduate Medical Journal, 51*(Suppl.), 27–32.

Garry, P. J., Goodwin, J. S., & Hunt, W. C. (1984). Folate and vitamin B12 status in a healthy elderly population. *Journal of American Geriatric Society, 32,* 719–727.

Garvey, M. J., Wesner, R., & Godes, M. (1988). Comparison of seasonal and nonseasonal affective disorders. *American Journal of Psychiatry, 145,* 100–102.

Gath, A. (1986). Hyperactive behavior and diet. *Adoption & Fostering, 10,* 55–56.

Gelenberg, A. J., Wojcik, J. D., Falk, W. E., Baldessarini, R. J., Zeisel, S. H., Schoenfeld, D., & Mok, G. S. (1990). Tyrosine for depression: A double-blind trial. *Journal of Affective Disorders, 19,* 125–132.

Gelenberg, A. J., Wojcik, J. D., Gibson, C. J., & Wurtman, R. J. (1983). Tyrosine for depression. *Journal of Psychiatric Research, 17,* 175–180.

Gelenberg, A. J., Wojcik, J. D., Growdon, J. H., Sved, A. F., & Wurtman, R. J. (1980). Tyrosine for the treatment of depression. *American Journal of Psychiatry, 137,* 622–623.

Gelman, D., King, P., Hager, M., Raine, G., & Pratt, J. (1985, October 14). The food-mood link. *Newsweek,* pp. 93–94.

Georgotas, A., & Cancro, R. (1988). *Depression and mania.* New York: Elsevier.

Ghadirian, A. M., Ananth, J., & Engelsmann, F. (1980). Folic acid deficiency and depression. *Psychosomatics, 21,* 926–929.

Gibson, C. J., & Wurtman, R. J. (1978). Physiological control of brain norephinephrine synthesis by brain tyrosine concentration. *Life Sciences, 22,* 1399–1406.

Gibson, R. S., & Seythes, C. A. (1984). Chromium, selenium, and other trace element intakes of a selected sample of Canadian menopausal women. *Biological Trace Element Research, 6,* 105–116.

Gilbert, R. M. (1984). Caffeine consumption. In G. A. Spiller (Ed.), *The methylxanthine beverages and foods: Chemistry, consumption, and health effects* (pp. 185–214). New York: Alan R. Liss.

Gillman, P. K., Bartlett, J. R., Bridges, P. K., Hunt, A., Patel, A. J., Kantamaneni, B. D., & Curzon, G. (1981). Indolic substances in plasma, cerebrospinal fluid, and frontal cortex of human subjects infused with saline or tryptophan. *Journal of Neurochemistry, 37,* 410–417.

Ginsberg, S. M., & Brown, G. W. (1982). No time for depression: A study of help-seeking among mothers of preschool children. In D. Mechanic (Ed.), *Symptoms, illness behavior, and help-seeking* (pp. 87–114). New York: Prodist.

Godfrey, P. S., Toone, B. K., Carney, M. W., Flynn, T. G., Bottiolieri, T., Laundy, M., Chanarin, I., & Reynolds, E. H. (1990). Enhancement of recovery from psychiatric illness by methylfolate. *Lancet, 336,* 392–395.

Goldberg, I. K. (1980). L-tyrosine in depression. *Lancet, 2,* 364.

Gordon, A. E., & Meldrum, B. S. (1970). Effect of insulin on brain 5-hydroxytryptamine and 5-hydroxy-indole-acetic acid of rat. *Biochemical Pharmacology, 19,* 3042–3044.

Gould, M. S., Wunsch-Hitzig, R., & Dohrenwend, B. P. (1980). Formulation of hypotheses about the prevalence, treatment, and prognostic significance of psychiatric disorders in children in the United States. In B. P. Dohrenwend, B. S. Dohrenwend, M. S. Gould, B. Link, R. Neugebauer, & R. Wunsch-Hitzig (Eds.), *Mental illness in the United States: Epidemiological estimates.* New York: Praeger.

Goyette, C. H., Conners, C. K., & Ulrich, R. F. (1978). Normal data on revised Conners parent and teacher rating scales. *Journal of Abnormal Child Psychology, 6,* 221–236.

Gray, G. E. (1986). Diet, crime, and delinquency: A critique. *Nutrition Reviews, 44*(Suppl.), 89–93.

Gray, G. E., & Leong, G. B. (1986). Serum folate levels in U.S. psychiatric inpatients. *Journal of Clinical Psychiatry, 47,* 98–99.

Greden, J. F. (1974). Anxiety or caffeinism: A diagnostic dilemma. *American Journal of Psychiatry, 131,* 1089–1092.

Greden, J. F., Fontaine, P., Lubetsky, M., & Chamberlain, K. (1978). Anxiety and depression associated with caffeinism among psychiatric inpatients. *American Journal of Psychiatry, 135,* 963–966.

Green, R. G. (1969). Reading disability. *Canadian Medical Association Journal, 100,* 586.

Greene, R., & Dalton, K. (1953). The premenstrual syndrome. *British Medical Journal, 1,* 1007–1016.

Greenwood, M. H., Friedel, J., Bond, A. J., Curzon, G., & Lader, M. H. (1974). The acute effects of intravenous infusion of L-tryptophan in normal subjects. *Clinical Pharmacology and Therapeutics, 16,* 445–464.

Greenwood, M. H., Lader, M. H., Kantameneni, B. D., & Curzon, G. (1975). The acute effects of oral tryptophan in human subjects. *British Journal of Clinical Pharmacology, 2,* 165–172.

Griffiths, R. R., & Woodson, P. P. (1988). Human coffee drinking: Reinforcing and physical dependence producing effects of caffeine. *Journal of Pharmacology and Experimental Therapeutics, 239,* 416–425.

Gross, M. D. (1984). Effect of sucrose on hyperkinetic children. *Pediatrics, 74,* 876–878.

Guaraldi, G. P., Fava, M., Mazzi, F., & La Greca, P. (1993). An open trial of methyltetrahydrofolate in elderly depressed patients. *Annals of Clinical Psychiatry, 5,* 101–105.

Hallstrom, T. (1969). Serum B_{12} and folate concentrations in mental patients. *Acta Psychiatry Scandinavia, 45,* 19–36.

Hammen, C. (1991). Generation of stress in the course of unipolar depression. *Journal of Abnormal Psychology, 100,* 555–561.

Hammen, C., Marks, T., deMayo, R., & Mayol, A. (1985). Self-schemas and risk for depression: A prospective study. *Journal of Personality and Social Psychology, 49,* 1147–1159.

Harley, J. P. (1981). Methodological issues in behavioral nutrition research. In S. A. Miller (Ed.), *Nutrition and behavior* (pp. 277–284). Philadelphia: The Franklin Institute Press.

Harley, J. P., Matthews, C. G., & Eichman, P. (1978). Synthetic food colors and hyperactivity in children: A double-blind challenge experiment. *Pediatrics, 62,* 975–983.

Harley, J. P., Ray, R. S., Tomasi, L., Eichman, P. L., Matthews, C. G., Chun, R., Cleeland, C. S., & Traisman, E. (1978). Hyperkinesis and food additives: Testing the Feingold hypothesis. *Pediatrics, 61,* 818–828.

Harper, A. E., & Gans, D. A. (1986, January). Claims of antisocial behavior from consumption of sugar: An assessment. *Food Technology,* 142–149.

Harrell, R. F., Capp, R. H., Davis, D. R., Peerless, J., & Ravitz, L. R. (1981). Can nutritional supplements help mentally retarded children? An exploratory study. *Proceedings of the National Academy of Science, 78,* 574–578.

Harrigan, J. A., Kues, J. R., Ricks, D. F., & Smith, R. (1984). Moods that predict coming migraine headaches. *Pain, 20,* 385–396.

Harrison, W. M., Rabkin, J. G., & Endicott, J. (1985). Psychiatric evaluation of premenstrual changes. *Psychosomatics, 26,* 789–799.

Hartmann, E. L. (1986). Effect of L-tryptophan and other amino acids on sleep. *Nutrition Reviews, 44*(Suppl.), 70–73.

Haslam, R. H. A. (1992). Is there a role for megavitamin therapy in the treatment of attention deficit hyperactivity disorder? *Advances in Neurology, 58,* 303–310.

Heninger, G. R., Mueller, P. S., & Davis, L. S. (1975). Depressive symptoms and the glucose tolerance test and insulin tolerance test. *Journal of Nervous and Mental Disease, 161,* 421–432.

Herbert, V. (1962). Experimental folate deficiency in man. *Transactions of the Association of American Physicians, 75,* 307–320.

Herrington, R. N., Bruce, A., Johnstone, E. C., & Lader, M. H. (1974). Comparative trial of L-tryptophan and amitriptyline in depression illnesses. *Psychological Medicine, 6,* 673–678.

Hickie, I., Lloyd, A., Wakefield, D., & Parker, G. (1990). The psychiatric status of patients with the chronic fatigue syndrome. *British Journal of Psychiatry, 156,* 534–540.

Hildebrandt, G., Rohmert, W., & Rutenfranz, J. (1974). 12- and 24-hr rhythms in error frequency of locomotive drivers and the influence of tiredness. *International Journal of Chronobiology, 2,* 175–180.

Hippchen, L. J. (1981). Some possible biochemical aspects of criminal behavior. *International Journal of Biosocial Research, 2,* 37–42.

Hippocrates. (1931). Aphorisms. In *Hippocrates* (W. H. S. Jones, Trans.; pp. 128–129), Cambridge, MA: Harvard University Press.

Honigfeld, G. (1964). Non-specific factors in treatment: 1. Review of placebo reactions and placebo reactors. *Diseases of the Nervous System, 25,* 145–156.

Horwitt, M. K., Hills, O. W., Harvey, C. C., Liebert, E., & Steinberg, D. L. (1949). Effects of dietary depletion of riboflavin. *Journal of Nutrition, 39,* 357–373.

Houser, H. B., & Bebb, H. T. (1981). Individual variation in intake of nutrients by day, month, and season and relation to meal patterns: Implications for dietary methodology. In National Research Council, Committee on Food Consumption Patterns (Ed.), *Assessing changing food consumption patterns* (pp. 155–179). Washington, DC: National Academy Press.

Hoza, B., & Pelham, W. E., Jr. (1993). Attention-deficit hyperactivity disorder. In R. T. Ammerman, C. G. Last, & M. Hersen (Eds.), *Handbook of prescriptive treatments for children and adolescents* (pp. 64–84). Boston: Allyn and Bacon.

Hrboticky, N., Leiter, L. A., & Anderson, G. H. (1985). Effects of L-tryptophan on short term food intake in lean men. *Nutrition Research, 5,* 595–607.

Hunter, R., Jones, M., Jones, T. G., & Matthews, D. M. (1967). Serum B_{12} and folate concentrations in mental patients. *British Journal of Psychiatry, 113,* 1291–1295.

Hurdle, A. D. F., & Williams, T. C. P. (1966). Folic-acid deficiency in elderly patients admitted to hospital. *British Medical Journal, 2,* 202–205.

Ibbotson, R. N., Dilena, B. A., & Horwood, J. M. (1967). Studies on deficiency and absorption of folates in patients on anticonvulsant drugs. *Australian Annals of Medicine, 16,* 144–150.

Ingram, R. E. (1990). Self-focused attention in clinical disorders: Review and a conceptual model. *Psychological Bulletin, 107,* 156–176.

Ingram, R. E., Lumry, A. B., Cruet, D., & Sieber, W. (1987). Attentional processes in depressive disorders. *Cognitive Therapy and Research, 11,* 351–360.

James, J. E., Stirling, K. P., & Hampton, B. A. M. (1985). Caffeine fading: Behavioral treatment of caffeine abuse. *Behavior Therapy, 19,* 593–604.

Janoff-Bulman, R. (1979). Characterological versus behavioral self-blame: Inquires into depression and rape. *Journal of Personality and Social Psychology, 37,* 1798–1809.

Jarvis, W. T. (1983). Food faddism, cultism, and quackery. In W. J. Darby, H. P. Broquist, & R. E. Olson (Eds.), *Annual Review of Nutrition, 3,* 35–52.

Jeejeebhoy, K. N., Chu, R. C., Marliss, E. B., Greenberg, G. R., & Bruce-Robertson, A. S. (1977). Chromium deficiency, glucose interlace and neuropathy reversed by chromium supplementation in a patient receiving long-term total parenteral nutrition. *American Journal of Clinical Nutrition, 30,* 531–538.

Jenkins, D. J. A., Wolever, T. M. S., Taylor, R. H., Barker, H. M., Fielden, H., Baldwin, J. M., Bowling, A. C., Newman, H. C., Jenkins, A. L., & Goff, D. V. (1981). Glycemic index of foods: A physiological basis for carbohydrate exchange. *American Journal of Clinical Nutrition, 34,* 352–366.

Jensen, K., Freunsgaard, K., Ahlfors, U. G., Pinkanen, T. A., Tuomikoski, S., Ose, E., Dencker, S. J., Lindberg, D., & Nagy, A. (1975). Tryptophan/imipramine in depression. *Lancet, 1,* 920.

Jensen, O. N., & Olesen, O. V. (1969). Folic acid concentrations in psychiatric patients. *Acta Psychiatry Scandinavia, 45,* 289–294.

Joseph-Vanderpool, J. R., Jacobsen, F. M., Murphy, D. L., Hill, J. L., & Rosenthal, N. E. (1993). Seasonal variation in behavioral responses to m-CPP in patients with seasonal affective disorder and controls. *Biological Psychiatry, 33,* 496–504.

Justice, P. M., Kamath, S., Langenberg, P. W., Sandstead, H. H., Milne, D. B., & Smith, G. F. (1988). Micronutrients status of children with down syndrome: A comparative study of the effect of megadoses of vitamins with minerals or placebo. *Nutrition Research, 8,* 1251–1258.

Kallstrom, B., & Nylof, R. (1969). Vitamin-B_{12} and folic acid in psychiatric disorders. *Acta Psychiatry Scandinavia, 45,* 137–152.

Kanarek, R. B., & Swinney, D. (1990). Effects of food snacks on cognitive performance in male college students. *Appetite, 14,* 15–27.

Kanarek, R. B., Glick, A. L., & Marks-Kaufman, R. (1991). Dietary influences on the acute effects of anorectic drugs. *Physiology & Behavior, 49,* 149–152.

Kariks, J., & Perry, S. W. (1970). Folic-acid deficiency in psychiatric patients. *Medical Journal of Australia, 1,* 1192–1195.

Kavale, K. A., & Forness, S. R. (1983). Hyperactivity and diet treatment: A meta-analysis of the Feingold hypothesis. *Journal of Learning Disabilities, 16,* 324–340.

Kazdin, A. E. (1988). *Child psychotherapy: Developing and identifying effective treatments.* New York: Pergamon Press.

Kennedy, H. G. (1988). Fatigue and fatigability. *British Journal of Psychiatry, 153,* 1–5.

Kershner, J., & Hawke, W. (1979). Megavitamins and learning disorders: A controlled double-blind experiment. *Journal of Nutrition, 109,* 819–826.

Keys, A., Brozek, J., Henschel, A., Mickelsen, O., & Taylor, H. L. (1950). *The biology of human starvation* (vol. 2). Minneapolis: University of Minnesota Press.

King, C. G., Bickerman, H. A., Bouvet, W., Harrer, C. J., Oyler, J. R., & Seitz, C. P. (1945). Aviation nutrition studies: Effects of in-flight and pre-flight meals of varying composition with respect to carbohydrate, protein and fat. *Journal of Aviation Medicine, 16,* 69–84.

Kinsbourne, M. (1994). Sugar and the hyperactive child. *The New England Journal of Medicine, 330,* 355–356.

Kirchenbaum, D. S., Tomarken, A. J., & Humphrey, L. L. (1985). Affect and adult self-regulation. *Journal of Personality and Social Psychology, 48,* 509–523.

Kirsch, I. (1985). Response expectancy as a determinant of experience and behavior. *American Psychologist, 40,* 1189–1202.

Kivela, S-L., Pahkala, K., & Eronen, A. (1989). Depression in the aged: Relation to folate and vitamins C and B_{12}. *Biological Psychiatry, 26,* 210–212.

Kozlovsky, A. S., Moser, P. B., Reiser, S., & Anderson, R. A. (1986). Effects of diets high in simple sugars on urinary chromium losses. *Metabolism, 35,* 515–518.

Krauchi, K., & Wirz-Justice, A. (1988). The four seasons: Food intake frequency in seasonal affective disorder in the course of a year. *Psychiatric Research, 25,* 323–338.

Krauchi, K., Wirz-Justice, A., & Graw, P. (1990). The relationship of affective state to dietary preference: Winter depression and light therapy as a model. *Journal of Affective Disorders, 20,* 43–53.

Krietsch, K., Christensen, L., & White, B. (1988). Prevalence, presenting symptoms, and psychological characteristics of individuals experiencing a diet-related mood-disturbance. *Behavior Therapy, 19,* 593–604.

Kroenke, K., Wood, D. R., Mangelsdorff, A. D., Meier, N. J., & Powell, J. B. (1988). Chronic fatigue in primary care: Prevalence, patient characteristics, and outcome. *Journal of the American Medical Association, 260,* 929–934.

Kruesi, M. J. P. (1986, January). Carbohydrate intake and children's behavior. *Food Technology,* 150–152.

Kumpulainen, J. T., Wolf, W. R., Veillon, C., & Mertz, W. (1979). Determination of chromium in selected United States diets. *Journal of Agricultural and Food Chemistry, 27,* 490–494.

Langseth, L., & Dowd, J. (1978). Glucose tolerance and hyperkinesis. *Food and Cosmetics Toxicology, 16,* 129–133.

Lapierre, K. A., Greenblatt, D. J., Goddard, J. E., Harmatz, J. S., & Shader, R. I. (1990). The neuropsychiatric effects of aspartame in normal volunteers. *Journal of Clinical Pharmacology, 30,* 454–460.

Larkin, J. E., & Pines, H. A. (1979). No fat persons need apply. *Sociology of Work and Occupations, 6,* 312–317.

Lauersen, N. H., & Stukane, E. (1983). *PMS: Premenstrual syndrome and you.* New York: Pinnacle Books.

Leathwood, P. D., & Pollet, P. (1983). Diet-induced mood changes in normal populations. *Journal of Psychiatric Research, 17,* 147–154.

Lecos, C. W. (1985, February). Sugar, how sweet it is—and isn't. *FDA Consumer,* 21–23.

Lehrman, K. (1987, September). Anorexia and bulimia: Causes and cures. *Consumers' Research,* 29–32.

Leibenluft, E., Fiero, P., Bartko, J. J., Moul, D. E., & Rosenthal, N. E. (1993). Depressive symptoms and the self-reported use of alcohol, caffeine, and carbohydrates in normal volunteers and four groups of psychiatric outpatients. *American Journal of Psychiatry, 150,* 294–301.

Lelord, G., Barthelemy, C., Martineau, N., Bruneau, J. P., Muh, G., & Callaway, E. (1988). Clinical and biological effects of vitamin B6 + magnesium in autistic subjects. In J. Leklem & R. Reynolds (Eds.), *Vitamin B6 responsive disorders in humans* (pp. 329–356). New York: Alan R. Liss.

Leon, A. S., Hunninghake, D. B., Bell, C., Rassin, D. K., & Tephly, T. R. (1989). Safety of long-term large doses of aspartame. *Archives of International Medicine, 149,* 2318–2324.

Lessof, M. H., & Brueton, M. H. (1984). Gastrointestinal reactions and food intolerance. In M. H. Lessof (Ed.), *Allergy: Immunological and clinical aspects* (pp. 175–218). New York: Wiley.

Levitt, A. J., & Joffe, R. T. (1989). Folate, B_{12}, and life course of depressive illness. *Biological Psychiatry, 25,* 867–872.

Levy, R. I. (1981). Declining mortality in coronary heart disease. *Arteriosclerosis, 1,* 312–325.

Lewinsohn, P. M., Hoberman, H., Teri, L., & Hautzinger, M. (1985). An integrative theory of depression. In S. Reiss & R. R. Bootzin (Eds.), *Theoretical issues in behavior therapy* (pp. 331–352). New York: Academic Press.

Lewinsohn, P. M., & Larson, D. W. (1982). The measurement of expectancies and other cognitions in depressed individuals. *Cognitive Therapy and Research, 6,* 437–436.

Lewis, D. A., Kathol, R. G., Sherman, B. M., Winokur, G., & Schlesser, M. A. (1983). Differentiation of depressive subtypes by insulin insensitivity in the recovered phase. *Archives of General Psychiatry, 40*, 187–170.

Lieberman, H. R., Corkin, S., Spring, B. J., Growdon, J. H., & Wurtman, R. J. (1983). Mood, performance, and pain sensitivity: Changes induced by food constituents. *Journal of Psychiatric Research, 1983*, 135–145.

Lieberman, H. R., Spring, B. J., & Garfield, G. S. (1986). The behavioral effect of food constituents: Strategies used in studies of amino acids, protein, carbohydrate, and caffeine. *Nutrition Reviews, 44*(Suppl.), 51–60.

Lieberman, H. R., Wurtman, J. J., & Chew, B. (1986). Changes in mood after carbohydrate consumption among obese individuals. *American Journal of Clinical Nutrition, 44*, 772–778.

Lindberg, D., Ahlfors, U. G., Dencker, S. J., Fruensgaard, K., Hansten, S., Jensen, K., Ose, E., & Pinkanes, T. A. (1979). Symptom reduction in depression after treatment with L-tryptophan or imipramine. *Acta Psychiatric Scandinavia, 60*, 287–294.

Lipton, M. A., & Wheless, J. C. (1980). Diet as therapy. In S. A. Miller (Ed.), *Nutrition and behavior* (pp. 213–234). Philadelphia: The Franklin Institute Press.

Lissner, L., Stevens, J., Levitsky, D., Rasmussen, K. M., & Strupp, B. J. (1988). Variation in energy intake during the menstrual cycle: Implications for food-intake research. *American Journal of Clinical Nutrition, 48*, 956–962.

Longhurst, J. E., & Mazer, G. E. (1988). The effects of a low glycemic diet on antisocial behavior in juvenile offenders. *International Journal of Biosocial Research, 10*, 123–136.

Lowe, T. L., Cohen, D. J., Miller, S., & Young, J. G. (1981). Folic acid and B_{12} in autism and neuropsychiatric disturbances of childhood. *Journal of the American Academy of Child Psychiatry, 20*, 104–111.

Lowenberg, M. E., Todhunter, E. N., Wilson, E. D., Feeney, M. C., & Savage, J. R. (1968). *Food & Man.* New York: Wiley.

Lucca, A., Lucini, V., Piatti, E., Ronchi, P., & Smeraldi, E. (1992). Plasma tryptophan levels and plasma tryptophan/neutral amino acids ratio in patients with mood disorder, patients with obsessive-compulsive disorder, and normal subjects. *Psychiatric Research, 44*, 85–91.

Lundh, L. (1987). Placebo, belief, and health. A cognitive-emotional model. *Scandinavian Journal of Psychology, 28*, 128–143.

Lyman, B. (1982). The nutritional values and food group characteristics of foods preferred during various emotions. *Journal of Psychology, 112*, 121–127.

Maddux, J. E. (1991). Self-efficacy. In C. R. Snyder & D. R. Forsyth (Eds.), *Handbook of social and clinical psychology* (pp. 57–58). New York: Pergamon Press.

Maddux, J. E., Norton, L. W., & Stoltenberg, C. D. (1986). Self-efficacy expectancy, outcome expectancy, and outcome value: Relative effects on behavioral intentions. *Journal of Personality and Social Psychology, 51*, 783–789.

Madras, B. K., Cohen, E. L., Messing, R., Munro, H. N., & Wurtman, R. J. (1974). Relevance of serum-free tryptophan to tissue tryptophan concentrations. *Metabolism, 23*, 1107–1116.

Maes, M., DeRuyter, M., Hobin, P., & Suy, E. (1986). The diagnostic performance of the L-tryptophan/competing amino acids ratio in major depression. *Acta Psychiatry Belgica, 86*, 257–265.

Maes, M., Vandewoude, M., Schotte, C., Martin, M., D'Hondt, P., Scharpe, S., & Blockx, P. (1990). The decrease available of L-tryptophan in depressed females: Clinical and biological correlates. *Progress in Neuro-Psychopharmacology & Biological Psychiatry, 14*, 903–919.

Manocha, S., Choudhuri, G., & Tandon, B. N. (1986). A study of dietary intake in pre- and post menstrual period. *Human Nutrition: Applied Nutrition, 40A*, 213–216.

Manu, P., Matthews, D. A., Lane, T. J., Tennen, H., Hesselbrock, V., Mendola, R., & Affleck, G. (1989). Depression among patients with chief complaint of chronic fatigue. *Journal of Affective Disorders, 17*, 165–172.

Mark, V., & Mark, J. P. (1989). *Brain power.* Boston: Houghton Mifflin Co.

Marshall, P. (1989). Attention deficit disorder and allergy: A neurochemical model of the relation between the illnesses. *Psychological Bulletin, 106,* 434–446.

Mattes, J. A. (1983). The Feingold diet: A current reappraisal. *Journal of Learning Disabilities, 16,* 319–323.

McCollum, E. V. (1957). *A history of nutrition.* Boston: Houghton Mifflin.

McKeon, P., Shelley, R., O'Regan, S., & O'Broin, J. (1991). Serum and red cell folate and affective morbidity in lithium prophylaxis. *Acta Psychiatry Scandinavia, 83,* 199–201.

McLoughlin, J. A., & Nall, M. (1988). Teacher opinion of the role of food allergy on school behavior and achievement. *Annals of Allergy, 61,* 89–91.

McNeal, E. T., & Cimbolic, P. (1986). Antidepressants and biochemical theories of depression. *Psychological Bulletin, 99,* 361–374.

Melamed, E., Glaeser, B., Growdon, J. H., & Wurtman, R. J. (1980). Plasma tyrosine in normal humans: Effects of oral tyrosine and protein-containing meals. *Journal of Neural Transmission, 47,* 299–306.

Mendels, J., Stinnett, J. L., Burns, D., & Frazer, A. (1975). Amine precursors and depression. *Archives of General Psychiatry, 32,* 22–30.

Messer, S. C., Morris, R. L., & Gross, A. M. (1990). Hypoglycemia and psychopathology: A methodological review. *Clinical Psychology Review, 10,* 631–648.

Michaud, C., Musse, N., Nicolas, J. P., & Mejean, L. (1991). Effects of breakfast-size on short-term memory, concentration, mood and blood glucose. *Journal of Adolescent Health, 12,* 53–57.

Mikkelsen, E. J. (1978). Caffeine and schizophrenia. *Journal of Clinical Psychiatry, 39,* 732–736.

Milich, R., & Pelham, W. (1986). Effects of sugar ingestion on the classroom and playgroup behavior of attention-deficit disordered boys. *Journal of Consulting and Clinical Psychology, 54,* 714–718.

Milich, R., Wolraich, M., & Lindgren, S. (1986). Sugar and hyperactivity: A critical review of empirical findings. *Clinical Psychology Review, 6,* 493–513.

Miller, H. L., Delgado, P. L., Salomon, R. M., Licinio, J., Barr, L. C., Charney, D. S. (1992). Acute tryptophan depletion: A method of studying antidepressant action. *Journal of Clinical Psychiatry, 53*(Suppl. #10), 28–35.

Miranda, J., & Persons, J. B. (1988). Dysfunctional attitudes are mood–state dependent. *Journal of Abnormal Psychology, 97,* 76–79.

Moffic, H. S., & Paykel, E. S. (1975). Depression in medical in-patients. *British Journal of Psychiatry, 126,* 346–353.

Moja, E. A., Cipollo, P., Castoldi, D., & Tofanetti, O. (1989). Dose-response decrease in plasma tryptophan and in brain tryptophan and serotonin after tryptophan-free amino acid mixtures in rats. *Life Sciences, 44,* 971–976.

Møller, S. E. (1990). 5-HT uptake inhibitors and tricyclic antidepressants: Relation between tryptophan availability and clinical response in depressed patients. *European Neuropsychopharmacology, 1,* 41–44.

Møller, S. E., Bech, P., Bjerrum, H., Bojholm, S., Butler, B., Folker, H., Gram, L. F., Larsen, J. K., Lauritzen, L., Loldrup, D., Munk-Andersen, E., Odum, K., & Rafaelsen, O. J. (1990). Plasma ratio tryptophan/neutral amino acids in relation to clinical response to paroxetine and clomipramine in patients with major depression. *Journal of Affective Disorders, 18,* 59–66.

Møller, S. E., Kirk, L., & Honoré, P. (1979). Free and total plasma tryptophan in endogenous depression. *Journal of Affective Disorders, 1,* 69–76.

Møller, S. E., Kirk, L., & Honoré, P. (1980). Relationship between plasma ratio of tryptophan to competing amino acids and the response to L-tryptophan treatment in endogenously depressed patients. *Journal of Affective Disorders, 2,* 47–59.

Monroe, S. M., Simons, A. D., & Thase, M. E. (1991). Onset of depression and time to treatment entry: Roles of life stress. *Journal of Consulting and Clinical Psychology, 59,* 566–573.

Montgomery, G. K. (1983). Uncommon tiredness among college undergraduates. *Journal of Consulting and Clinical Psychology, 51,* 517–525.

Morrison, J. D. (1980). Fatigue as a presenting complaint in family practice. *Journal of Family Practice, 5,* 795–801.

Murphy, D. L., Baker, M., Goodwin, F. K., Miller, L., Kotin, J., & Bunney, W. E. (1974). L-tryptophan in affective disorders: Indoleamine changes and differential clinical effects. *Psychopharmacology, 34,* 11–20.

Muscettolo, G., Galzenati, M., & Balbi, A. (1982). SAMe versus placebo: A double blind comparison in major depressive disorders. In E. Costa & G. Racagni (Eds.), *Typical and atypical antidepressants. Clinical Practice* (pp. 151–156). New York: Raven Press.

National Center for Health Statistics. (1978). *The national ambulatory medical care survey: 1975 summary* (pp. 22–26). Hyattsville, MD: Author.

National Research Council. (1983). *Selenium in nutrition* (Rev. ed.). Report of the Subcommittee on Selenium, Committee on Animal Nutrition, Board on Agriculture, Washington, DC: National Academy Press.

National Research Council. (1984). *National survey data on food consumption: Uses and recommendations.* Washington, DC: National Academy Press.

Neimeyer, G. J., & Kosch, S. G. (1988). An overview of assessment and treatment of premenstrual syndrome. *Journal of Counseling and Development, 66,* 397–399.

Neims, A. H. (1986). Individuality in the response to dietary constituents: Some lessons from drugs. *Nutrition Reviews, 44*(Suppl.), 237–241.

Nielsen, A. C., & Williams, T. A. (1980). Depression in ambulatory medical patients. *Archives of General Psychiatry, 37,* 999–1004.

Nightingale, S. L. (1990). Tryptophan recall expanded. *Journal of the American Medical Association, 263,* 2421.

O'Dowd, M. A., & Zofnass, J. S. (1991). Neuropsychiatric and psychosocial factors in the rehabilitation of patients with aids. In J. Mukand (Ed.), *Rehabilitation for patients with HIV disease* (pp. 199–216). New York: McGraw-Hill.

Oren, D. A., & Rosenthal, N. E. (1992). Seasonal affective disorders. In E. S. Paykel, *Handbook of affective disorders.* New York: The Guilford Press.

Oser, B. L., & Ford, R. A. (1981). Caffeine: an update. *Drug and Chemical Toxicology, 41,* 311–319.

Owasoyo, J. O., Neri, D. F., & Lamberth, J. G. (1992). Tyrosine and its potential use as a countermeasure to performance decrement in military sustained operations. *Aerospace Medical Association, 63,* 3640369.

Pardridge, W. M. (1977). Regulation of amino acid availability to the brain. In R. J. Wurtman & J. J. Wurtman (Eds.), *Nutrition and the Brain,* Vol. 1; pp. (141–204). New York: Raven Press.

Pardridge, W. M., Connor, J. D., & Crawford, I. L. (1975). Permeability changes in the blood-brain barrier: causes and consequences. *CRC Critical Reviews of Toxocology, 3,* 159–199.

Pare, C. M. B., Young, D. P. U., Price, K., & Stacey, R. S. (1969). 5-Hydroxytryptamine noradrenaline and dopamine in brainstem, hypothalamus and caudate nucleus of controls and patients committing suicide by coal gas poisoning. *Lancet, II,* 133–135.

Passeri, M., Ventura, S., Abate, G., Cucinotta, D., & La Greca, P. (1991). Oral 5-methyltetrahydrofolate (MTHF) in depression associated with Senile Organic Mental Disorders (OMD's): A double-blind, multicenter study vs trazodone (TRZ). *European Journal of Clinical Investigation, 21,* 24.

Pauling, L. (1968). Orthomolecular psychiatry. *Science, 160,* 265–271.

Pauling, L. (1970). *Vitamin C and the common cold.* San Francisco: W. H. Freeman.

Pelham, W. E. (1989). Behavior therapy, behavioral assessment, and psychostimulant medication in treatment of attention deficit disorders: An interactive approach. In J. Swanson & L. Bloomingdale (Eds.), *Attention deficit disorders IV: Current concepts and emerging trends in attentional and behavioral disorders of childhood* (pp. 169–202). London: Pergamon Press.

Pelham, W. E., Gnagy, E. M., Greenslade, K. E., & Milich, R. (1992). Teacher ratings of DMS-III-R symptoms for the disruptive behavior disorders. *Journal of the American Academy of Child and Adolescent Psychiatry, 31,* 210–218.

Peterson, C., Schwartz, S. M., & Seligman, M. E. (1981). Self-blame and depressive symptoms. *Journal of Personality and Social Psychology, 41,* 253–255.

Pi-Sunyer, F. X. (1988). Obesity. In M. E. Shils & V. N. Young (Eds.), *Modern nutrition in health and disease* (pp. 799–816). Philadelphia: Lea & Febiger.

Pivonka, E. E. A., & Grunewald, K. K. (1990). Aspartame- or sugar-sweetened beverages: Effects on mood in young women. *Journal of the American Dietetic Association, 90,* 250–254.

Popkin, S., Zetin, M., Stamenkovic, V., Kripke, D. F., & Bunney, W. E., Jr. (1986). Seasonal affective disorder: Prevalence varies with latitude and climate. *Clinical Neuropharmacology, 9*(Suppl. 4), 181–183.

Powers, H. W. S. (1973). Dietary measures to improve behavior and achievement. *Academic Therapy, 9,* 203–214.

Prange, A. J., Wilson, I. C., Lynn, C. W., Alltop, L. B., & Stikeleather, R. A. (1974). L-tryptophan in mania. *Archives of General Psychiatry, 30,* 56–62.

Prinz, R. J., & Riddle, D. B. (1986). Associations between nutrition and behavior in five-year-old children. *Nutrition Reviews, 44*(Suppl.), 151–157.

Prinz, R. J., Roberts, W. A., & Hantman, E. (1980). Dietary correlates of hyperactive behavior in children. *Journal of Consulting and Clinical Psychology, 48,* 760–769.

Prokop, O., & Prokop, L. (1955). Fatigue and falling asleep at the steering wheel. *Deutsche Zeitschrift für die Gesamte Gerichtliche Medizin, 44,* 343–355.

Pruess, J. B., Fewell, R. R., & Bennett, F. C. (1989). Vitamin therapy and children with Down's syndrome: A review of research. *Exceptional Children, 55,* 336–341.

Pyszczynski, T., Holt, K., & Greenberg, J. (1987). Depression, self-focused attention, and expectancies for positive and negative future life events for self and others. *Journal of Personality and Social Psychology, 52,* 994–1001.

Randolph, T. G. (1974). Allergy as a causative factor of fatigue, irritability, and behavior problems of children. *The Journal of Pediatrics, 31,* 560–572.

Rao, B., & Broadhurst, A. D. (1976). Tryptophan and depression. *British Medical Journal, 1,* 460.

Rapp, D. (1978). Does diet affect hyperactivity? *Journal of Learning Disabilities, 11,* 56.

Reda, M. A., Carpiniello, B., Secchiaroli, L., & Blanco, S. (1985). Thinking, depression, and antidepressants: Modified and unmodified beliefs during treatment with amitryptiline. *Cognitive Therapy and Research, 9,* 135–143.

Reid, R. L. (1985). Premenstrual syndrome. *Current problems in obstetrics, gynecology and fertility, 8,* 1–57.

Reynolds, E. H., Preece, J. M., Bailey, J., & Coppen, A. (1970). Folate deficiency in depressive illness. *British Journal of Psychiatry, 117,* 287–292.

Reynolds, E. H., Preece, J. M., & Johnson, A. L. (1971). Folate metabolism in epileptic and psychiatric patients. *Journal of Neurology and Psychiatry, 34,* 726–732.

Reynolds, E. H., & Stramentinoli, G. (1983). Folic acid, S-adenosylmethionine and affective disorder. *Psychological Medicine, 13,* 705–710.

Rhode, P., Lewinsohn, P. M., & Seeley, J. R. (1990). Are people changed by the experience of having an episode of depression? A further test of the scar hypothesis. *Journal of Abnormal Psychology, 99,* 264–271.

Riley, C. J., & Shaw, D. M. (1976). Total and nonbound tryptophan in unipolar illness. *Lancet, 2,* 1249.

Rimland, B. (1974). An orthomolecular study of psychotic children. *Orthomolecular Psychiatry, 3,* 371–377.

Rimland, B. (1983). The Feingold diet: An assessment of the reviews by Mattes, by Kavale, and Forness and others. *Journal of Learning Disabilities, 16,* 331–333.

Rimland, B. (1988). Controversies in the treatment of autistic children: Vitamin and drug therapy. *Journal of Child Neurology, 3,* S68–S72.

Rimland, B., Callaway, E., & Dreyfus, P. (1978). The effects of high doses of vitamin B_6 on autistic children: A double-blind crossover study. *American Journal of Psychiatry, 135,* 472–475.

Riskind, J. H., & Rholes, W. S. (1984). Cognitive accessibility and the capacity of cognitions to predict future depression: A theoretical note. *Cognitive Therapy and Research, 8,* 1–12.

Riskind, J. H., Rholes, W. S., Brannon, A. M., & Burdick, C. A. (1987). Attributions and expectations: A confluence of vulnerabilities in mild depression in a college student population. *Journal of Personality and Social Psychology, 53,* 349–354.

Roberts, H. J. (1990a). *Aspartame (Nutrasweet): Is it safe?* Philadelphia: The Charles Press.

Roberts, H. J. (1990b). Aspartame, tryptophan, and other amino acids as potentially hazardous experiments. *Southern Medical Journal, 83,* 1110–1111.

Robinson, L. A., Berman, J. S., & Neimeyer, R. A. (1990). Psychotherapy for the treatment of depression: A comprehensive review of controlled outcome research. *Psychological Bulletin, 108,* 30–49.

Roccatagliata, G. (1986). *A history of ancient psychiatry.* Westport, CT: Greenwood Press.

Rose, W. C., Haines, W. J., & Warner, D. T. (1954). The amino acid requirements of man. *Journal of Biological Chemistry, 206,* 421–430.

Rosen, L. A., Booth, S. R., Bender, M. E., McGrath, M. L., Sorrell, S., & Drabman, R. S. (1988). Effects of sugar (sucrose) on children's behavior. *Journal of Consulting and Clinical Psychology, 56,* 583–589.

Rosen, L. N., Targum, S. D., Terman, M., Bryant, M. J., Hoffman, H., Kasper, S. F., Hamovit, J. R., Docherty, J. P., Welch, B., & Rosenthal, N. E. (1990). Prevalence of seasonal affective disorder at four latitudes. *Psychiatric Research, 31,* 131–144.

Rosenthal, N. E., Genhart, M. J., Caballero, B., Jacobsen, F. M., Skwerer, R. G., Coursey, R. D., Rogers, S., & Spring, B. J. (1989). Psychobiological effects of carbohydrate- and protein-rich meals in patients with seasonal affective disorder and normal controls. *Biological Psychiatry, 25,* 1029–1040.

Rosenthal, R., & Jacobson, L. (1968). *Pygmalion in the classroom: Teacher expectation and pupil's intellectual development.* New York: Holt, Rinehart & Winston.

Rosenthal, N. E., Lewy, A. J., Wehr, T. A., Kern, H. E., & Goodwin, F. K. (1983). Seasonal cycling in a bipolar patient. *Psychiatric Research, 8,* 25–31.

Rosenthal, N. E., Sack, D. A., Gillin, J. C., Lewy, A. J., Goodwin, F. K., Davenport, Y., Mueller, P. S., Newsome, D. A., & Wehr, T. A. (1984). Seasonal affective disorder: A description of the syndrome and preliminary findings with light therapy. *Archives of General Psychiatry, 41,* 72–80.

Ross, H. M. (1986). Orthomolecular psychiatry, then, now and tomorrow. *Journal of Orthomolecular Medicine, 1,* 110–112.

Ross, M., & Olson, J. M. (1981). An expectancy-attribution model of the effects of placebos. *Psychological Review, 88,* 408–437.

Rossignol, A. M. (1985). Caffeine-containing beverages and premenstrual syndrome in young women. *American Journal of Public Health, 75,* 1335–1337.

Rossignol, A. M., & Bonnlander, H. (1990). Caffeine-containing beverages, total fluid consumption, and premenstrual syndrome. *American Journal of Public Health, 80,* 1106–1110.

Rossignol, A. M., Zhang, J., Chen, Y., & Xiang, Z. (1989). Tea and premenstrual syndrome in the People's Republic of China. *American Journal of Public Health, 79,* 67–69.

Royak-Schaler, R., & Feldman, R. H. (1984). Health behaviors of psychotherapists. *Journal of Clinical Psychology, 40,* 705–710.

Rubinow, D. R., Hoban, M. C., & Grover, G. N. (1987). Menstrually-related mood disorders. In D. Nerozzi, F. K. Goodwin, & E. Costa (Eds.), *Hypothalamic dysfunction in neuropsychiatric disorders* (pp. 335–346). New York: Raven Press.

Russ, M. J., Ackerman, S. H., Banay-Schwartz, M., Shindledecker, R. D., & Smith, G. P. (1990). Plasma tryptophan to large neutral amino acid ratios in depressed and normal subjects. *Journal of Affective Disorders, 19,* 9–14.

Ryan, V. C., Rao, L. O., & Rekers, G. (1990). Nutritional practices, knowledge, and attitudes of psychiatric healthcare professionals: Unexpected results. *The Psychiatric Hospital, 21,* 125–127.

Ryan-Harshman, M., Leiter, L. A., & Anderson, G. H. (1987). Phenylalanine and aspartame fail to alter feeding behavior, mood and arousal in men. *Physiology and Behavior, 39,* 247–253.

Scally, M. C., Ulus, I. H., & Wurtman, R. J. (1977). Brain tyrosine level controls striatal dopamine synthesis in haloperidon-treated rats. *Journal of Neural Transmission, 43,* 103.

Scanlon, D., & Strauss, L. (1991). *Diets that work for weight control or medical needs.* Los Angeles: Lowell House.

Schiffman, S. S., Buckley, C. E., Sampson, H. A., Massey, E. W., Barniuk, J. N., Follette, J.

V., & Warwick, Z. S. (1987). Aspartame and susceptibility to headache. *New England Journal of Medicine, 317,* 1181–1185.

Schiffman, S. S., Crofton, V. A., & Beeker, T. G. (1985). Sensory evaluation of soft drinks with various sweeteners. *Physiology and Behavior, 34,* 369–377.

Schildkraut, J. J. (1965). The catecholamine hypothesis of affective disorders: A review of supporting evidence. *American Journal of Psychiatry, 122,* 509–522.

Schneider, H. A. (1963). What has happened to nutrition? In D. J. Ingle (Ed.), *Life and disease* (pp. 155–169). New York: Basic Books.

Schoenthaler, S. J. (1982). The effect of sugar on the treatment and control of antisocial behavior: A double-blind study of an incarcerated juvenile population. *International Journal of Biosocial Research, 3,* 1–9.

Schoenthaler, S. J. (1983a). The Alabama diet-behavior program: An empirical evaluation at the Coosa Valley Regional Detention Center. *International Journal of Biosocial Research, 4,* 79–87.

Schoenthaler, S. J. (1983b). Diet and crime: An empirical examination of the value of nutrition in the control and treatment of incarcerated juvenile offenders. *International Journal of Biosocial Research, 4,* 25–39.

Schoenthaler, S. J. (1983c). The effect of citrus on the treatment and control of antisocial behavior: A double-blind study of an incarcerated juvenile population. *International Journal of Biosocial Research, 5,* 107–117.

Schoenthaler, S. J. (1983d). The Los Angeles Probation Department diet-behavior program: An empirical examination of six institutions. *International Journal of Biosocial Research, 5,* 88–98.

Schoenthaler, S. J. (1983e). The Northern California diet-behavior program: An empirical examination of 3,000 incarcerated juveniles in Stanislaus County Juvenile Hall. *International Journal of Biosocial Research, 4,* 99–106.

Schreibmen, L., Loos, L. M., & Stahmer, A. C. (1993). Autistic disorder. In R. T. Ammerman, C. G. Last, & M. Hersen (Eds.), *Handbook of prescriptive treatments for children and adolescents* (pp. 9–27). Boston: Allyn & Bacon.

Secker-Walker, R. H., Morrow, A. L., Kresnow, M., Flynn, B. S., & Hochheiser, L. I. (1991). Family physicians' attitudes about dietary advice. *Family Practice Research Journal, 11,* 161–170.

Shannon, W. R. (1922). Neuropathic manifestations as a result of anaphylactic reaction to foods contained in their dietary. *American Journal of the Diseases of Children, 24,* 89–94.

Shaw, D. M., Tidmarsh, S. F., Thomas, D. E., Briscoe, M., Dickerson, J. W. T., & Chung-A-On, K. O. (1984). Senile dementia and nutrition. *British Medical Journal, 288,* 792–793.

Shulman, R. (1967). A survey of vitamin B_{12} deficiency in an elderly psychiatric population. *British Journal of Psychiatry, 113,* 241–251.

Siever, L. J., & Davis, K. L. (1985). Overview: Toward a dysregulation hypothesis of depression. *American Journal of Psychiatry, 147,* 1017–1031.

Silverstone, T., & Goodall, E. (1986). Serotonergic mechanism in human feeding: The pharmacological evidence. *Appetite, 7,* 85–87.

Simonson, E., Brozek, J., & Keys, A. (1948). Effects of meals on visual performance and fatigue. *Journal of Applied Psychology, 1,* 270–278.

Simopoulos, A. P. (1987). Characteristics of obesity: An overview. *Annals of the New York Academy of Science, 499,* 4–13.

Slutsker, L., Hoesley, F. C., Miller, L., Williams, L. P., Watson, J. C., & Fleming, D. W. (1990). Eosinophilia-myalgia syndrome associated with exposure to tryptophan from a single manufacturer. *Journal of the American Medical Association, 264,* 213–217.

Smith, A., Leekam, S., Ralph, A., & McNeil, G. (1988). The influence of meal composition on post-lunch changes in performance efficiency and mood. *Appetite, 10,* 195–203.

Smith, A., Ralph, A., & McNeill, G. (1991). Influences of meal size on post-lunch changes in performance efficiency, mood, and cardiovascular function. *Appetite, 16,* 85–91.

Smith, A. P., & Miles, C. (1986a). Acute effects of meals, noise and nightwork. *British Journal of Psychology, 77,* 377–387.

Smith, A. P., & Miles, C. (1986b). The effects of lunch on cognitive vigilance tasks. *Ergonomics, 29*, 1251–1261.

Smith, A. P., & Miles, C. (1986c). Effects of lunch on selective and sustained attention. *Neuropsychobiology, 16*, 117–120.

Smith, B., & Prockop, D. J. (1962). Central-nervous-system effects of ingestion of L-tryptophan by normal subjects. *The New England Journal of Medicine, 267*, 1338–1341.

Smith, S. E., Pihl, R. O., Young, S. N., & Ervin, E. R. (1987). A test of possible cognitive and environmental influences on the mood lowering effect of tryptophan depletion in normal males. *Psychopharmacology, 91*, 451–457.

Smith, S. L., & Sauder, C. (1969). Food cravings, depression, and premenstrual problems. *Psychosomatic Medicine, 31*, 281–287.

Sneath, P., Chanarin, I., Hodkinson, H. M., Mcpherson, C. K., & Reynolds, E. H. (1973). Folate status in a geriatric population and its relation to dementia. *Ageing, 2*, 177–182.

Speer, F. (1958). The allergic tension-fatigue syndrome in children. *International Archives of Allergy, 12*, 207–214.

Sprague, R. L. (1981). Measurement and methodology of behavioral studies: The other half of the nutrition and behavior equation. In S. A. Miller (Ed.), *Nutrition and Behavior* (pp. 269–276). Philadelphia: Franklin Institute Press.

Spring, B. (1986). Effects of foods and nutrients on the behavior of normal individuals. In R. J. Wurtman & J. J. Wurtman (Eds.), *Nutrition and the Brain* (pp. 1–48). New York: Raven Press.

Spring, B., Chiodo, J., & Bowen, D. J. (1987). Carbohydrates, tryptophan, and behavior: A methodological review. *Psychological Bulletin, 102*, 234–256.

Spring, B., Chiodo, J., Harden, M., Bourgeois, M. J., Mason, J. D., & Lutherer, L. (1989). Psychobiological effects of carbohydrates. *Journal of Clinical Psychiatry, 50*(Suppl. 5), 27–33.

Spring, B., Lieberman, H. R., Swope, G., & Garfield, G. S. (1986). Effects of carbohydrates on mood and behavior. *Nutrition Reviews, 44*(Suppl.), 51–70.

Spring, B., Maller, O., Wurtman, J., Digman, L., & Cozolino, L. (1983). Effects of protein and carbohydrate meals on mood and performance: Interactions with sex and age. *Journal of Psychiatric Research, 17*, 155–157.

Stare, F. J., & McWilliams, M. (1981). *Living nutrition.* New York: Wiley.

Stasiak, E. A. (1982). Nutritional approaches to altering criminal behavior. *Journal of Behavior, Technology, Methods, and Therapy, 28*, 110–115.

Stegink, L. D., Filer, L. J., Jr., & Baker, G. L. (1988). Repeated ingestion of aspartame-sweetened beverage: Effect on plasma amino acid concentrations in normal adults. *Metabolism, 37*, 246–251.

Stewart, T. W., Harrison, W., Quitkin, F., & Baker, H. (1984). Low B6 levels in depressed out-patients. *Biological Psychiatry, 19*, 613–616.

Stone, A. A., & Neale, J. M. (1984). Effects of severe daily events on mood. *Journal of Personality and Social Psychology, 46*, 137–144.

Strain, G. W., Strain, J. J., & Zumoff, B. (1985). *International Journal of Obesity, 9*, 375–380.

Stuff, J. E., Garza, C., Smith, E. O., Nichols, B. L., & Montandon, C. M. (1983). A comparison of dietary methods in nutritional studies. *The American Journal of Clinical Nutrition, 37*, 300–306.

Sutherland, H. (1892). Menstruation and insanity. In D. H. Tuke (Ed.), *A dictionary of psychological medicine* (pp. 801–803). New York: Arno Press.

Sved, A. F. (1983). Precursor control of the function of monoaminergic neurons. In R. J. Wurtman & J. J. Wurtman (Eds.), *Nutrition and the brain* (vol. 6, pp. 223–275). New York: Raven Press.

Swanson, F. M., & Kinsbourne, M. (1980). Food dyes impair performance of hyperactive children on a laboratory learning test. *Science, 207*, 1485.

Swanwick, G., Manley, P., & McKeon, P. (1992). Lithium, affective disorder and folate-A review. *Lithium, 3*, 175–179.

Sydenstricker, V. P. (1941). The clinical manifestations of nicotinic acid and riboflavin deficiency (pellagra). *Annals of Internal Medicine, 14*, 1499–1517.

Takahashi, K., Asano, Y., Kohsaka, M., Okawa, M., Sasaki, M., Honda, Y., Higuchi, T., Yamazaki, J., Ishizuka, Y., Kawaguchi, K., Ohta, T., Hanada, K., Sugita, Y., Maeda, K., Nagayama, H., Kotorii, T., Egashira, K., & Takahashi, S. (1991). Multi-center study of seasonal affective disorders in Japan. A preliminary report. *Journal of Affective Disorders, 21,* 57–65.

Tamerin, J. S., & Mendelson, J. H. (1969). The psychodynamics of chronic inebriation: Observation of alcoholics during the process of drinking in an experimental group setting. *American Journal of Psychiatry, 125,* 886–889.

Teff, K. L., Young, S. N., & Blundell, J. E. (1989). The effect of protein or carbohydrate breakfasts on subsequent plasma amino acid levels, satiety and nutrient selection in normal males. *Pharmacology, Biochemistry and Behavior, 34,* 829–837.

Teff, K. L., Young, S. N., Marchand, L., Botez, M. I. (1989). Acute effect of protein or carbohydrate breakfasts on human cerebrospinal fluid monamine precursor and metabolite levels. *Journal of Neurochemistry, 52,* 235–241.

Thayer, R. E. (1987). Energy, tiredness, and tension: Effects of a sugar snack versus moderate exercise. *Journal of Personality and Social Psychology, 52,* 119–125.

Thayer, R. E. (1989). *The biopsychology of mood and arousal.* New York: Oxford University Press.

Thayer, R. E., Takahashe, P. J., & Pauli, J. A. (1988). Multidimensional arousal states, diurnal rhythms, cognitive and social processes, and extraversion. *Personality and Individual Differences, 9,* 15–24.

Thomson, J., Rankin, H., Ashcroft, G. W., Yates, C. M., McQueen, J. K., & Cummings, S. W. (1982). The treatment of depression in general practice: A comparison of L-tryptophan, amitriptyline, and a combination of L-tryptophan and amitriptyline with placebo. *Psychological Medicine, 12,* 741–751.

Thornton, W. E., & Thornton, B. P. (1978). Folic acid, mental function, and dietary habits. *Journal of Clinical Psychiatry, 39,* 315–322.

Tizard, B. (1966). Repetitive auditory stimuli and the development of sleep. *Electroencephalographic Clinical Neurophysiology, 20,* 112–121.

Todhunter, E. N. (1962). Development of knowledge in nutrition. *Journal of the American Dietetic Association, 41,* 335–340.

Tolonen, M., Halme, M., & Sarna, S. (1985). Vitamin E and selenium supplementation in geriatric patients. *Biological Trace Element Research, 7,* 161–168.

Trites, R. C., Ferguson, H. B., & Tryphonas, H. (1980). Diet treatment for hyperactive children with food allergies. In R. M. Knights & D. Bakken (Eds.), *The rehabilitation, treatment, and management of learning disabilities* (pp. 151–163). Baltimore: University Park Press.

Trunnell, E. P., Turner, C. W., & Keye, W. R. (1988). A comparison of the psychological and hormonal factors in women with and without premenstrual syndrome. *Journal of Consulting and Clinical Psychology, 97,* 429–436.

Tryphonas, H., & Trites, R. (1979). Food allergy in children with hyperactivity, learning disabilities, and/or minimal brain dysfunction. *Annals of Allergy, 42,* 22–27.

Turkel, H. (1975). Medical amelioration of Down's syndrome incorporating the orthomolecular approach. *Journal of Orthomolecular Psychiatry, 4,* 102–115.

U.S. Department of Agriculture, Human Nutrition Information Service. (1981). *Provisional table on the nutrient content of bakery foods and related items* (rev). Washington, DC: U.S. Government Printing Office.

U.S. Department of Agriculture, Human Nutrition Information Service. (1988). *Provisional table on the dietary fiber content of selected foods.* Washington, DC: U.S. Government Printing Office.

Valcuikas, J. A., Lilis, R., Wolff, M. S., & Anderson, H. A. (1978). Comparative neurobehavioral study of a polybrominated biphenyl-exposed population in Michigan and a nonexposed group in Wisconsin. *Environmental Health Perspective, 23,* 199–210.

van Praag, H. M. (1980). Central monitoring metabolism in depressions: I. Serotonin and related compounds. *Comprehensive Psychiatry, 21,* 30–43.

van Praag, H. M. (1981). Management of depression with serotonin precursors. *Biological Psychiatry, 16,* 291–310.

van Praag, H. M. (1985). Monoamines and depression: The present state of the art. In R.

Plutchik & H. Kellerman (Eds.), *Biological foundations of emotion* (pp. 335–356). New York: Academic Press.

van Praag, H. M., Korf, J., & Puite, J. (1970). 5-hydroxytryptamine levels in the cerebrospinal fluid of depressed patients treated with probenecid. *Nature, 225,* 1259–1260.

van Praag, H. M., & Lemus, C. (1986). Monamine precursors in the treatment of psychiatric disorders. In R. J. Wurtman & J. J. Wurtman (Eds.), *Nutrition and the Brain* (Vol. 7; pp. 89–139). New York: Raven Press.

Varley, C. K. (1984). Diet and the behavior of children with attention deficit disorder. *Journal of the American Academy of Child Psychiatry, 23,* 182–185.

Velten, E. C. (1968). A laboratory task for induction of mood states. *Behavior Research and Therapy, 6,* 473–482.

Virkkunen, M. (1986). Reactive hypoglycemic tendency among habitually violent offenders. *Nutrition Reviews, 44*(Suppl.), 94–103.

Voigt, E. D., Engel, P., & Klein, H. (1968). On the daily operation of physical work capacity. *Internationale Zietschrift für Angewandte Physiologie Einschliesslich Arbeitsphysiologie, 25,* 1–12.

Von Hilsheimer, G. (1974). *Allergy, toxins, and the learning disabled children.* San Rafael, CA: Academic Therapy.

Wadden, T. A., & Stunkard, A. J. (1987). Psychopathology and obesity. *Annals of the New York Academy of Science, 499,* 55–65.

Watson, G. (1965). Differences in intermediary metabolism in mental illness. *Psychological Reports, 17,* 563–582.

Watson, D., & Clark, L. A. (1984). Negative affectivity: The disposition to experience aversive emotional states. *Psychological Bulletin, 96,* 465–490.

Watson, D., Clark, L. A., & Carey, G. (1988). Positive and negative affectivity and their relation to anxiety and depressive disorders. *Journal of Abnormal Psychology, 97,* 346–353.

Watson, D., Clark, L. A., & Tellegen, A. (1988). Development and validation of brief measures of positive and negative affect: The PANAS scales. *Journal of Personality and Social Psychology, 54,* 1063–1070.

Watson, G., & Currier, W. D. (1960). Intensive vitamin therapy in mental illness. *The Journal of Psychology, 49,* 67–81.

Watson, D., & Pennebaker, J. W. (1989). Health complaints, stress, and distress: Exploring the central role of negative affectivity. *Psychological Bulletin, 96,* 234–254.

Weathers, C. (1983). Effects of nutritional supplementation on IQ and certain other variables associated with Down's syndrome. *American Journal of Mental Deficiency, 88,* 214–217.

Wehr, T. A., & Rosenthal, N. E. (1989). Seasonality and affective illness. *American Journal of Psychiatry, 146,* 829–839.

Weingarten, H. P., & Elston, D. (1990). The phenomenology of food cravings. *Appetite, 15,* 231–246.

Weissman, M. M., & Myers, J. K. (1978). Affective disorders in a U.S. urban community: The use of research diagnostic criteria in an epidemiological survey. *Archives of General Psychiatry, 35,* 1304–1311.

Wessely, S., & Powell, R. (1989). Fatigue syndromes: A comparison of chronic "postviral" fatigue with neuromuscular and affective disorders. *Journal of Neurology, Neurosurgery, and Psychiatry, 52,* 940–948.

Westbrook, M. T., & Viney, L. L. (1982). Psychological reactions to the onset of chronic illness. *Social Science Medicine, 16,* 899–905.

Whitlock, F. A. (Ed.). (1982). *Symptomatic affective disorders.* New York: Academic Press.

Wilder, J. (1947). Sugar metabolism in its relation to criminology. In R. M. Linder & R. V. Seliger (Eds.), *Handbook of correctional psychology* (pp. 98–129). New York: Philosophical Library.

Wilkinson, D. G. (1981). Psychiatric aspects of diabetes mellitus. *British Journal of Psychiatry, 138,* 1–9.

Willett, W. (1990). *Nutritional epidemiology.* New York: Oxford University Press.

Williams, J. J., & Cram, D. M. (1978). Diet in the management of hyperkinesis. *Canadian Psychiatric Association Journal, 23,* 241–248.

Williams, R. D., Mason, H. L., Wilder, R. M., & Smith, B. F. (1940). Observations on induced thiamine (vitamin B$_1$) deficiency in man. *Archives of Internal Medicine, 66,* 785–799.

Winokur, A., Maislin, G., Phillips, J. L., & Amsterdam, J. D. (1988). Insulin resistance after oral glucose tolerance testing in patients with major depression. *American Journal of Psychiatry, 145,* 325–330.

Winstead, G. K. (1976). Coffee consumption among psychiatric inpatients. *American Journal of Psychiatry, 133,* 1447–1450.

Witschi, J. C. (1990). Short-term dietary recall and recording methods. In W. Willett (Ed.). *Nutritional epidemiology* (pp. 52–68). New York: Oxford University Press.

Wolf, E. M. B., With, J. C., & Lohman, T. G. (1979). Nutritional practices of coaches in the big ten. *Physical Sports Medicine, 7,* 112–124.

Wolraich, M., Milich, R., Stumbo, P., & Schultz, F. (1984). Effects of sucrose ingestion on the behavior of hyperactive boys. *Pediatrics, 106,* 675–682.

Wolraich, M. L., Milich, R., Stumbo, P., & Schultz, F. (1985). Effects of sucrose ingestion on the behavior of hyperactive boys. *Journal of Pediatrics, 106,* 675–681.

Wurtman, J. J. (1989). Carbohydrate craving, mood changes, and obesity. *Journal of Clinical Psychiatry, 49*(Suppl.), 37–39.

Wurtman, J. J., Brzezinski, A., Wurtman, R. J., & Laferrere, B. (1989). Effect of nutrient intake on premenstrual depression. *American Journal of Obstetrics and Gynecology, 161,* 1228–1235.

Wurtman, J., Wurtman, R., Mark, S., Tsay, R., Gilbert, W., & Growdon, J. (1985). d-fenfluramine selectively suppresses carbohydrate snacking by obese subjects. *International Journal of Eating Disorders, 4,* 89–99.

Wurtman, J., Wurtman, R., Reynolds, S., Tsay, R., & Chew, B. (1987). Fenfluramine suppresses snack intake among carbohydrate cravers but not among noncarbohydrate cravers. *International Journal of Eating Disorders, 6,* 687–699.

Wurtman, R. J. (1983). Neurochemical changes following high-dose aspartame with dietary carbohydrates [Letter to the editor]. *New England Journal of Medicine, 309,* 429–430.

Wurtman, R. J. (1985). Aspartame: Possible effect on seizure susceptibility [Letter to the editor]. *Lancet, 2,* 1060.

Wurtman, R. J. (1987). Nutrients affecting brain composition and behavior. *Integrative Psychiatry, 5,* 226–257.

Wurtman, R. J., Hefti, F., & Melamed, E. (1981). Precursor control of neurotransmitter synthesis. *Pharmacological Reviews, 32,* 315–335.

Wurtman, R. J., Larin, F., Mostafapour, S., & Fernstrom, J. D. (1974). Brain catechol synthesis: Control by brain tyrosine concentration. *Science, 185,* 183–184.

Wurtman, R. J., & Wurtman, J. J. (1986). Carbohydrate cravings, obesity and brain serotonin. *Apetite, 7*(Suppl.), 99–103.

Wurtman, R. J., & Wurtman, J. J. (1989). Carbohydrates and depression. *Scientific American,* January, 68–75.

Wurtman, R. J., Wurtman, J. J., Growdon, J. H., Henry, P., Lipscomb, A., & Zeisel, S. H. (1981). Carbohydrate craving in obese people: Suppression by treatments affecting serotoninergic neurotransmission. *International Journal of Eating Disorders, 1,* 2–15.

Yokogoshi, H., Roberts, C. H., Caballero, B., & Wurtman, R. J. (1984). Effects of aspartame and glucose administration on brain and plasma levels of large neutral amino acids and brain 5-hydroxyindoles. *The American Journal of Clinical Nutrition, 40,* 1–7.

Young, S. N. (1986a). The clinical psychopharmacology of tryptophan. In R. J. Wurtman & J. J. Wurtman (Eds.), *Nutrition and the brain* (vol. 7; pp. 49–88). New York: Raven Press.

Young, S. (1986b). The effect of altering tryptophan levels on aggression. *Nutrition Reviews, 44*(Suppl.), 112–121.

Young, S. N. (1991a). Some effects of dietary components (amino acids, carbohydrate, folic acid) on brain serotonin synthesis, mood, and behavior. *Canadian Journal of Pharmacology, 69,* 893–903.

Young, S. N. (1991b). Use of tryptophan in combination with other antidepressant treatments: A review. *Journal of Psychiatry & Neuroscience, 16,* 21–246.

Young, S. N., Ervin, F. R., Pihl, R. O., & Finn, P. (1989). Biochemical aspects of tryptophan depletion in primates. *Psychopharmacology, 98,* 508–511.

Young, S. N., & Ghadirian, A. M. (1989). Folic acid and psychopathology. *Progress in Neuropsychopharmacology & Biological Psychiatry, 13,* 841–863.

Young, V. R., Hussein, M. A., Murray, E., & Scrimshaw, N. S. (1971). Plasma tryptophan response curve and its relation to tryptophan requirements in young adult men. *Journal of Nutrition, 101,* 45–60.

Young, S. N., Smith, S. E., Pihl, R. O., & Ervin, F. R. (1985). Tryptophan depletion causes a rapid lowering of mood in normal males. *Psychopharmacology, 87,* 173–177.

Yuwiler, A., Brammer, G. L., Morley, J. E., Raleigh, M. J., Flannery, J. W., & Geller, E. (1981). Short-term and repetitive administration of oral tryptophan in normal men. *Archives of General Psychiatry, 38,* 619–626.

Yuwiler, A., Oldendorf, W. H., Geller, E., & Braun, L. (1977). Effect of albumin binding and amino acid competition on tryptophan uptake into brain. *Journal of Neurochemistry, 28,* 1015–1023.

Zametkin, A. J., & Rapoport, J. L. (1987). Neurobiology of attention deficit disorder with hyperactivity: Where have we come in 50 years. *Journal of the American Academy of Child Adolescent Psychiatry, 26,* 676–686.

Index

Academy of Orthomolecular Psychiatry, 147
ADHD (attention-deficit hyperactivity
    disorder)
    research design, 12
    symptoms of, 147–148
    treatments for, 167–168
        elimination of food-induced allergies,
            151–155
        Feingold diet, 37, 149
        restriction of sugar, 55–56, 150–151
        vitamin therapy, 151
Adolescents. See ADHD (attention-deficit
    hyperactivity disorder); Children, disor-
    ders in
Allergies, food, 151–155
Amino acids, 20–21, 38, 41–43, 75 Table
    5.2. See also LNAAs (large neutral amino
    acids); Tryptophan
Antisocial behavior, 158–161
Aspartame, 18, 78–80
Assessment devices, 29–31
Attention-deficit hyperactivity disorder. See
    ADHD (attention-deficit hyperactivity
    disorder)
Autism, 155–156

Blood–brain barrier, and LNAAs, 43–44
B_1 (thiamin), 7 Table 1.1, 8 Table 1.2, 99
B_6 (pyridoxine), 7 Table 1.1, 8 Table 1.2,
    99, 155–156
B_{12} (cyanocobalamin), 7 Table 1.1, 8 Table
    1.2, 99–101

Caffeine, 22–26
    eliminating, from diet, 14–16, 25, 93–
        95, 136–139
    and PMS, 122–123, 167
Carbohydrate cravings
    and obesity, 114–117, 167
    and PMS, 120–122, 167
    problems with defining, 123–124
    and seasonal affective disorder (SAD),
        110, 112, 167
Carbohydrates, effect of, on. See also Car-
    bohydrate cravings; Sucrose
    depression, 56–59, 67–69, 89–96
    mood, 80–83
    task performance, 87
Cartier, Jacques, 6
Casal, Gaspar, 6–7

Case studies (dietary intervention)
    Linda, 165–167
    Nancy, 163–164
Catecholamines, 38
    dietary control of, 46–49
CDDI (Christensen Dietary Distress Inven-
    tory), 139–141, 164, 169–176
Cerri, Guiseppi, 6–7
Challenge phase (methodological issue), 26
Children, disorders in. See also ADHD
    (attention-deficit hyperactivity disorder)
    autism, 155–156
    Down's syndrome, 156–158
    juvenile delinquency, 158–161
Christensen Dietary Distress Inventory
    (CDDI), 139–141, 164, 169–176
Chromium, 51–53
Correlational research design, 12
Cyanocobalamin (B_{12}), 7 Table 1.1, 8 Table
    1.2, 99–101
Cyclical changes (methodological issue),
    27–29

Deficiency diseases, 6–10
Depression. See also Mood, dietary influ-
    ences on
    dietary intervention in treatment of, 89–
        96, 136–144, 163–167
        folic acid, 134–136
        L-tryptophan, 127–132
        selenium, 136
        tryptophan, 96–98, 165
        tyrosine, 133–134
        vitamins, 134–136, 165
    and fatigue, 56–60
    and low energetic arousal, 60–69
D-fenfluramine, and carbohydrate cravings,
    115–116, 122
Diet. See Dietary intervention; Foods
Dietary analysis systems, 31–32
Dietary intake (methodological issue), 29–
    32
Dietary intervention
    and ADHD, 167–168
        elimination of food-induced allergies,
            151–155
        Feingold diet, 37, 149
        restriction of sugar, 55–56, 150–151
        vitamin therapy, 151
    and autism, 155–156
    case studies

Dietary intervention (*Continued*)
   Linda, 166–167
   Nancy, 163–164
   and depression. *See* Depression, dietary
      intervention in treatment of
   and Down's syndrome, 156–158
   identifying responders to, 139–141, 164,
      169–176
   implementing, 141–144
   and juvenile delinquency, 158–161
Dietary record (assessment device), 30
Dopamine. *See* Catecholamines
Dose level (methodological issue), 26–27
Dose-response procedures, 27, 39–41
Double-blind procedure, defined, 17–18
Down's syndrome, 156–158
Dysfunctional cognitions, 63–65, 67–69

Energetic arousal, low, 60–67. *See also*
   Fatigue
   and carbohydrates, 67–69
Eosinophilia-myalgia, 133
Expectancy effects, 16–18, 55–56
Experimental research design, 12–13

Fatigue, 56–60. *See also* Energetic arousal,
   low
Feingold diet, 37, 149, 167–168
Folic acid, 7 Table 1.1, 8 Table 1.2, 101–
   108
   in treatment of depression, 134–136
Food faddism, 3–4
Food-frequency questionnaire (assessment
   device), 30–31
Foods, 3–6, 18–21, 24–27, 29–32. *See also*
   Dietary intervention; Mood, dietary influences on; Task performance, dietary influences on
   allergies induced by, 151–155
   and deficiency diseases, 6–10
   and expectancies, 16–18, 55–56
   idiosyncratic responses to, 14–16
   metabolic effects of. *See* Neurotransmit-
      ters, dietary control of
Funk, Casimir, 7

Gender differences, in. *See also* Women
   ADHD (attention-deficit hyperactivity
      disorder), 148
   autism, 155
   cyclical changes, 27–28
   obesity, 113–114, 117
   tryptophan-depletion research, 77
Glucose intolerance, 52–53
Goldberger, Joseph, 7

Hippocrates, quoted, 5
Hyperactivity. *See* ADHD (attention-deficit
   hyperactivity disorder)
Hypoglycemia, 50–51, 159–161

Idiosyncratic response (methodological issue), 14–16

Juvenile delinquency, 158–161

Lind, James, 6
LNAAs (large neutral amino acids)
   ratio of, to tryptophan, 45–46, 50, 97,
      116–117
   transportation of, 43–44, 48–49
L-tryptophan, 127–132. *See also*
   Tryptophan
Lunch, effect of, on
   mood, 81–83
   task performance, 86–87

Mania, 132–133
Meals. *See* Foods
Methodology, issues affecting
   challenge phase, 26
   cyclical changes, 27–29
   dietary intake, 29–32
   dose level, 26–27
   expectancy, 16–18
   idiosyncratic response, 14–16
   placebo identification, 18–19
   prior nutritional status, 19–20
   time course of behavioral effect, 21–24
   washout phase, 24–25
   whole foods versus single nutrients, 20–
      21
   withdrawal effect, 25–26
Microcomputer dietary analysis systems,
   31–32
Monoamines. *See* Catecholamines;
   Serotonin
Mood, dietary influences on. *See also*
   Depression
   aspartame, 18, 78–80
   carbohydrates, 80–83
   tryptophan, 20–21, 73–78
   tyrosine, 78
   vitamins, 99–108

Negative affect, 65–69
Neurotransmitters, dietary control of, 37–
   39, 50–53

catecholamines, 46–48
  model, 48–49
  serotonin, 39–44, 49–50, 114–117
    model, 45–46
Norepinephrine. See Catecholamines
Nutrients. See Foods
Nutrition. See Foods
Nutritional status, prior (methodological issue), 19–20

Obesity, 112–117, 167
Orthomolecular psychiatry, 147

Pauling, Linus, 147
PBB (polybrominated biphenyls), 13–14
Pellagra, 6–7, 9
Peptides, 38
Placebo identification (methodological issue), 18–19
PMS (premenstrual syndrome), 167
  defined, 118
  symptoms of, 119–123
Polybrominated biphenyls (PBB), 13–14
Premenstrual syndrome. See PMS (premenstrual syndrome)
Pyridoxine (B₆), 7 Table 1.1, 8 Table 1.2, 99, 155–156

Quasi-experimental research design, 13–14

Research designs, 12–14

S-adenosyl methionine (SAM), 107–108
SAD (seasonal affective disorder), 109–112, 167
SAM (S-adenosyl methionine), 107–108
Schizophrenia, 132
Scurvy, 6
Seasonal affective disorder (SAD), 109–112, 167
Selenium, 136
Self-efficacy expectations, 62–63, 67–69
Self-focus of attention, 61–62, 66–69
Serotonin, 38, 75–78. See also L-tryptophan
  dietary control of, 39–44, 49–50, 114–117
    model, 45–46

Sucrose, 22–26. See also Dietary intervention
  eliminating, from diet, 14–16, 25–26, 93–95, 136–139
  implicated in "Twinkie defense," 158
  and placebos, 18
Sugar. See Sucrose

Task performance, dietary influences on, 83–87
Thiamin (B₁), 7 Table 1.1, 8 Table 1.2, 99
Time course of behavioral effect (methodological issue), 21–24
Tryptophan, 132–133. See also LNAAs (large neutral amino acids); L-tryptophan
  effect of, on
    carbohydrate cravings, 115–116
    depression, 96–98, 165
    mood, 20–21, 73–78
    task performance, 85–86
  and serotonin synthesis, 39–43
24-hour recall (assessment device), 29–30
"Twinkie defense," 158
Tyrosine
  and catecholamine synthesis, 46–49
  effects of, 78, 85–86, 133–134

Unipolar depression. See Depression

Vitamin deficiency diseases, 6–10
Vitamins
  discovery of, 6–10
  effect of, on mood, 99–108
  in treatment of
    ADHD, 151
    autism, 155–156
    depression, 134–136, 165
    Down's syndrome, 156–158
Vitamin supplements, exaggerated claims about, 5–6

Washout phase (methodological issue), 24–25
Whole foods versus single nutrients (methodological issue), 20–21
Withdrawal effect (methodological issue), 25–26
Women. See also Gender differences, in
  menstrual cycle of, 28–29
  nutritional intake of, 89, 90 Table 6.1
  and PMS, 118–123, 167

About the Author

Larry Christensen, PhD, received his graduate degree from the University of Southern Mississippi and is a member of the American Psychological Association and the American Psychological Society. He advanced through the ranks of assistant, associate, and full professor at Texas A&M University and recently accepted a position as Chair of the Psychology Department at the University of South Alabama. He has taught courses in research methods, psychological statistics, social psychology, and the psychology of nutrition. He is past president of the Southwestern Psychological Association and served as committee judge for the Gordon Allport Intergroup Relations Prize. Dr. Christensen has authored or coauthored more than 55 scientific articles. His books include *Experimental Methodology*, *Introduction to Statistics for the Social and Behavioral Sciences* (with C. Stoup), and *The Food–Mood Connection: Eating Your Way to Happiness.*